QUASI-STATES: SOVEREIGNTY, INTERNATIONAL RELATIONS, AND THE THIRD WORLD

Cambridge Studies in International Relations is a joint initiative of Cambridge University Press and the British International Studies Association (BISA). The series will include a wide range of material, from undergraduate textbooks and surveys to research-based monographs and collaborative volumes. The aim of the series is to publish the best new scholarship in International Studies from Europe, North America and the rest of the world.

CAMBRIDGE STUDIES IN INTERNATIONAL RELATIONS

QUASI-STATES:
SOVEREIGNTY, INTERNATIONAL RELATIONS, AND THE THIRD WORLD

ROBERT H. JACKSON
Department of Political Science,
University of British Columbia

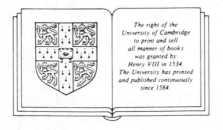

The right of the
University of Cambridge
to print and sell
all manner of books
was granted by
Henry VIII in 1534.
The University has printed
and published continuously
since 1584.

CAMBRIDGE UNIVERSITY PRESS
Cambridge
New York Port Chester Melbourne Sydney

Published by the Press Syndicate of the University of Cambridge
The Pitt Building, Trumpington Street, Cambridge CB2 1RP
40 West 20th Street, New York, NY 10011, USA
10 Stamford Road, Oakleigh, Melbourne 3166, Australia

First published 1990

Printed in Great Britain by
Redwood Press Limited, Melksham, Wiltshire

British Library cataloguing in publication data
Jackson, Robert H.
  Quasi-states: sovereignty, international relations and
  the third world. – (Cambridge studies in international
  relations; v.12).
  1. Developing countries. Politics and government
  I. Title
  320.9172′4

Library of Congress cataloguing in publication data
Jackson, Robert H.
  Quasi-states: sovereignty, international relations, and the Third
  World / Robert H. Jackson.
     p.   cm. – (Cambridge studies in international relations: 12)
  Includes bibliographical references.
  ISBN 0 521 35310 6
  1. Sovereignty.   2. Developing countries   Foreign relations.
  3. International relations.   I. Title.   II. Series.
  JX4041.J28   1990
  341.26—dc20   89–77369   CIP

ISBN 0 521 35310 6

For Margie

CONTENTS

ACKNOWLEDGEMENTS

The genesis of this book was the realization in earlier work that many Third World states are to an exceptional degree creatures and beneficiaries of international morality and international law. Preliminary articles on this theme regarding African states were written jointly with Carl Rosberg and published in *World Politics* (1982) and the *Journal of Modern African Studies* (1986). I owe him a considerable intellectual debt. James Mayall suggested that I should develop these prototype ideas in a general study of international relations. I was fortunate to receive early comments on a proposal for such a book from two readers for Cambridge University Press, one of whom was Roy Jones, which helped to clarify my thinking at an early stage and overcome initial false starts. Some parts of chapters 2 and 3 were first delivered as papers at the 1985 and 1986 meetings of the British International Studies Association and later published in the *Review of International Studies* (October 1986) and *International Organization* (Autumn 1987). I am grateful to the editors and anonymous readers for their help in making revisions. I also wish to thank staff and students in the Department of International Relations at the University of Keele for their reactions to a preliminary draft of chapter 6 presented in February 1988. A different version of chapter 7 was delivered at the 1989 joint meeting of the American and British International Studies Associations in London. I am grateful to Michael Donelan and Jack Donnelly, the discussants, for their very helpful criticisms. An overview of the final argument was presented to John Vincent's postgraduate seminar on international relations at Nuffield College, Oxford, in April 1989. I thank all who contributed to the discussion which followed. I would especially like to acknowledge the generosity of Alan Cairns, Kal Holsti, and Alan James who on short notice set aside their own work and provided comments on an earlier draft which were invaluable in making revisions. I have only myself to blame for any errors of fact or judgement which remain.

The manuscript was completed during 1988–9 while I held an Izaak

Walton Killam Memorial Fellowship on sabbatical leave from the University of British Columbia. I am most grateful to the Trustees for their generous award. I would also like to acknowledge the Donner Canadian Foundation which provided research funding at an earlier stage and Mark Zacher, Director of the UBC Institute of International Relations, who gave intellectual encouragement at every stage. Final revisions were made during April and May 1989 while I was a Visiting Fellow at the Centre of International Studies, London School of Economics and Political Science. I am grateful to Michael Leifer, the Director, for his hospitality during my stay in London. Steve Smith of the University of East Anglia, the managing editor of this series, and Michael Holdsworth of Cambridge University Press responded with good humour and encouragement when on several occasions the manuscript failed to arrive as promised.

Petula Muller and Nancy Mina contributed their cheerful expertise in navigating the manuscript through the high-tech world of computers and laser printers.

My greatest debt is to my wife Margie and daughter Jenny who overlooked my inattention to the practical aspects of our family life, not least the 1988 Canadian income tax returns, while I was preoccupied with writing and rewriting successive drafts. I dedicate this work to my wife with gratitude and affection.

Vancouver
June, 1989

INTRODUCTION

This book investigates the international normative framework that upholds sovereign statehood in the Third World. I call it 'negative sovereignty' and contrast it with the older structure of 'positive sovereignty' that emerged in Europe along with the modern state and was expressed by Western imperialism and colonialism. The new regime is an explicit repudiation of the old. I refer to the sovereign units supported by this framework as 'quasi-states' to call attention to the fact that they lack many of the marks and merits of empirical statehood postulated by positive sovereignty. I have sought answers to five primary questions: What is the *modus operandi* of the negative sovereignty regime? How did it come into existence historically? What are the consequences of negative sovereignty not only for international politics but also for the domestic conditions of quasi-states? What are the implications for international relations theory? Finally, what are the prospects for quasi-states?

It may be helpful at the outset to clarify my approach. First, I am concerned not with all aspects of Third World states or even most aspects but only with one: their sovereign aspect. I believe, however, that negative sovereignty is a crucial and overlooked institution which not only helps sustain many of these states but also impinges on human rights and socioeconomic development within them.

Third world states have been studied to date largely in terms of sociological or political economy approaches which emphasize underlying cultural or material circumstances rather than overarching moral and legal norms. The original image of 'The Third World' portrayed in Peter Worsley's well known book by that name was sociological.[1] The basic referent of the term ever since has been the underdeveloped countries of the non-Western world. One of these dominant approaches is modernization theory: Third World states understood in terms of 'tradition' and 'modernity' and the socioeconomic processes – such as technological innovation, industrialization, urbanization, literacy, education, and so forth – by which countries change from the

1

former condition to the latter. Another prevalent approach is under-development theory: Third World states seen as confined to a peripheral condition of neocolonial dependency by a Western dominated capitalist world economy which leaves them with very limited freedom to develop on their own. In international relations the latter image, with its emphasis on global class divisions, is sometimes referred to as 'structuralism' in contrast to the traditional state-centric or 'pluralist' image of the international system.[2] The structuralist image obviously would be less compelling if there were no underdeveloped states. Most of these states are very different sociologically from developed states and particularly those of the West and seem to require analytical orientations that take account of this.

Nowhere in these schemes is much attention given to international legitimacy and law, however. For Marxists this is a second order phenomenon denoted by the term 'superstructure' while for behaviouralists it is merely 'formal legality'. Structuralists see the primary forces of international relations in terms of underlying material conditions which transcend international boundaries. Behaviouralists usually consider formal rules and institutions of the state as secondary effects of cultural and social norms which are assumed to be fundamental in animating and shaping political life. Neither can say whether or not sovereignty is important because it is insignificant by definition and excluded from analysis by and large.

The term 'Third World' may not be entirely apt for dealing with quasi-states since it is often used to signify a globe divided vertically in terms of wealth and class rather than horizontally in terms of sovereign populated territory. It is also valued-loaded and ideological: it has usually been a positive term evoking the socioeconomic needs and claims of non-Western populations but it is becoming a negative term signifying corrupt and abusive elites that rule over them. This shift in connotation is a reflection of post-independence authoritarianism in many ex-colonial states which disappointed original expectations of democracy. And yet 'Third World' also usually denotes territorial jurisdictions which were formed under colonial rule and emerged into the light of day by an international legal transaction – decolonization – whereby sovereignty was transferred from European states to indigenous governments. Today these jurisdictions not only possess equal sovereignty under international law but also claim positive entitlements to external aid so that they may eventually become as developed as the states of the First World. We need a mode of analysis that calls our attention to the international normative and legal order which supports them.

2

Second, although 'sovereignty' is essentially a legal condition of states, this is not a legal study. However, I believe it is necessary to unite international law and politics to understand properly the subject of sovereign statehood. The state, after all, is constituted and operates by means of law in significant part. My emphasis is on the rules of the sovereignty regime but I take a general institutional approach. 'Rules' include not only international 'law' properly so-called but also principles, standards, conventions, practices and the like.[3] The analysis of rules is usually associated with jurisprudence and this book can be considered a study in international jurisprudence pertaining to the Third World. However, as indicated, it is jurisprudence from a political scientist's rather than a lawyer's viewpoint. Lawyers, as I understand them, seek knowledge of the rules that constitute particular legal orders and their validity. Academic international lawyers try to determine the authenticity, sources and elements of international law – as a glance at any good textbook reveals.[4] The main point is to establish with as much certainty as possible what the law is in particular domains in order to give instruction to the legal student or practitioner. For example, textbooks in public international law explicate the standing rules of international life which are current at the time and make professional judgements on their legal validity, as when Ian Brownlie opines that self-determination is now part of the *jus cogens* of the law of nations.[5]

Political scientists are interested in rules not to determine their current legal status but to ascertain the extent to which they shape political life. Knowledge of rules assists in explaining how and why political actors operate the way they do. Rules of conduct are prescriptive: they are laid down, acted on, invoked, applied, and so on.[6] For purposes of this discussion Dorothy Emmet's general definition of 'rule' can suffice: 'a directive that acts of a certain kind should or should not be done on certain kinds of occasion by a person, a certain kind of person, or anyone . . . To study human society is, then, to take account of conduct which is partly at least rule directed.'[7] The subject of this approach is 'not just regularities in conduct, but *regulated* conduct'.[8] The international system is a rule-based order at least in part. 'International society', the 'community of states', and the 'constitution of world politics' are expressions which attempt to capture this normative feature of international relations.

Institutions and the rules and offices of which they consist do not have the ontological status of natural facts: they are made and manipulated by men. Convention and nature are utterly different categories.[9] The modern state, as Jacob Burckhardt once put it, is 'a work of art'.[10]

3

Almost a century earlier Edmund Burke wrote: 'Commonwealths are not physical, but moral essences. They are artificial combinations and ... arbitrary productions of the human mind.'[11] Not only the familiar embodiment of statehood domestically – constitutions, legislatures, courts, elections, parties, bureaucracies, local government, and much else – but also the expression of sovereignty internationally – mutual recognition, diplomacy, international law, and the like – are works of political agents built up pragmatically and passed on historically.

Institutionalists consequently tend to view the relations of states as a sphere of volition rather than determination by social forces or natural laws. International relations is a study of initiatives, communications, responses, transactions, exchanges and similar decisions that must inevitably be not only instrumental but also moral because deciding means that it could have been otherwise. Decisionmakers are therefore responsible for their actions. The power or authority to make decisions is ordinarily denied to those who are not deemed to be capable of assuming responsibility. The world could therefore be other than it is and our actions and decisions are implicated in whatever it happens to be. There is no escape from responsibility although it falls more heavily on the shoulders of those with the greatest power and authority to shape events among whom statesmen are usually in the first rank. My approach, like that of Hedley Bull, is accordingly based on human will and not on structural-functional analysis, class analysis or any other methodology which discounts choices and their consequences or suggests that international relations somehow operate over the heads of statesmen.[12]

I find it useful to analyse the states-system by employing the metaphor 'game' which by definition is a rule-constituted and rule-governed activity.[13] In a game it is necessary to know at least the basic rules not only to play but also to be a spectator and figure out what is going on. Otherwise confusion results – as when Americans try to understand cricket in terms of baseball and Parliament in terms of Congress, or Britons attempt the reverse. This book is about a version of the sovereignty game that has been instituted since about 1960 primarily to incorporate a multitude of new and often very weak states into the international community. The rules of this novel game are significantly different from those which existed previously. And to understand this game in terms of the old rules can lead to misunderstanding. The expansion of international society throughout the Third World would have been impossible without also changing the rules of the old sovereignty game which justified overseas empire and made membership in the community of states contingent on capable and to some extent 'civilized' government – as defined by the West. I investigate the rules of this new sovereignty game: what they are, how they originated, how they work, why they exist, what their consequences have been both for international society and for the new states themselves, what they imply concerning international relations theory, and what their future might be.

My study is simply an attempt, following the lead of others, to think the new sovereignty regime through to some conclusions.[14] I try to make explicit the changing assumptions and beliefs about the right to sovereignty in the Third World and the international reasoning involved in decolonization, self-determination, human rights, and development. In many places this involves reflecting on institutions, laws, treaties, conferences, declarations, resolutions, and so forth which embody this right in international relations. The study discloses an image of Third World states as consisting not of self-standing structures with domestic foundations – like separate buildings – but of territorial jurisdictions supported from above by international law and material aid – a kind of international safety net. In short, they often appear to be juridical more than empirical entities: hence quasi-states. The analysis also lends support to the institutionalist argument that rules and laws – including international law – can have substantial independent effects on political life some of which may be contrary to what was originally expected.

Institutional practices or rules of the game always involve predilections which advantage some and disadvantage others. There is no such thing as completely impartial rules: in favouring certain plays rules tend to invite certain kinds of players. It is not only the case that institutions are as good or as bad as those who operate them but also that they tend to encourage certain operators and operations. Institutions always involve what E. E. Schattschneider refers to as 'the mobilization of bias'.[15] If we accept and validate them we also must accept the biases they contain. In the case of the negative sovereignty game this bias, not surprisingly, usually works in favour of sovereigns and against their citizens. Perhaps surprisingly it also sometimes works in favour of Third World sovereigns and against their First and Second World counterparts.

Since this book focuses on the normative presuppositions underlying the negative sovereignty game it could be considered an enquiry into the political theory of international relations.[16] This raises a third point concerning my approach which is one of philosophical 'idealism' as exemplified particularly by the work of R. G. Collingwood and Michael Oakeshott. (The rather different international relations meaning of the word is considered below.) Without digressing into their philosophies perhaps it will suffice to say that the emphasis accordingly is on moral and legal ideas involved in the existence and relations of sovereign states. International equality, self-determination, non-discrimination, anti-colonialism, international aid, human rights, among others are instances of ideas entangled in the negative sovereignty regime: they are 'operative ideals', to use A. D. Lindsay's term, which indicate how international relations ought to be conducted in the late twentieth century.[17] Insofar as they have been institutionalized they are also facts which disclose how those relations are conducted.

The philosophical point of idealism is that ideas (or thoughts) and realities (or facts) are not separate categories but form a single whole.[18] There may be a physical reality but there is no political reality independent of human thought and action. Collingwood expresses this in terms of a distinction between history and science (or nature): 'the activity by which man builds his own constantly changing historical world is a free activity. There are no forces other than this activity which control it or modify it or compel it to behave in this way or in that, to build one kind of world rather than another.' He hastens to add that this does not of course mean that man is 'free to do what he pleases' for he is always constrained by the situation which consists of other men and their ideas which may or may not be in harmony with his own.[19] In other words, complete freedom or complete restraint are rarely if ever encountered in human conduct.

Statesmen are free within the situation they find themselves which consists externally of other states and internally of their subjects. This obviously is a circumstance of constrained choice, with the constraints varying from one time or place to the next from the nearly hegemonous position of the superpower to the almost confined situation of the micro-state. Sovereign statehood itself constitutes both constraints and opportunities. The *grundnorm* of such a political arrangement is the basic prohibition against foreign intervention which simultaneously imposes a duty of forbearance and confers a right of independence on all statesmen. Since states are profoundly unequal in power the rule is obviously far more constraining for powerful states and far more liberating for weak states. It can be and from time to time has been violated, of course, which is indicative of a volitional and not a deterministic world. The essentially normative character of nonintervention and indeed all constitutive rules of sovereign statehood is indicated by a vocabulary which typically includes such words as 'must', 'should', 'ought', 'permitted', 'prohibited', 'entitled', 'obligated', and so forth. This is the prescriptive vocabulary of freedom and

6

responsibility of which sovereign statehood is a particularly important manifestation.

Political institutions can nevertheless have a life of their own seemingly independent of the human agents who invent or operate them. One can speak intelligibly of constitutional 'fate' implying that once a certain arrangement of rules is institutionalized certain circumstances of choice are destined to follow. Some things are possible; others are ruled out. The structure of choice may seem inevitable. This most definitely is the case with sovereign statehood which is now so ingrained in the public life of humankind and imprinted in the minds of people that it seems like a natural phenomenon beyond the control of statesmen or anybody else. When schoolchildren are repeatedly shown a political map of the world which represents the particular locations of named states in different continents and oceans they can easily end up regarding such entities in the same light as the physical features such as rivers or mountain ranges which sometimes delimit their international boundaries. It is nevertheless the case that not only the map itself but also the sovereign jurisdictions it represents are a totally artificial political arrangement which could be altered or even abolished. An historical atlas indicates the actual changes which have taken place over the centuries as a result of wars, peace treaties, negotiations, arbitrations, and other international relations and if it goes back far enough it reveals a world which is no longer structured in terms of sovereign statehood. Far from being natural entities, modern sovereign states are entirely historical artifacts the oldest of which have been in existence in their present shape and alignment only for the past three or four centuries. Prior to that time human populations in Europe where the modern state was invented and elsewhere organized themselves politically along rather different institutional lines: mostly in terms of empire and suzerainty.

'Idealism' does not mean that the analyst is in any way 'idealistic' or attempting to read *his* values into a subject. An 'idealist' in this philosophical meaning is not the naive opposite of a hard headed 'realist' in the usual international relations meaning of the term. Philosophical 'idealism' does not preclude 'realism' in international studies which consists in the idea that power, interests, prudence, and other instrumental considerations shape world politics. But an international relations realist who is a philosophical idealist is one who rejects any notion of states and their interactions as independent of human wills and desires: the international system conceived as a mechanism like the solar system. Things can go wrong, of course, since human actions and particularly politics often have unintended consequences. But this

7

is not the same as natural laws which operate above or beneath human consciousness. Hans J. Morgenthau is a good example of a realist who conceives of international relations in philosophically idealist terms as the instrumental calculations and miscalculations of statesmen: what he calls 'power politics'.[20] The human world is composed significantly of ideas and the world of states is no exception. We cannot meaningfully study international relations without investigating the operative ideals which give shape to them whether intentionally or inadvertantly. The negative sovereignty regime is a basic change of mind about how the international system ought to operate and the institutionalization of that idea.

A fourth point concerns the study of international relations specifically. This is not an analysis of the national interests or foreign policies of new states. Nor is it an account of their international alliances – what Robert Mortimer aptly terms the 'Third World coalition'.[21] Neither is it a study of Third World diplomacy, although 'the dialogue between states' – as Adam Watson puts it – does figure in the new sovereignty game insofar as it is an established institution of international society.[22] Such studies, however, do not deal generally with the constitution of international society or specifically with sovereignty. Lastly, it is not primarily a work of international history, although chapters 3 and 4 survey the sovereignty regimes of the modern era and the emergence of negative sovereignty during the episode of decolonization.

As indicated, this is basically a study in international political theory following the example of Martin Wight and others who focus in various ways on the 'society' of states and conceive of international relations as therefore involving not only power and agency but also rules, institutions, norms, practices, and the like. I explore in chapter 7 the presuppositions of ex-colonial states to see how far they conform to the predominant paradigms of international relations theory, namely 'realism' or power politics and 'rationalism' or international legitimacy and law.[23] 'Realism' signifies the idea that states are human agencies which interact not in respect to international law or other norms but solely or at least primarily out of regard for their national interests – reason of state. In classical realism states or rather statesmen are postulated as instrumental agents with wills and powers of their own and their relations are understood very considerably if not entirely in terms of power and the balance of power.

According to classical 'rationalism', however, statesmen are authorities who possess noninstrumental rights and duties either by natural law or by international custom and contract – positive law – or both.

They create international society rather like individuals contract civil society and therefore resemble citizens or any other 'right-and-duty bearing unit', as F. W. Maitland once put it.[24] They are subjects of international law. Rationalists generally believe that citizenship in the states-system is a good thing by and large because it contributes to international order and civilization. A rights-based and law-governed system of international relations is preferable to one grounded only in national interest and the balance of power because it adds moral and legal restraints to that of prudence. It therefore helps to preserve and protect the populations of states and their civil and socioeconomic goods which are the ultimate values served by international society if not the most immediate ones.

Although realism and rationalism place their emphasis on categorically different devices of international regulation they both postulate the state as an inherently liveable and therefore valuable place. A 'realistic rationalist' is one who recognizes that such values are the ultimate justification of statehood and must be protected by every means possible including both arms and norms. The postulated inherent value of statehood has always been challenged by reality, of course. Political goods are a standard of appraisal and statesmen have always fallen short of these standards in their actual behaviour. However, the gap between standards and conduct probably has never been any greater than it is today. We live in a world in which the concrete benefits of sovereign statehood for the people involved are highly unequal from one country or region to the next. Decolonization has added significantly to this inequality by bringing into existence a large number of sovereign governments which are limited in their capacity or desire to provide civil and socioeconomic goods for their populations. They are supported by international society like all others, however. The actual outcome in such cases is therefore a reversal of the postulated traditional relationship noted above whereby international relations serves the ultimate purpose of protecting the political goods of sovereign states. This argument is made at some length in the chapters which follow.

This raises a fifth and more difficult point concerning value judgements. There is no escaping values because they are embedded in the very fabric of political life, both domestic and international. The community of states itself embodies certain values which an analysis such as this cannot and should not avoid although it need not subscribe to them and probably should take a sceptical view of them. The cardinal value is of course independence which is the foundation on which the entire scheme rests. Virtually all the principles and practices of a

9

sovereign states-system derive either directly or indirectly from this desideratum. The logic of such a system is the international expression of liberalism: sovereign states are the equivalent of free individuals. One can recognize this without being a liberal, however. Insofar as both the costs and the benefits of independence are examined, my analysis, if anything, might be considered a critique of international liberalism. However, this is not the hidden agenda. It is simply where the argument has led me.

Since independent statehood is revealed as a mixed blessing in the following chapters it might be inferred that colonialism or paternalism are the underlying value premises of the study. Although this is not the case a word of explanation is probably necessary. The argument is not that independence is bad or that colonialism is good which is the reversal of the usual value orientation today and would merely be reverting to the value orientations of yesterday. Rather, it is that independence in itself is neither good nor bad: there are no categorical goods in international relations or indeed in any other spheres of political life. Whether a particular rule or institution or practice or policy is of value or not always depends on circumstances. To believe otherwise is to surrender to dogma. Unfortunately, the uncritical and widespread faith in self-determination or equal sovereignty today often has this character.

Third World sovereignty is a delicate subject to investigate because it raises difficult and indeed troubling questions which touch on some of the major taboo subjects of our time involving culture, poverty, and race. The Third World has recently emerged from an extended period of Western imperial domination and it may seem unfair or at least premature to raise questions about the advantages and disadvantages of independence for the people involved. One such question is whether all countries stand to benefit more or less equally from independence and if not whether other institutions – such as associate statehood – would for some be more beneficial in their circumstances? Another is how far the sufferings of some citizenries are the responsibility of their rulers? A third is whether all sovereign governments are subject to the same standards of human rights? What we have today and have had for the past three or four decades is the ascendancy of a doctrine that the current arrangement and distribution of sovereign statehood if it is not yet good for everybody everywhere will eventually prove to be if those developed states who are in a position to make it possible act responsibly. The main focus should therefore be on their conduct. Third World governments being less powerful and experienced and so often finding themselves in a disadvantaged position *vis-à-vis* developed countries should not be subjected to the same probing kind of analysis and criticism which academics routinely direct at First or Second World governments. The prohibition usually derives from such doctrines as cultural relativism, socioeconomic determinism, or antiracism.

However, there is no overruling reason why such issues should not be studied. To exempt the conduct of certain governments (or individuals) from scrutiny solely on the *a priori* grounds of their different culture or material conditions or race is to acquiesce in a form of prejudice. Such considerations are important and they may justify or excuse the conduct of certain governments or other agents. And one cannot but agree that greater power always carries with it increased responsibilities. But recognizing that there may be extenuating circumstances such as poverty which limit responsibility is entirely different from deciding beforehand that such conditions demand that the subject should not be investigated. This is to decide on ideological rather than empirical grounds and it amounts to evasion or avoidance of questions which may be difficult to handle nowadays but are crucially important nevertheless if we wish to understand the nature of the contemporary international system.

In raising this issue explicitly my normative focus of concern is the citizenries of many Third World states whose adverse circumstances are well known but often attributed to almost anything except the actions and omissions of their own governments and the sovereign states-sytem which legitimates and supports them. Some way of giving these citizenries a voice above and beyond that of their rulers is urgently needed and I hope this monograph can make a small contribution to that end. This is my agenda.

This brings me to a final issue which concerns terminology. The adjectives 'negative' and 'positive' do not signify 'bad' and 'good'. They simply denote rights of nonintervention (freedom from) and capabilities to act or to deter (freedom to) which are analytical and not evaluative usage consistent with contemporary political theory.[25] To be free from the interventions of others is not at all the same as being in a position to deter such interventions or to engage in them. These two types of liberty are categorically different. Not only that: in international relations historically both freedoms tend to be possessed by most states. However, they have become separated as a result of decolonization: quasi-states possess negative sovereignty by definition but usually rather limited positive freedom. This has created a novel set of international relations problems and predicaments as I attempt to indicate in various chapters which follow.

11

The argument takes the form of connected essays which seek to uncover different facets of the divorce of positive and negative sovereignty in international relations. Chapters 1 and 2 explicate the character of quasi-states and the *modus operandi* of the negative sovereignty game. The two chapters which follow outline the historical background of positive and negative sovereignty and the emergence of quasi-states as a consequence of particular ideas about self-determination involved in decolonization. Chapters 5 and 6 investigate the consequences of negative sovereignty for the socioeconomic and civil conditions of certain Third World states. Chapter 7 considers the implications of negative sovereignty for the theory of international relations. The conclusion offers some final thoughts on the future of quasi-states. I hope the argument is written in a style which is sufficiently plain to enable the reader to agree or disagree, or agree in part, as the case may be. If it provokes controversy I should consider it a success.

1 STATES AND QUASI-STATES

PROLOGUE

Let us begin with a brief imaginary journey in our time machine and interview a man in the street in 1936. Suppose he is an Englishman and it is Lower Regent Street, London, in the heart of the British Empire. As it happens, he is a career civil servant in a senior position at the Colonial Office. We introduce ourselves as historians from the late twentieth century and ask for an interview. Fortunately, he is used to eccentrics and immediately agrees.

The conversation comes round to the British Empire. He enquires how it is doing. We say it no longer exists. Obviously taken aback, he asks what happened to it. We reply that it was wound down in the fifties and sixties. He evidently has some difficulty believing this and asks what became of the numerous colonies in Asia, Africa, and Oceania? We tell him that colonialism came into disrepute during and after a second world war against Germany and Japan from which the United States and the Soviet Union emerged as rival superpowers. Britain's colonies and also those of France, Holland, Belgium, Portugal, and all other overseas imperial powers had subsequently become independent states.

He asks how it was possible to decolonize so soon throughout the world? We reply that it was relatively easy: by transferring sovereignty to indigenous politicians. He persists in wanting to know how independence could be granted to so many different colonial peoples at various stages of development. How did they so quickly become conversant with the language, institutions, and techniques of modern self-government? Were they prepared for the transfer of power? Some were, we reply, and some were not. It did not matter, however, because they all acquired the right of self-determination which is now universally recognized by international law. Sovereignty could no longer be withheld on the grounds that indigenous politicians were not yet sufficiently experienced in modern statecraft or the colonial

13

populations were not adequately prepared and equipped for independent citizenship or, indeed, on any other traditional empirical grounds. Their right of self-determination was considered absolute and the former right of Europeans to rule them was completely abandoned – except by the white South Africans. We point out that they had become a pariah state with world opinion totally aligned against them.

He cannot believe that the far-flung British Empire, consisting in the mid-thirties of some forty colonies on several continents at various stages of political and economic development, could have been dismantled as rapidly and uniformly as we claim. He could foresee a sovereign India – it had been on the verge of acquiring independence since the twenties. Perhaps Ceylon (Sri Lanka) might be independent, although he thought it would be vulnerable to Indian imperialism if it were to lose its British status. Conceivably more of the League Mandates in the Middle East could be self-governing, as was already the case with Iraq. He suspected they would be just as unstable, however. And he could see how constitutionally more advanced crown colonies such as the Gold Coast (Ghana) might possibly be brought to effective self-government in a somewhat shorter time than anticipated – although he rather doubted it. But the independence of the numerous disparate British dependencies scattered across Asia, Africa, and Oceania – that was inconceivable.

How were the formidable obstacles of political and economic backwardness overcome so quickly? Were all colonies developed to the point of being capable of self-government? We pointed out that colonies were not raised up before independence, at least not to some common international standard. Instead, the legal requirement that they be developed to this point was abandoned. Although their post-independence records have of course varied and there have been some remarkable success stories, particularly in Asia, in general living conditions have been less satisfactory than was originally expected at the time of decolonization. In many former colonies, particularly those of Sub-Saharan Africa, living conditions have significantly deteriorated since decolonization amidst recurrent civil strife, political corruption and economic mismanagement compounded by various external factors such as declining commodity prices and rising interest rates.

That every colony could be granted independence at more or less the same time regardless of domestic conditions – if that is what we are saying – goes against everything the Colonial Office believes concerning the distinctiveness of individual dependencies and the enormous variations in development between them. It defies major assumptions

14

of imperial theory and international law concerning the necessity of dependency status to ensure good government in those numerous parts of the world which are not ready for self-government. Why just the other day Margery Perham – 'that meddling Oxford Donna' – in one of her pontificating essays in *The Times* called for indirect rule and the gradual development of local government as the only reasonable path to progress in Africa. Even her well known 'internationalism' does not extend beyond the League of Nations idea of 'trusteeship' which she thinks ought to be the mainspring of British colonial policy.[1] Do we really expect him to believe that all this changed? It would be nothing less than a revolution. Nevertheless, we insisted it has occurred.

The sudden change was possible, we thought, because it was essentially normative. It was not a case of developing the colonies to the point of satisfying classical positive criteria of sovereign self-government. Under the strong and increasing pressure of international egalitarianism this requirement was abandoned and every colony almost without exception sooner or later was granted independence by the colonial powers. They were generally recognized by the international community and became members of the United Nations – the successor to the League. There were now some 160 members of that body as compared to about 50 when it was founded in 1945. Most of the increased membership consists of former European colonies. There was even a significant number of 'micro-states' – mostly small islands, such as Fiji or the Seychelles. Even the tiny former British riverine territory in West Africa still known as The Gambia was now independent. The Gambia? He evidently has some difficulty imagining such a world.

What was behind this revolutionary international change? This question continues to be debated by historians. There is no definitive answer and we could only offer a few conjectures. The war certainly was a major cause, particularly its reduction of the military power of Britain and France. But we thought the thesis should not be carried too far. The power of Western Europe was still very great. Indeed, since the war the countries of this region not only formed a major military alliance with the United States against the Soviet Union but also achieved a significant measure of economic community among themselves which gave them joint economic weight greater than that of any other world region. Three of its members including Britain and France were still among the five leading capitalist powers of the world.

The new postwar rivalry between the United States and the Soviet Union which came to be known as the 'cold war' was a significant

15

background factor that affected the capacity of the colonial powers to maintain their empires. The international environment was receptive to anti-colonial ideologies which were reinforced by domestic ideologies promoting enfranchisement of racial and ethnic minorities in Western states. Self-determination, perhaps the leading idea involved, was institutionalized as a primary international value in the Charter of the UN. And it was in that world body, particularly its General Assembly, that the doctrine was not only voiced but also incorporated into various Declarations and Resolutions which acquired moral and legal force. The European colonial powers were unable to sustain widespread belief in the legitimacy of colonialism. Rather than endure perpetual and growing international criticism, they began to decolonize. The more they decolonized, of course, the greater was the number of new states which vociferously opposed colonialism until eventually, for all intents and purposes, it disappeared. By 1960 virtually total decolonization was inevitable. By 1980 it was essentially complete.

Although the causes of this change continue to be debated this cannot alter the fact that it has occurred and that the world today is more or less as we describe it: without any significant formal overseas empires. We talked about this transformation for a while. He eventually tired of the joke, however, and politely broke off the conversation with the excuse that he must return to his office. Evidently a former Governor of Nigeria – somebody by the name of Sir Donald Cameron – was giving a briefing that afternoon on the continuing virtues of indirect rule as a vehicle of political development in British colonies.[2]

INTERNATIONAL CONSTITUTIONAL CHANGE

The difficulties in this imaginary dialogue derive from divergent and even contradictory ideas and expectations concerning the relations of Britain (and of Europe more generally) to the non-Western parts of the world. Our colonial official has a conception based on the international system of his time and of the previous half century and more. The prewar framework of international law and legitimacy drew a sharp distinction between Europeans or people of European descent and non-Europeans: only the former were unquestionably entitled to sovereign statehood. The latter were assumed not to be qualified at least *prima facie*, and the burden of proof was on them to justify it in terms of standards defined by Western civilization. The postwar framework draws no such distinction and assumes the opposite: that all colonial peoples are entitled to be independent regardless of their culture, race, wealth, geography, or any similar criterion. Today the

16

difficulties of perception are the reverse: we find it hard to imagine a world in which extensive territories and populations outside the West are dependencies and subjects of Western imperial powers. Indeed, it is difficult not only to imagine but also to accept. The difference of international outlook between our generation and that of our grand-parents is fundamental.

In the mid-1930s vast regions in Asia, Africa, and Oceania were still part of the domestic jurisdictions of certain Western states which had established formal empires over these areas.[3] Consequently, in addition to formally equal relations between sovereign states there were also formally unequal relations between metropolitan powers and their various colonies, protectorates, and mandated or trust terri-tories overseas. Imperial relations therefore were external but not yet international. The British Empire by international law was a single state but in political and economic fact it was a far flung assortment of colonial dependencies at different stages of development with varying degrees of local autonomy under a single metropolitan authority: the Westminster parliament. This arrangement was widely regarded as legitimate and even natural in view of the enormous distances which separated European and non-European peoples – not only geographi-cal distances but also economic, political, cultural, technological, scien-tific, and even emotional and psychological.

In the decades since 1945 the international world has been formally levelled into one and only one constitutional category: sovereign states. No Western government now possesses domestic jurisdiction over extensive populated territories overseas. Virtually every note-worthy dependency and most of those which are not even noteworthy have become sovereign states with membership in the United Nations and the right to engage in international relations on a basis of equality with all other states including their former colonial masters. The con-stitutional levelling that occurred within Western domestic societies has also taken place internationally and for most of the same reasons which have to do with the doctrine of equal rights and equal dignity of all mankind. Alien rule is now not only unjustifiable but unthinkable – especially if it involves racial differences between rulers and ruled and the rulers are white. Hence the illegitimacy of South Africa. The crucial principle of the contemporary international constitution as it applies to formerly dependent areas of the world is universal and categorical self-determination of the indigenous people. To be a sovereign state today one needs only to have been a formal colony yesterday. All other considerations are irrelevant. Even the size of the colony either in population or in territory is not a criterion, as numerous micro-states

17

indicate. All that is required is the evident desire of the population to be independent. I say 'evident' because it is usually attributed to a population rather than expressed by them, as in a referendum.

The termination of formal international hierarchy has not brought an end to international differentiation or stratification, however. On the contrary, we draw many distinctions between independent countries which are reflected by the various adjectives used to describe sovereign states today. They are not legal differences, however. The globe is usually seen as divided in two fundamentally different ways: first there is the East–West conflict defined by the nuclear balance of power behind which shelter rival ideologies and ways of life. It is at the moment undergoing fundamental reappraisal on both sides owing to political and economic reforms in the Soviet bloc and will become far less significant if the parties can agree to reduce their arms and increase their reciprocity in other ways. However, this division is only the most recent manifestation of the balance of power which has always divided powerful states. Very possibly some similar division will take its place, perhaps based more on economic, technological, and scientific rivalry than military.

Today in addition however there is a North–South gap between states disclosed by profoundly unequal standards of living which cannot be altered fundamentally by international agreements and diplomacy. This division is likely to persist indefinitely regardless of international decisions to the contrary because it is rooted in deep-seated cultural, material, and even psychological conditions of sovereign states. If these domestic conditions are to be changed it will very likely be only by the efforts of governments supported by citizens and sustained over long periods. New words have been coined to differentiate countries in these terms. The ex-colonies initially became known as the 'new' or 'emergent' states of Asia, Africa, and Oceania. Together with some Latin American countries they now constitute a 'Third World' of impoverished states in contrast to a 'First World' of the Western industrial democracies. Whereas before the second world war most states were more or less 'developed' and the terminology was not used to differentiate states, the characterization of countries as 'less developed', 'developing', and 'developed' is now universal.

Distinctions between more and less 'developed' states have been refined and elaborated by a global statistical enterprise organized to measure and report on the comparative performance of countries. International society has acquired a capacity for data gathering and analysis which was almost nonexistent before the second world war. A case in point is the World Bank which publishes annual *World Development Reports* that contain aggregate socioeconomic statistics and analysis on almost all the countries of the world. They are compared in terms of population, GNP per capita, inflation, life expectancy, growth of production, external debt, industry, agriculture, food, health, nutrition, and various other socioeconomic indicators. The result is a ranking of sovereign states according to the following categories: low-income, lower middle-income, upper middle-income, high-income oil exporters, industrial market economies, and nonreporting states (some Soviet bloc countries). These reports amount to world league tables which reveal a range of living conditions and capabilities among states that is enormous. The reference group in relation to which these categories are defined and all countries evaluated is the 'developed' states. This suggests strongly that the unit of socioeconomic analysis today is the sovereign state and the standard of evaluation is the comparatively high level of performance achieved by Western industrialized countries including Japan.

Informal distinctions between states are also drawn today in terms of civil conditions. There has been in recent decades a remarkable increase of international awareness, concern and action regarding human rights. Since the Universal Declaration of Human Rights in 1948 international humanitarianism has been promoted by various international bodies with the result that legal instruments and remedies for protecting human rights are now available which never existed previously. Although they are gravely inadequate in a world of sovereign states, their existence nevertheless reveals explicit standards of domestic state conduct which half a century ago were largely and erroneously taken for granted among Western states and presumed not yet attainable by most non-Western peoples. In addition, countless international humanitarian organizations exist today that never existed previously, perhaps exemplified best by Amnesty International. Rather like the World Bank reports but without the same blessing of statesmen and looking at different data of human well-being the annual reports of Amnesty International are a record of the human rights performance of virtually all of the contemporary states of the world. They also disclose a wide divergence in the performance of sovereign governments from one extreme where the highest standards of human rights protection achieved to date are regularly enforced to the opposite pole where they are routinely neglected or violated. The unit of analysis is again the sovereign state and the standard of evaluation is the comparatively high level of human rights protection accomplished by the Western democracies. Consequently, although

19

formal hierarchy between states has been abolished informal ranking of a very significant kind has been greatly expanded.

Without overlooking for a moment significant improvements in the socioeconomic and civil conditions of many non-Western populations since decolonization I believe it is plausible to argue that the international change briefly outlined above is primarily juridical. Some non-Western states have developed very substantially and rapidly, of course, including in particular the Newly Industrializing Countries (NICs) of Asia and the oil producing countries. And some Latin American states are becoming economically significant in global terms. Developmental breakthroughs are occurring and will undoubtedly continue to occur. The global fulcrum of economic power has begun to move away from its historical centres in Western Europe and North America which are facing increased competition from these regions. The North consequently is no longer an exclusively European or even white club and in the future it will undoubtedly become far more multiracial and multicultural than it is today. Our children will not automatically equate economic, technological, and scientific advance with European civilization as our parents did. Although it is perhaps less evident, civil and political rights are also discernible where they were not in evidence previously: authoritarianism has been brought to an end on the Mediterranean periphery of Western Europe and democratic reforms are being initiated in Eastern Europe and the Soviet Union. Democracy and human rights have been demanded in China recently and democratic elections were held in South Korea and Pakistan. Democratic government has been evident for some time in other Asian countries, most notably in India – although political violence has by no means been eliminated. Democratization has also made headway in some Latin American countries even though human rights have been under threat in that region. Humanitarian awareness is increasing around the world today and similar developments cannot therefore be ruled out in other places.

Yet, if the statistics of the World Bank and Amnesty International are anything to go by (and they are basically what we have to go by) a global faultline still runs along approximately the same frontier which formerly separated sovereign states and colonies. The world is divided between a minority of states whose populations enjoy comparatively high living standards (which are increasing), and a majority whose inhabitants subsist at far lower levels which in some cases are little changed from colonial times and may even have declined. The number of states among the developed and developing minority is expanding but the number of people within the underdeveloped majority where birthrates are generally far higher is also increasing. The gap is civil as well as material: indeed, authoritarian governments which threaten or violate human rights are probably as numerous as underdeveloped countries. In one respect everything has changed: there are no longer any significant dependencies in the world but only equal sovereign states. In another respect, however, there has been far less change: the world's population remains divided along more or less the same North–South lines as previously. What has basically changed therefore are the international rules of the game concerning the obligation to be a colony and the right to be a sovereign state. The moral assumptions behind these rules have also changed in the direction of international equality and democracy.

STATES AND QUASI-STATES

The ex-colonial states have been internationally enfranchised and possess the same external rights and responsibilities as all other sovereign states: juridical statehood. At the same time, however, many have not yet been authorized and empowered domestically and consequently lack the institutional features of sovereign states as also defined by classical international law. They disclose limited empirical statehood: their populations do not enjoy many of the advantages traditionally associated with independent statehood. Their governments are often deficient in the political will, institutional authority, and organized power to protect human rights or provide socioeconomic welfare. The concrete benefits which have historically justified the undeniable burdens of sovereign statehood are often limited to fairly narrow elites and not yet extended to the citizenry at large whose lives may be scarcely improved by independence or even adversely affected by it. These states are primarily juridical. They are still far from complete, so to speak, and empirical statehood in large measure still remains to be built. I therefore refer to them as 'quasi-states'.

International society can enfranchise states which usually requires general recognition of a government's independence. But international society cannot empower states to anything like the same extent since this for the most part involves internal relationships. State-building is primarily a domestic process occurring over a long period of time that can only be brought about by the combined wills, efforts, and responsibilities of governments and populations. The community of states at most can only assist or hinder it. Nevertheless, as we will see, one of the defining characteristics of quasi-states is the undertaking of contemporary international society to promote their

21

development – or at least to compensate them for their current condition of underdevelopment rather like poor citizens in welfare states.

This difference between states and quasi-states has been noted by others. Colonies were granted 'independence' without necessarily possessing 'freedom' – to borrow a useful distinction from John Plamenatz.[4] He explains it as follows:

> The colonies now claiming independence are not societies of the same kind as the thirteen colonies which signed the Declaration of Independence in 1776 . . . If capacity for freedom is our test, the thirteen revolted colonies . . . were fit for self-government; or at least not less fit than the country they rebelled against. It is by no means clear that the colonies now clamouring for independence are all fit for self-government in the same way.[5]

It is clearer today than it was in 1960 – when these remarks were published – that numerous emergent states did not, and many still do not, disclose substantial and credible statehood by the empirical criteria of classical positive international law.[6] Their lack of freedom has not been a barrier to their independence, however. Quasi-states enjoy equal sovereignty, as Hedley Bull and Adam Watson point out, but they lack established institutions capable of constraining and outlasting the individuals who occupy their offices: 'still less do they reflect respect for constitutions or acceptance of the rule of law'.[7] This means that the real benefits of independence which is what freedom amounts to have not yet arrived for most of their citizens.

Since the concept of 'quasi-state' is crucial to this study it is important to be as clear as possible about its meaning to avoid misunderstanding. My argument is not that the empirical characteristics of quasi-states are new. On the contrary, some states have always been less substantial and capable than others. History offers many examples of large or strong states and small or weak states and indeed of ramshackle or derelict states both inside Europe and outside. Prior to German and Italian unification in the nineteenth century there was still a considerable number of what one historian refers to as 'pygmy' states in Europe.[8] There were also dilapidated and splintering empires under self-indulgent dynasties, such as the Habsburgs and Ottomans. And many states outside Europe were easy prey for expanding European imperialism. There is no shortage of examples. The history of the modern state is in no small part a history of rulers who are illegitimate, governments that are disorganized or incompetent, and subjects who are indifferent, isolated, alienated, cowed, or in rebellion. Furthermore, although there is undoubtedly greater substantial inequality between sovereign states today than ever before it is not international inequality *per se* that is new. Inequality between states is a persistent feature of international relations as Robert Tucker points out in an important essay on the subject.[9] In the past, however, small and weak states had to survive as best they could by their own efforts and those of whatever allies they were able to enlist in their support. Some survived, some succumbed. International history is in large measure the story of this struggle. This is the traditional reality of the states-system as a *power* or balance of power system which continues to define the dominant theory of international relations: 'realism'. Hans J. Morgenthau's theory of 'power politics' or Martin Wight's definition of classical international theory as 'the theory of survival' are well known responses to this historical reality.[10]

What has changed is not the empirical conditions of states but the international rules and institutions concerning those conditions. Briefly, the freedom or positive sovereignty of states expressed by the traditional balance of power system has been interfered with and subjected to new normative regulations: weak, marginal, or insubstantial states are now exempted from the power contest at least in part and treated as international protectorates. This is clearer in the case of military rivalry but new international economic regulations also differentiate between states and quasi-states today. The weakness or backwardness of countries is no longer a justification for conquest or colonialism. Nor is it a justification for international support of anti-government rebels in derelict Asian or African states – unlike nineteenth-century Europe, for example, where the 'spectacle' of a 'ramshackle' Austro-Hungarian Empire 'which denied freedom to its subject peoples' provided grounds for foreign intervention in the eyes of John Stuart Mill and other liberals.[11] International development assistance is usually advocated sometimes coupled with demands for human rights protection but sovereignty is not interfered with or even questioned.

Therefore, it is not empirical differences and variations among states that is novel – although these are probably greater today than ever before owing to the globalization of international society. Rather, it is the way that inequality and underdevelopment is conceived, evaluated, and responded to by international society that has changed. Ramshackle states today are not open invitations for unsolicited external intervention. They are not allowed to disappear juridically – even if for all intents and purposes they have already fallen or been pulled down in fact. They cannot be deprived of sovereignty as a result of war, conquest, partition, or colonialism such as frequently happened in the past. The juridical cart is now before the empirical

23

horse. This is entirely new. The result is a rather different sovereignty regime with an insurance policy for marginal states. In short, quasi-states are creatures and their elites are beneficiaries of non-competitive international norms. It is this which is new and indeed unprecedented in the long history of the sovereign states-system.

Instead of being a threat to sovereignty and perhaps even statehood, political weakness and economic underdevelopment are now considered reasons for exemption from the more strenuous classical international competition between states. They are also valid grounds for positive assistance from international society. What is different, therefore, is the existence of an international society that has presided over the birth of numerous marginal entities, guarantees their survival, and seeks at least to compensate them for underdevelopment if not to develop them into substantial independent countries. Before the present century there was no special international regime that catered for small or weak states. All sovereign states today including some which are far more chaotic than the Austro-Hungarian or Ottoman Empires ever were – such as Chad or Lebanon – enjoy an unqualified right to exist and high prospects for survival despite their domestic disorganization and illegitimacy. This categorical right derives from new international norms such as anti-colonialism, ex-colonial self-determination, and racial sovereignty underwritten by egalitarian and democratic values which like so much else have their origins in Western social and political movements.

Consequently, for some states today there is an entirely different *constitutional* mechanism which has largely displaced the military or diplomatic security arrangements of the past. Ex-colonial self-determination has led to a new kind of territorial legitimacy and the freezing of the political map in much of the Third World. The rules of sovereign statehood have changed in the direction of far greater international toleration and accommodation of marginal governments than has been the case since the emergence of Western-dominated universal international society in the mid nineteenth century.[12] Whereas in the past such entities were usually dominated by effective states and often demoted to an inferior international status as political dependencies and barred from the club of sovereign states, today they are admitted as equal members. Their admission has brought into existence a community of states of unprecedented diversity of membership, from the leading military and economic powers at one extreme to a lengthening list of specks on the map at the other, and assorted regimes of greater or lesser substance and credibility in between. Never have disparities between the outward forms and the inward substance of sovereign states been any greater than they are today. This has changed the character of the sovereignty game fundamentally and irrevocably, as I argue in the next chapter.

Quasi-states and their external support structures reflect a novel doctrine of negative sovereignty which was fashioned expressly for the independence of the Third World. This regime was instituted because it was the only way numerous underdeveloped colonies could rapidly be made independent. If balance of power and self-help criteria of classical positive international law had been retained in the determination of new statehood, fewer countries would have gained independence and probably many would still be colonies today. Decolonization would have been postponed until empirical grounds for self-government and therefore authentic freedom had been achieved which in many cases would have taken a long time. In some cases it would have been delayed indefinitely. However, this prospect was denied once colonialism became illegitimate in the decade and a half following 1945 when the community of states adopted the principle of self-determination as an unqualified human right of all colonial peoples. It became impossible to insist, as Plamenatz puts it, that some countries 'ought to be deprived of their independence in order to be made capable of freedom'.[13] The new doctrine justified the independence of every colony which desired it and thereby established a radically different basis of sovereign statehood on the ex-colonial peripheries of the world. It was now possible to possess juridical statehood while as yet disclosing little evidence of empirical statehood. It was also possible – as it never had been in the past – to make demands on international society for assistance to become developed and it was difficult to ignore such demands without denying the real problems and difficulties of the new members of an expanded community of states.

Quasi-states are therefore disclosed by a new positive international society which fostered the independence of such states and caters for their survival and development. If we imagine this superstructure in terms of arrows of assistance and support between states or between international organizations and states, many are pointed towards the Third World and away from the First World or from the UN and other international agencies involved in development. Materially the arrows represent bilateral and multilateral public aid flows, technical assistance, international borrowing at concessional rates of interest, debt relief, technology transfer, food aid, humanitarian relief, refugee assistance, and much else. In some important respects these efforts by the society of states are attempts to compensate for the differentiating

25

if not discriminating effects of international economics whose arrows are pointed in the opposite direction towards the developed and developing capitalist economies – just as domestic welfare states were constructed in part to compensate for the inequality effects of market economies. Normatively the arrows represent emergent standards of international morality and legality which underwrite the foregoing transactions and presuppose nonreciprocity between developed and underdeveloped countries. The latter are presumed not yet able to take equal advantage of traditional economic rules of the states-system such as free trade or free flowing international capital. Some of these new economic principles and practices are summed up in the novel conception of 'international development law'.[14] One can therefore conceive of quasi-states in part as a focus of struggle between traditional forces of competitive international economics and new post-colonial international society which is attempting to shore up marginal states deemed unable to compete successfully.

In short, quasi-states are creatures of changes in the rules of membership and modes of operation of international society which were deliberately made to replace the institutions of European overseas colonialism. The correct level of analysis for understanding these problematical entities consequently is not the state as such but the states-system and particularly its new accommodating norms. Hence the following chapters focus on the rules of the negative sovereignty game rather than the stratagems or tactics of its players. However, at a more fundamental level quasi-states reveal the same egalitarian and democratic values as other twentieth-century enfranchisement and liberation movements concerning disadvantaged class, racial, and ethnic minorities. A close parallel in time is the civil rights movement in the United States which has virtually identical moral imperatives and some comparable institutional features.[15] Quasi-states are therefore part of a more general process of self-determination which has affected domestic as well as international politics in the latter half of the twentieth century.

NEGATIVE SOVEREIGNTY AND POSITIVE SOVEREIGNTY

Embedded in the foregoing remarks is a concept of negative and positive sovereignty that shapes the analysis in the chapters which follow. It is derived from the cognate ideas of negative and positive liberty made famous by Isaiah Berlin.[16] Liberty is possessed by individuals, of course, whereas sovereignty is a property of states. In applying Berlin's distinction to international relations I make no claim that individuals are strictly analogous to states: the domestic analogy. On the contrary, the analogue is useful in disclosing differences as well as resemblances between individuals and states that raise special problems for international relations which do not exist in interpersonal relations.

Negative liberty is defined by Berlin as 'the area within which a man can act unobstructed by others'.[17] It affords individuals 'freedom from' interference and therefore presupposes individual self-determination. Under conditions of negative freedom one has immunities from others and is therefore 'at liberty'. There is a sphere of action which is one's own. 'Over himself, over his own body and mind, the individual is sovereign.' Interference with an individual's negative liberty ordinarily is justified – according to J. S. Mill – only if he harms or threatens to harm another. 'His own good, either physical or moral, is not a sufficient warrant'.[18] This presupposes that individuals are rational agents and can be held accountable for their actions – unless there are valid grounds such as insanity which override the principle. Mill believed in individual sovereignty not only for its own sake but for the utilitarian contribution that unfettered individuals could make to the greater good of all.

Negative sovereignty can also be defined as freedom from outside interference: a formal-legal condition.[19] Non-intervention and sovereignty in this meaning are basically two sides of the same coin. This is the central principle of the classical law of nations: the sphere of exclusive legal jurisdiction of states or international *laissez faire*. Negative sovereignty as regards quasi-states primarily involves decolonization: it is the distinctive liberty acquired by former colonies as a consequence of the international enfranchisement movement mentioned above. It is a formal-legal entitlement and therefore something which international society is capable of conferring. Negative sovereignty is the legal foundation upon which a society of independent and formally equal states fundamentally rests. One can therefore think of independence and nonintervention as the distinctive and reciprocal rights and duties of an international social contract between states. When it is held it is held absolutely in the sense that it is not dependent on any conditions other than the compact itself which does not require positive action but only observance and forbearance: the basic postulate of the classical liberal rule of law. It is the central principle of public international law and the main focus of international jurisprudence.

Negative sovereignty differs from negative liberty in important respects, however. It cannot presuppose the same satisfactions or benefits as negative liberty owing to fundamental differences between

27

states and individuals. Individuals are equipped to enjoy immunities simply by being or at least by being adult and not physically or mentally disabled. The sovereign individual is intrinsically and demonstrably valuable. Populations considered as states may or may not be able to derive benefits from national autonomy, however, depending on what their independent government is or is not willing or able to do for them. Individuals are sole agents but states are large and complex organizations consisting of many agents, both rulers and ruled, which creates problems of mutual capability and responsibility. Sovereignty only presupposes governments which are *deemed* capable and responsible. Although this has never been completely accurate empirically, it was a reasonable simplifying assumption historically when international society consisted of Western states that shared not only a common cosmopolitan culture but more or less the same levels of development which enabled them to reciprocate without undue difficulty. It is more problematical nowadays in a global international society because states are more varied culturally and unequal economically, technologically, and militarily than they have ever been.

Moreover, a sovereign government unlike a free individual is Janus-faced: it simultaneously faces both outward at other states and inward at its population. The responsibility of an individual consists entirely in externally oriented actions: it is owed to others. But the responsibility of a sovereign government is both external to other sovereigns and internal to its citizens. The harm principle for an individual, according to Mill, concerns only the harm that can be done to other individuals which would infringe on their negative liberty. But the harm principle for a state concerns not only infringements on the sovereignty of other states but also on the liberty of its citizens. An independent individual who respects Mill's principle can only hurt himself, but an independent government who is responsible to other sovereigns can still harm his subjects either deliberately or through negligence or incompetence. A sovereign not only can commit many more crimes and torts than an individual but there is no higher authority to arrest him, bring him to trial and – if guilty – punish him. This is why attempts have been made to establish an international law of human rights which would overrule sovereign rights in certain circumstances.

There is consequently a dilemma in negative sovereignty rooted in the divisibility of states which does not exist in negative liberty owing to the indivisibility of persons. In short, because there can be quasi-states whereas there are no quasi-persons, negative sovereignty and national self-determination are not categorical goods like negative liberty and individual self-determination. Instead, they are more ambiguous. It is impossible to believe in sovereign states in the same unqualified way that Mill believed in sovereign individuals. International liberalism is more contradictory and ambivalent than domestic liberalism and its analysis is consequently more complicated.

Positive liberty, according to Berlin, 'consists in being one's own master'. It is 'freedom to': being active and self-directive; choosing, pursuing, and realizing goals. It points towards the acquisition and enjoyment of capacities and not merely immunities; it presupposes agencies and conditions which are enabling. Positive freedom implies that there are some individuals and perhaps many who might be at liberty but who lack the necessities – education, training, skills, tools, money and so forth – to take advantage of it. This sort of reasoning is particularly evident nowadays in affirmative action programmes which seek to extend substantive benefits to people who otherwise would not qualify for them. This is justified on the grounds that negative liberty cannot by itself enable them to be their own masters owing to disadvantages not of their own making, such as class or race or sex. The authentically autonomous individual is one who has far greater control of his destiny than mere freedom from the interference of others makes possible. This is the view of Marx and indeed all who find negative liberty unsatisfactory as a basis for realizing the good life.

Positive sovereignty likewise presupposes capabilities which enable governments to be their own masters: it is a substantive rather than a formal condition. A positively sovereign government is one which not only enjoys rights of nonintervention and other international immunities but also possesses the wherewithal to provide political goods for its citizens. It is also a government that can collaborate with other governments in defence alliances and similar international arrangements and reciprocate in international commerce and finance. Positive sovereignty is the means which enable states to take advantage of their independence usually indicated by able and responsible rulers and productive and allegiant citizens. Positive sovereignty, as Schwarzenberger puts it, is not a legal but a political attribute if by 'political' is understood the sociological, economic, technological, psychological, and similar wherewithal to declare, implement, and enforce public policy both domestically and internationally.[20] It is the distinctive overall feature of a 'developed' state. Consequently it is a stronger characteristic of some states than of others.

Since states are never at rest owing to cultural transformation, scientific and technological innovation, and ultimately the passage of time positive sovereignty is a relative and changing rather than an absolute condition, unlike negative sovereignty.[21] There can be no complete self-mastery either for a state or for an individual: it is always a matter of degree. Even a superpower is limited in what it can accomplish and it is a wise American or Soviet President who realizes this. But the variation is far greater today than fifty years ago owing to decolonization which has resulted in the independence of states at all levels of development and underdevelopment. Consequently, although sovereigns everywhere today enjoy negative rights of nonintervention only some possess the wherewithal to take advantage of their independence. And whereas international society can provide governments with negative sovereignty through the act of general recognition, this is not the case with positive sovereignty which depends primarily on the actions and resources of governments and their populations.

Variations in substance and capabilities among states are far greater than among individuals and the gap between negative and positive sovereignty consequently is much wider than that between negative and positive liberty. It is not a question of size or even power: there have always been large and small, powerful and weak states. Denmark is a dwarf compared to Germany and has suffered historically from German invasion and occupation. But the Danish government can otherwise provide for its population as well as any state and better than most. Sovereignty for Danes is a tangible good. It is not a question of being a dwarf or a giant among states. Rather, it is a question of being a state in organized domestic reality and not merely by international law as indicated, for example, by per capita living standards of the population. Denmark, or for that matter, Iceland or New Zealand or Singapore are substantial and credible realities whose small populations enjoy living standards which are far in excess of those in most larger and more populous states of the world. In short, individuals can do more good and less harm with negative liberty – which is perhaps why classical liberalism gives limited attention to positive freedom – than states can effect with negative sovereignty – which likewise is perhaps why classical positive international law, a branch of liberalism, confined the possession of sovereignty to developed or 'civilized' countries. Today the response is different: underdevelopment serves as legitimate grounds for international assistance. Incapacity and inequality have been turned into positive international rights.

This gap between negative and positive sovereignty is universally perceived by international relations today due to new standards and expectations of the society of states concerning the development of its members. These, in turn, are linked to the existence of highly capable and relatively civil states located mainly although no longer exclusively in one quarter of the globe which highlight the comparative inadequacy of quasi-states. The gap was not considered significant in international relations before the development of highly organized and comparatively civil European states in the nineteenth century. As will be discussed in chapter 3, the old pre-nineteenth-century 'Grotian' law of nations embraced political systems with little regard for differences of culture or degrees of organization and disorganization. It was mid nineteenth century positive international law reflecting the comparative modernization of European states which first perceived the gap and responded by denying sovereignty to most non-Western political systems.[22] They were reduced to Western dependencies of one kind or another. The old colonial regime withheld independence from underdeveloped countries until they were considered 'fit' for self-government. The new post-colonial regime extends independence as a matter of right in the expectation or at least hope of subsequently assisting them to develop their capacities of self-government and thereby enable them to deliver civil and socioeconomic goods to their populations. International aid is justified on the affirmative action grounds that independence is necessary but not sufficient to enable ex-colonial states to become their own masters. Consequently, the positive norms and activities of contemporary international organization can be understood as an attempt (to date not very successful) to compensate for the shortage of positive sovereignty of quasi-states.

What is most significant in all of this is not variations in empirical statehood which have always existed but changes of international norms and expectations concerning underdevelopment. What was once considered a *prima facie* ground for denying membership in international society is now regarded as a claim to additional international support and assistance: sovereignty plus. The following chapter outlines the contrasting *modus operandi* of these very different sovereignty regimes.

2 A NEW SOVEREIGNTY REGIME

SOVEREIGN STATEHOOD

Sovereignty in international relations signifies constitutional independence of other states. In the words of Alan James, 'all that constitutional independence means is that a state's constitution is not part of a larger constitutional arrangement'.[1] The Gold Coast, a British colony, was not sovereign because it was not legally independent of Great Britain. Indeed, it was constitutionally part of the British Empire. Ghana, the sovereign successor to the Gold Coast since 1957, is legally independent not only of Britain but of all other sovereign states.

⌐Sovereignty, according to James, 'is a legal, absolute, and unitary condition'.[2] Legal in that a sovereign state is not subordinate to another sovereign but is necessarily equal to it by international law – although, of course, not necessarily by international fact. Absolute in that sovereignty is either present or absent. When a country is sovereign it is independent categorically: there is no intermediate condition. In international law such statuses as 'trusteeship' and 'associate statehood' have been conceived and even recognized. They do not signify semi-sovereignty, however. They are different legal categories altogether. 'In this matter, there can, in principle, be no half-way house, no question of relative sovereignty'.[3]Unitary in that a sovereign state is a supreme authority within its jurisdiction. This is the case whether or not a state has a unitary or a federal constitution, because in either case it is a sole authority in its external relations with other states. Otherwise it would be more than one state each of which would have the attribute of unitariness. As it happens, in federal states external affairs is the responsibility of the national government. It could not be otherwise without inviting ambiguity about the locus of sovereignty. The Canadian federal government's steadfast but not always successful determination to deny the Province of Quebec even the appearance of any right to engage in foreign affairs is illustrative.

Sovereign statehood, as previously indicated, is only one of several

32

kinds of international status which have existed historically. Today it is virtually the only kind. This was not the case in the recent past, however. Before the advent of quasi-states various other forms existed which were associated, in one way or another, with European colonialism. Most of them could be found within the elaborate constitutional framework of the British Empire which included entities such as 'colonies' (settled, conquered or ceded), 'protectorates' (including 'colonial protectorates', 'international protectorates', and 'protected states'), 'mandates' or 'trust territories', and 'condominia'. Many British dependencies were constitutional amalgams. The Gold Coast, for example, was a multiple dependency consisting of a settled colony (Gold Coast Colony), a conquered colony (Ashanti), a protectorate (Northern Territories), and a trust territory (British Togoland). Although each of these statuses differed in institutional shape, they all disclosed the common condition of legal subordination to a foreign power. They were a denial of sovereignty. The Gold Coast was a dependency not only by British law but also by international law.

The language of sovereign statehood is categorical and not contingent. This is consistent with legal language generally. To say that sovereignty is an absolute condition, for example, is the same as saying that marriage or any other formal relationship is absolute: one either is or is not a married person, a baptized Catholic, a Bachelor of Arts, a United States citizen, and the like. Legal language is different from sociological language in the same way that marriage differs from sexual relations, baptism from submersion, a BA from learning, or citizenship from residence. The first category in every case invokes a status, whereas the latter is merely descriptive. The same can be said of sovereign statehood: constitutional independence differs categorically from physical separation and colonial status is not the same as economic dependency. Sovereign states are legally but not necessarily physically insular and today most of them are economically dependent or interdependent. These are divergent categories and to confuse them is to commit what Gilbert Ryle appropriately terms a 'category mistake'. The social science of international relations has unfortunately increased the possibility of mixing the language of sociology (or political economy) with that of jurisprudence (or political theory) thereby inviting conceptual muddle. This is particularly the case as regards sovereignty: such terms as 'independence', 'imperialism', and 'colonialism', have been dislodged from their legal moorings and are today thoroughly infused with sociological and even ideological meanings. The problem of ambiguity is by no means recent, however, and is inherent, for example, in the issue of qualifying for sovereignty on empirical grounds.

In classical international law government effectiveness was a central ground of sovereign statehood. Sovereignty was, as James Crawford puts it, 'merely the location of supreme power within a particular territorial unit, necessarily came from within and did not require the recognition of other States or princes'.[5] It was simply there. Demonstrated capacity for self-government created credibility and respect which warranted recognition: sovereigns preceded sovereignty. In the now rather dated words of Hans Kelsen: 'A national legal order begins to be valid as soon as it has become, on the whole, efficacious, and ceases to be valid as soon as it loses this efficacy'.[6] If this were still true today many Third World states probably would not exist.

The grounds – sovereigns – and the title – sovereignty – are categorically different, however. States historically were empirical realities before they were legal personalities. A government could acquire sovereignty in virtue of being an inescapable reality in the surrounding international landscape which other sovereigns were obliged to recognize sooner or later: the positive sovereignty of the Soviet Union and China after their communist revolutions which some Western states regarded as illegitimate and for a time refused to recognize are twentieth-century examples; the freedom of Holland and Portugal from Spain before the latter recognized them as sovereign are seventeenth-century examples. Today, however, rulers can acquire independence solely in virtue of being successors of colonial governments: the negative sovereignty of many more or less nominal Third World states. The states of sub-Saharan Africa did not as a rule become free of the European empires and later claim independence. On the contrary, they were granted independence by those empires regardless of their empirical conditions and they exist today more by their universal right of independence than by their demonstrable reality.

THE OLD SOVEREIGNTY GAME

Since sovereignty is essentially a legal order defined by rules it can very appropriately be understood in terms of a game. One can intelligibly employ the metaphor only in the analysis of rule-articulated political orders: games are activities constituted and regulated by rules. It is useful to distinguish two logically different but frequently confused kinds of rules: constitutive (civil) and instrumental (organizational).[7] Constitutive rules define the game: number of players, size and shape of playing field, time of play, prohibited actions, and so on. Instrumental rules, on the other hand, are precepts, maxims, strata-

34

gems, and tactics which are derived from experience and contribute to winning play. They are prudential or opportunistic considerations put into practice by players or teams, such as instructions given by a coach: for example, to keep a straight bat in cricket or to choke up on the bat in baseball. However, neither belong at all to the rule books (constitutions) of these games. They are, for example, categorically different from the constitutive rule of both games that if after being hit the ball is caught before it strikes the ground the batsman or batter is out.

The classical sovereignty game is of course constituted by various laws, practices, customs, conventions, and prescriptions which promote international civility and are generally acknowledged by sovereign states. For example, traditional public international law belongs to the constitutive part of the game in that it is significantly concerned with moderating and civilizing the relations of independent governments. Diplomacy also belongs insofar as it aims at reconciling and harmonising divergent national interests through international dialogue. On the other hand, foreign policy is among the major instruments used by statesmen in playing the sovereignty game: that is, pursuing their interests. Reason of state or national interest therefore is not part of the constitution of international society. Rather, it is an attribute of states and integral to the instrumental part of the game. Diplomacy also belongs to the instrumental part insofar as it involves machinations and intrigues aimed at furthering national interests. History gives examples of both constitutional and Machiavellian diplomacy and this ambiguity is registered in the current semantics of the term. This study concerns mainly the constitutive rules of the sovereignty game and is interested in instrumental facets only insofar as they disclose the character, conditions, consequences, or biases of the game.

The constitutive rules of the sovereignty game are a response to the unavoidable and undeniable reality of a world of states: plurality. They are entailed by constitutional independence: legal equality of states, mutual recognition, jurisdiction, non-intervention, making and honouring of treaties, diplomacy conducted in accordance with accepted practices, and in the broadest sense a framework of international law including the law of war which attempts to confine even violent conflict between states within a rule-bounded playing field that protects noncombatants and other spectators. In short, the rules include every convention and practice of international life which moderate and indeed civilize the relations of states: a world theorized for the first time by Hugo Grotius.[8] And consistent with the rules of other competitive games those of sovereignty for the most part restrict or confine state behaviour – to demarcated jurisdictions – usually by means of prohibitions, i.e. non-intervention. Indeed, the classical international game of sovereignty like the rule of law or constitutional government within states is basically a game of liberty. It is a central institution of the political world of liberalism. A crucial difference and major feature of the sovereignty game, however, is the absence of referees with authority to enforce the rules; this is left to the players themselves. Consequently, the game is more prone to disorder and breakdown.

Who can play the game? One must be legally entitled: the players, or teams, are sovereign states and only sovereign states. Obviously, there are always many more spectators than players and there is consequently a high value on sovereignty. The title 'player' or 'team' is governed by rules of recognition which acknowledge who can play. The number of sovereigns has never been large. It is an exclusive game. From about the middle of the nineteenth century until the second world war, as already indicated, only Europeans or their descendants held the title apart from a few important and isolated exceptions. Since that time the rules of recognition have been changed to allow non-European governments onto the international playing field but not necessarily into the same league or division. Although the rules are still restrictive today and there are many peoples who desire independence but are denied, they are far more accommodating than they were fifty or a hundred years ago. This is a basic constitutional change which has created a rather different game as I explain below.

The classical sovereignty game exists to order the relations of states, prevent damaging collisions between them, and – when they do occur – regulate the conflicts and restore the peace. Playing is doing what a sovereign does in relation to other sovereigns within the constitutive rules of the game: pursuing foreign policy goals. This is what attracts the spectators – who are scarcely interested in the rule book and only take an interest in rule violations by the visiting team – and invites the experts and consultants who purport to master the prudence and technique of foreign policy. This is the high-stakes part of the game played down through the centuries by statesmen with greater or lesser skill and success. The legitimate foreign policy interest of a state is logically that of advantage and gain but certainly not to the point of destroying the game which is about independence and the political goods derived from it. Ultimately the national interest of sovereign states is protection and preservation of their own way of life. If they elect also to proselytize it must be within the rules of the game. This would exclude crusades, *jihads*, state sponsored terrorism, the global communist revolution, forcibly making the world safe for democracy, and any other actions in contempt of sovereignty.

Winning and losing is a more limited concept than playing. Some unfortunate or inept or weak states will lose games, of course, and may as a result be deprived of independence. Some losers may even be broken up – the partition of Poland in 1795. Others may be reduced to protectorates or colonies and effectively barred from the game – as happened to many traditional Asian and African rulers in their encounter with the West. This is not inimical to the game itself, however, which cannot insure against losing. Finality is a notion as ill-suited to the sovereignty game as it is to most political games which usually are never-ending. Although there are major and minor teams, stronger and weaker players, and today first, second, and third divisions, there can be no perennial or final winners and losers without destroying the game or turning it into something else. If that happened there would, of course, no longer be a sovereign states-system founded on plurality. Instead, there would be universal empire or world government based on one overriding authority, its logical and historical opposite. The constitutive rules of the sovereignty game as well as some of the instrumental calculations – such as the balance of power – precisely acknowledge international plurality and exist to prevent global hegemony. Some states and their alliances have always dominated large areas of the field of play – what Peter Calvocoressi terms 'super-sovereign or suzerain states'.[9] But no single state or alliance has ever commanded the entire field and subjected all other states to its exclusive authority – although over the centuries several have made the attempt.

Moreover, disregarding the rules in an effort to win amounts to destroying the game by transforming it into a fight. But in international relations 'fighting' is a narrower concept than one might think. Warfare, for example, is not fighting as long as it conforms to the laws and practices of war as generally accepted among states. War is part of the game and historically a very important part indeed. Here we encounter the game at its most realistic. The main point of the constitutive rules historically is not to prevent or to banish warfare, which is unrealistic, but to civilize it as much as possible. 'There is a difference between claiming sovereign autonomy and claiming world domination; between regarding another political entity as an adversary to be worsted or defeated, and regarding it as an enemy to be utterly vanquished or even destroyed.'[10] This remark captures the character of warfare conducted within the rules of the sovereignty game.

In the classical game which still exists in the more developed parts of the world, players as indicated are logically and in many cases histori- cally prior to the game. They are rulers of substantial political systems who are endowed with domestic authority and power and are there- fore credible internationally: empirical statehood. They are natural rivals in virtue of their proximity and conflicting interests. Inter- national relations is partly a zero-sum game: this is particularly evident historically in conflict over territory. It is also partly a collaborative engagement – for example, among allies defending common interests. As indicated, states vary considerably in size and power, which often obliges rulers of small states to seek alliances with large. In the classical game, however, variations in capability *per capita* are far less and render small powers valuable allies. Small states obviously can also be as civil as large. Size alone cannot determine quality among states any more than among men as Emerich Vattel observed in his famous remark that a dwarf is still a man.

A sovereign state, as noted previously, consists traditionally of a bordered territory occupied by a settled population under effective and at least to some extent civil – that is 'civilized' – government. Successful states provide their populations with shelter against external and internal threats enabling not only an orderly and safe but also poten- tially a prosperous and cultivated way of life to be carried on. Sover- eign states are traditionally postulated, therefore, as inherently valuable and capable entities which provide conditions for the good life. This is their justification in classical political theory. Like the rules of the road or any other laws of liberty which presuppose the value of agents, international rules exist to prevent collisions and therefore injury or damage to postulated intrinsically valuable states.

The inherent value of states is also disclosed by their military as- pects. Among the defining properties of states historically are arms: they are organized, equipped, and prepared for war even if they only wish to avoid it. This can be a sign that they are livable rather than desolate places. Sovereigns are 'in the state and posture of gladiators', Hobbes wrote, not because they are war mongerers but because they defend the industry, arts, sciences, and other goods of their subjects.[11] Whereas most of the benefits of European states originally were re- stricted rather narrowly to rulers and leading subjects upon whom they depended – the dynastic state – later in the course of political and economic development they were extended to the citizenry at large – the nation-state. However, even the earliest recognizable sovereigns were justified by providing order: without them, according to Bodin, 'one should have neither intercourse, commerce, nor alliance'.[12]

States, like turtles, would not have hard shells if they were not habitable. If people had shells they would not have invented states.

In the classical theory of sovereign statehood, as noted in the introduction, there are consequently two predominant paradigms: realism and rationalism.[13] The first postulates states as power organizations with conflicting national interests and without the morality of individuals: *raison d'état*. Reduced to essentials, the state is a war machine which exists to produce national security. This is the familiar discourse of Machiavelli and other classical realists. In Michael Oakeshott's terms it is the state conceived as an 'enterprise association' or *universitas*: an organization with an overriding national interest in security and survival.[14] The second paradigm postulates states as subjects of international law: sovereign governments are international legal persons. This is the idiom of Grotius, Vattel, and other classical rationalists. It is international relations conceived as a society – *societas* – consisting of independent governments under common rules which apply equally and impartially to all.[15] The state is a legal person or citizen of international society and the rules are international law in the broadest sense: the international equivalent of the rules of the road. Sovereignty is the right to sail the metaphorical ship of state on the open oceans regulated by international law without being told where to head but only how to proceed.

This is the traditional image of the state in the old sovereignty game. The original players were governments which had successfully asserted sovereignty in the past, had never surrendered it or succumbed to another state, and consequently had a strong historical right to play the game. When the United States achieved freedom from the British Empire through its war of independence or when Japan avoided Western imperialism, empirical statehood and the derivative positive title to sovereignty was demonstrated. When, however, virtually the entire African continent was partitioned and colonized by European states in the late nineteenth century this is precisely what native rulers were unable to demonstrate. Consequently, Africa became a field of play of European rather than indigenous states and to speak of 'European Africa' as many then did was entirely consistent with international reality. African rulers were reduced by cession and conquest to dependencies that were denied all rights to participate in the game. Only Ethiopia and Liberia managed to avoid colonization and achieve fringe player status. They were forerunners of a new international phenomenon: quasi-states.

In short, international law hitherto acknowledged two statuses: sovereign states and various formal dependencies. Although the

39

League of Nations began to change the rules of the game, sovereignty and empirical statehood were still roughly aligned in most cases. The second status was eliminated following the second world war by outlawing colonialism and inventing new rules of sovereign statehood for ex-colonies based on a novel doctrine of self-determination. Many colonial entities were thereby transformed legally into states. In reality, of course, they scarcely changed at all. Indeed, some regressed by too rapidly replacing European officials with less experienced indigenous personnel. International society now contained one and only one *official* class which masked enormous differences and variations in the substance and credibility of statehood around the world. This change understandably had an impact on how the sovereignty game is played. The analogy with competitive sports becomes misleading at this point because the new third division states are not simply less skilled and successful at playing the same sovereignty game, they are in fact playing a somewhat different game than first and second division states with novel rules adapted to their special circumstances. The new rules provide them with constitutional advantages – like handicaps given to poor golfers.

A NEW SOVEREIGNTY GAME

Third World sovereigns expect and enjoy the same rights as all others. They are jealous about their independence and consequently the game for them is no less a game of liberty than it is for others. However, they ground their claim to independence in a novel doctrine that invokes the right of self-determination of territories which previously were colonial jurisdictions. They also demand special considerations and rights defined by their adverse circumstances which established states do not claim. This creates an unprecedented form of international nonreciprocity as I explain below. The new sovereignty game involves basically two normative innovations: self-determination of ex-colonies, and development entitlements of impoverished countries. These norms reinforce the sovereignty of otherwise weak and vulnerable Third World governments and therefore amount to a kind of sovereignty plus. In addition, however, the contemporary society of states has been articulating a norm of human rights which limits the autonomy of all sovereigns including those in the Third World. It is consequently resisted by many whose domestic conduct is open to question by human rights organizations. The unintended effect of this norm is to differentiate between states in terms of humanitarianism, with many Third World governments classified as inadequate protectors of human rights.

Categorical self-determination of former colonies is the fundamental innovation which established the negative sovereignty regime: it is the moral imperative in decolonization which underwrites the independence and territorial integrity of most Third World states. It also serves as a bulwark against demands for self-determination by domestic ethnonational groups. Ex-colonial self-determination therefore established not only the categorical right to independence of colonial populations but the inviolability of the existing ex-colonial territories also. It consecrates the ex-colonial boundaries and ironically is the triumph of the European definition of the non-European world – as indicated by the current map of Asia, Africa, and Oceania which is scarcely altered from colonial times and bears only limited resemblance to the pre-existing political situation. The sovereigns have changed and the Europeans have left but the territorial jurisdictions they created are exactly as before in most cases.

'Self-determination of peoples' is acknowledged by the UN Charter (Article 1) and has been reiterated by many subsequent treaties, declarations, and resolutions of the international community. Who today is entitled to self-determination? Who qualify as 'peoples'? It is no longer a positive right of *national* self-determination – very few new states are 'nations' either by long history or common ethnicity or successful constitutional integration. Instead, it is the negative right of ex-European colonies – which usually contain different peoples but are not peoples themselves – to constitutional independence under an indigenous government regardless of conditions or circumstances. This new abstract right is less demanding than the old concrete requirement and that is of course the point: to enfranchise colonies and banish colonialism from international relations. It is an anti-colonial liberating principle.

Numerous peoples which were not colonies could not claim this new right of self-determination and have accordingly been barred from entering the international community. Many which still aspire to independence are consequently frustrated by the rules of the new sovereignty game which not only exclude them but give no sign of allowing them to play in the future. The accidents of imperial history consign them to the role of unwilling spectators even where they may actually be in effective control of territory – as in the case of Eritrea. Baluchis, Biafrans, Eritreans, Tigreans, Ewes, Gandans, Karens, Katchins, Kurds, Moros, Pathans, Sikhs, Tamils, and many other ethnonationalities are the abandoned peoples of the contemporary community of states. The moral language of the game refers to them disparagingly as 'separatists', 'secessionists', or 'irredentists' which strongly suggests

41

that they are illegitimate and not likely to be admitted to the clubhouse in the foreseeable future. Self-determination has become a conservative right of quasi-states.

The new statesmen are understandably united and determined to bar ethnonationalities from the club because if they were admitted it would involve loss of jurisdiction over the territories in question and remaking of international frontiers which, in turn, would threaten international order. In such a zero-sum game many existing sovereigns would be losers because the territory in dispute is already under their jurisdiction. Palestinians are among the very few dispossessed nationalities that have achieved an anomalous quasi-sovereignty in the current international regime mainly because the state which presently controls their homeland is itself of uncertain legitimacy internationally. Israelis of necessity play the old positive sovereignty game in defiance of the new rules. The politics of the Middle East leave them little choice.

There is a more fundamental reason why colonial jurisdictions have been perpetuated and indigenous ethnonationalities in the vast majority of cases barred from international society. If they were admitted, most existing Third World states would crumble into far smaller particularisms. These entities might be more coherent domestically than existing quasi-states and there probably would be fewer civil conflicts. However, they would fragment existing international society into a far greater number of jurisdictions than exist now. Instead of fifty states, Africa would contain more than ten or twenty times as many – depending on how 'peoples' were defined.[16] This would be an unmanageable number and would expose the continent to far greater risks of external control than it faces at present. Self-determination consequently has become an international categorical imperative which discloses the weakness of the post-colonial states whose governments claim it and whose territories are defined and preserved by it.

The major difference between the new rules and the old, therefore, is that they apply to many political entities which have not met traditional tests of empirical statehood and probably would not exist as sovereign states otherwise. In the late twentieth century numerous artificial ex-colonial entities are postulated, created and protected by this international norm. What started out as a claim of the people against the state and in the case of colonies as a justification for self-government, has ended up as a sovereign right.

In recent decades the world community has also been instituting unprecedented positive entitlements of sovereign states. Today one can speak of a development assistance regime based on a distinction between 'developed' and 'underdeveloped' states with dramatically unequal capacities and needs. This regime has been targeted primarily and extensively at the Third World since the 1960s. It is evident in numerous multilateral and bilateral public aid programmes as well as proliferating activities of private international aid organizations. And it presupposes a new type of sovereign state which is independent in law but insubstantial in reality and materially dependent on other states for its welfare. Today underdevelopment is not only a fact, however, but also the ground for a claim to positive assistance from the international community in general and from wealthy states in particular. These claims are conceived by certain moral theorists as subsistence rights in parallel with traditional security rights of states and equally as significant.[17] There is an emerging academic literature on international distributive justice which seeks answers to the question, among others, whether affluent states have obligations to share their wealth with poor countries.[18]

Even if underdeveloped states cannot yet be said to possess unequivocal subsistence rights their socioeconomic demands and expectations tell us something crucially important not only about the difficult material circumstances and basic socioeconomic needs of their populations but also about the character and *modus operandi* of the new international regime which is trying to shore them up. International development is an extension of self-determination from the negative or political to the positive or socioeconomic realm: not only the freedom from nonintervention but also the entitlement to material assistance: sovereignty plus. In practice this usually translates into international financial and technical assistance for underdeveloped countries including debt relief and exemptions from the more exacting requirements of financial and trading rules in recognition of their special needs and circumstances.

The old sovereignty game made no positive socioeconomic provision for sovereign states which were assumed to be self-reliant, more or less equally developed, and therefore authentically free agents. The main point was to avoid discrimination either for or against sovereign states which were considered capable of fending for themselves and entitled only to benefit from rules which were equal for all. Nondiscrimination signified equal trading rights and reciprocity: the so-called level playing field as established, for instance, by the Most Favoured Nation principle of classical international law. States possessed sovereignty by their merits or deserts and international justice was necessarily commutative. Such free-standing and free-trading entities did not require positive discrimination or sovereignty plus. However, the existence of underdeveloped states obviously confounds this logic: a playing field that is level for teams of more or less equal talents and capacities is not level if they are profoundly unequal which is the case today in relations between developed and underdeveloped countries. Historically this inequality was reconciled by colonization of the underdeveloped. In other words inequality was legitimated and legalized. Contemporary norms of international democracy forbid this and so it is responded to by international efforts to establish special positive rules, organizations and possibly rights – an international development regime – for those in need.

At the same time, however, classical negative rights of nonintervention are still retained by all states, developed and underdeveloped alike. The development claims advanced by many Third World governments and their advocates do not presuppose any curtailment of their traditional security rights. The new ethics of international development are obviously difficult to reconcile with historical liberties of sovereign statehood. If developed states have obligations to come to the assistance of underdeveloped states – as is often claimed – they certainly have no corresponding rights to ensure that their assistance is properly and efficiently used by governments of the latter. Developed states have no such rights because it would violate the sovereignty of underdeveloped states and could amount to foreign intervention. There is a fundamental incompatibility, therefore, between classical liberal rules of reciprocity and commutative justice and contemporary doctrines of nonreciprocity and distributive justice. The problem is that underdeveloped states claim both security rights and development rights and the international community desires to acknowledge both claims but the classical rules of a sovereign states-system get in the way. This is an asymmetrical relationship unknown in traditional international relations: the bearers of rights and the holders of obligations are differentiated in a way that contradicts the historical reciprocity and equality of states: southern governments have only rights and northern only duties. The former have no obligations to use foreign aid properly or productively. The latter have no right to demand it. Some of the problems which arise from this contradictory international morality are discussed in chapter 5.

The new sovereignty game is also complicated by the emergence of a cosmopolitan regime which seeks to establish the legal status of humans in international relations against that of the sovereign Leviathan. This norm is not part of the sovereignty game but is a reaction to it: human rights are intended to curb sovereign rights. One of the most noteworthy innovations in international law during the postwar era has been the codification of human rights in the Universal Declaration of Human Rights and various other international covenants, conventions, and declarations regarding racial discrimination, religious intoleration, torture, and so forth. In addition, there has been a proliferation of international humanitarian organizations, based mainly in the West but operating worldwide, as exemplified by Amnesty International, the International Committee of the Red Cross, the International Commission of Jurists, the Minority Rights Group, the International League of Human Rights, and numerous others. This is a significant development which tells us something about the civil or rather uncivil conduct of sovereign states and our attitudes to it today.

Recent international humanitarian law, necessarily reflecting the global divisions between the individualist West and collectivist East, and the developed North and underdeveloped South, embraces not only civil and political but also social and economic rights. The West has historically placed emphasis on civil and political liberties which have their origins in traditional doctrines of natural rights and natural law that reach back to European antiquity. The Soviet Union and its allies have promoted a contrary doctrine of socioeconomic rights as a way of asserting the legitimacy of their contrasting social system and avoiding criticism of their dismal record of civil rights protection; although this is changing in the Gorbachev era and the Soviet Union and some other East European countries are now explicitly recognizing and increasingly protecting civil and political rights. Many Third World governments also tend to assert socioeconomic rights as human rights which adds moral force to their development claims and distracts attention from their questionable conduct as regards civil and political liberties. Socioeconomic rights also enhance their power while such liberties restrict it.

However, it is misleading to equate the two categories and the fact that current international law does equate them tells us more about international politics than about human rights. Only civil and political liberties are 'human rights' properly so-called and traditionally acknowledged by international law: that is, universal moral entitlements – 'natural rights' – such as the right to life, freedom of movement, *habeus corpus*, freedom from torture and so forth. Everyone everywhere can take a life or have it taken from him, confine or be confined, cause or suffer physical torment, and generally take or refrain from action which interferes with others. Even in the most underdeveloped countries anybody who is capable of action can forbear from threatening, confining, torturing, or abusing people in other ways. Human rights in international relations are immunities primarily against sovereign

45

governments. Every government can guarantee such rights at least in principle because it requires only responsible and resolute *conduct*. Failure to protect human rights accordingly is misconduct and indefensible everywhere.)

Social and economic rights require something in addition to human conduct. This is the case with subsistence, employment, education, health care, pensions, and all other claims for material benefits. Stanley Benn suggests that such 'welfare-promoting' rights are more aptly termed 'needs'.[19] For example, it makes no sense to talk of health care rights in underdeveloped countries which are severely short of doctors, nurses, hospitals, and other medical resources, technologies, and facilities. This is not merely owing to underdevelopment, however, because it also makes no sense to talk of such things as 'rights' in developed countries as is evident in the moral predicament involved in giving access to scarce artificial kidney machines. There is always a limit to material goods even in a rich society whereas there is no limit to human decency in any society. I therefore consider as 'human rights' only those natural rights which are universal and have been traditionally regarded as such. Social and economic claims to development or subsistance if they are rights at all can only be positive rights of sovereign states. As indicated, I classify them as components of the international development regime outlined previously.

Human rights in current international law are subject to the consent of sovereigns, however. The cosmopolitan society of humankind is legally – not to mention politically – inferior to the international society of sovereign states. Independent governments are free to decide whether or not to be signatories to human rights instruments. They may feel under a moral obligation to sign. They may come under political pressure to sign. They may believe it is in their interests to sign. They are under no legal obligation to do so, however. Although there is a growing moral imperative in international society to protect human rights which derives from the domestic standards and international influence of Western democracies, sovereign rights still have priority over human rights in international law. Since most Third World states are not only underdeveloped but also authoritarian and therefore unconstrained domestically, they are inclined to deny human rights.

Serious and frequent human rights violations are not likely to occur in successful democracies in normal circumstances such as times of peace when governments are subject to popular control.[20] Indeed, other things being equal, such states are likely to be not only signatories to international human rights law but also leading advocates of

46

global humanitarianism. In authoritarian states, however, where constitutional and legal restraints on the exercise of power are far less
effective and may even be nonexistent, international human rights law
obviously is more intrusive and has a higher cost in terms of domestic
government freedom of action. The probability of subscription and
compliance is accordingly lower. In many Third World countries, as
Amnesty International reports annually indicate, human rights are
routinely violated by governments.[21] The focus of international humanitarian concern on such states reflects their comparative lack of
domestic human rights protections. But the resistance of their rulers to
international humanitarianism, their assertion of the priority of sovereign rights over human rights, and their affirmation of social and
economic rights undoubtedly indicates not only their jealousy regarding sovereignty but their insecurity and vulnerability also. Currently,
moreover, there is no effective general right of 'humanitarian intervention' in international law to override sovereign rights.[22] Nor could
there be without fatally undermining the sovereignty game which
must embody the contrary right of nonintervention to exist.

In principle, as indicated, Third World states are as accountable to
human rights norms as any other governments insofar as they consist
of adult and sane human beings. In practice, however, many are
recently independent by historical standards and have as yet limited
experience of self-rule. Their governments regularly find themselves in
more difficult circumstances than their First World counterparts. Their
authority may be disregarded, defied, or even unknown in some
quarters. They are underdeveloped and frequently disjointed which
means they cannot always protect human rights even if they desire it.
They may not be able to control their own agents who might operate
with considerable independence as local freelancing despots. These
characteristics are suggestive not only of states but also of societies in
which political civility is not yet completely institutionalized. Human
rights violations would be less surprising in such circumstances. International humanitarian efforts have not compensated for the civil weak-
nesses of certain independent countries and they are unlikely to do so
in the foreseeable future. However, they are an indication of one of the
most significant dilemmas of the new sovereignty game between sovereign rights and human rights which is discussed in chapter 6.

A NOVEL INTERNATIONAL FRAMEWORK

The argument spelled out in the remainder of the book can
now be summarized. Third World independence has resulted in the

formation for the first time of two simultaneous games of sovereignty within a universal international society: the continuing demanding 'hardball' (or 'fastpitch') game based on positive sovereignty, and a new, softer, third division game derived from negative sovereignty. The first and prior game includes not only the familiar East–West military contest which is the successor to the traditional balance of power system but also a competition for global leadership in science, technology, and economics. The new game is the North–South 'dialogue' which is the successor of Western colonialism. It is in many respects a collaborative regime fashioned to replace the imperial orders which governed non-Western areas in the past. Numerous quasi-states which might not exist otherwise have found a protected niche within this sphere. What is fundamentally changed, therefore, is not the geographical distribution of power in the world. Rather, it is the moral and legal framework of the states-system and the way that underdeveloped parts of the world are supported externally. Contemporary international society can be distinguished from its ancestors by a strong democratic desire to incorporate all ex-colonies as sovereign states regardless of their level or prospects of empirical statehood.

Moreover, there are many states today which claim material support from other states in addition to the usual rights of independence. An attempt is being made for the first time in modern history to establish responsibilities for the welfare of people which extend beyond national borders and to promote it by cooperation between rich and poor states. Even if international development support for the latter has been woefully inadequate to the need so far, these claims cannot be questioned on moral and increasingly even legal grounds and such states are not expected to fend entirely for themselves. Contemporary international society is therefore expected to be not only a civil association for all states but in addition a joint enterprise association to assist its poorer members. This remarkable although as yet far from successful enterprise arguably would be unnecessary if there were no quasi-states.

Finally and in response to the frequently adverse civil conditions of many countries around the world the community of states is also attempting to establish international standards of human rights which sovereign governments are urged to observe. These efforts run up against the strong emphasis on sovereign rights, however, and are often resisted by nondemocratic governments in the entirely rational belief that they will undermine their power and authority. Self-determination has liberated indigenous governments in Third World states

48

but has at the same time subjected many populations to unstable and illiberal regimes which often use their sovereign rights to deny or at least neglect human rights. This ironic outcome was not supposed to happen.

3 SOVEREIGNTY REGIMES IN HISTORY

SOVEREIGNTY: FACT OR NORM?

There is an old controversy in international relations as to whether 'sovereignty' is intrinsic to states – a fact – or a status acknowledged by other statesmen. Does the world today consist of about 170 distinct and separate organized political realities called 'states'? Is sovereignty constituted by that reality? Or is the globe a framework of jurisdictions defined according to common principles of international law? Is sovereignty a rule or rather a set of rules of an international society and therefore extrinsic to states? In short, are sovereign states self-standing realities and rugged individualists or are they constituents of an international community and responsible citizens or, again, are they somehow both at the same time?

The political entities we have come to know as 'states' appeared first in Western Europe. The original foundations were the region's geographical and demographic configuration as 'population islands' in an ocean of forest and heath. States were the 'scaffolding' erected on these islands by ambitious rulers facing strenuous international competition. The states-system is at the root of 'the European miracle' in which that continent and particularly its northwestern extremity historically outdistanced the rest of the world not only in science and technology but also in political economy and statecraft. 'The states-system was an insurance against economic and technological stagnation . . . A large part of the system's dynamic was an arms race.'[1] Of course, European states were rarely the efficient machines rulers wanted or the equitable institutions philosophers desired. On the contrary, they were frequently ramshackle and arbitrary. But they were also increasingly less disorganized and illusory than political systems elsewhere. The proof was the eventual hegemony of Europe over the rest of the world.

Sovereign states first came into view when medieval Christendom fractured under the combined impact of the Renaissance and the Reformation. Anarchy was exploited by the new prince who in the

50

words of Martin Wight 'suppressed the feudal barons and challenged the Pope . . . a narrower and at the same time a stronger unit of loyalty than medieval Christendom'.[2] New kings and new kingdoms marched forward together, the latter as handiwork of the former. By the seventeenth century when modern international law was first theorized by Grotius 'the emerging territorial state was a creature of personal rule' and the 'three hundred-odd independent sovereignties' in Germany alone were testimony to initial 'patrimonial conception of the state'.[3] In his unrivalled study of the Italian Renaissance Burckhardt summed up the political change as follows: 'a new fact appears in history – the State as the outcome of reflection and calculation'.[4] For Burckhardt the new Italian princes were essentially 'illegitimate', but power always seeks justification of some kind. The leading principle of legitimacy in the new international order undoubtedly was *Rex est imperator in regno suo*: the King is Emperor within his own realm. Under this claim 'independence *de facto* was ultimately translated into a sovereignty *de jure*'.[5] Sovereignty is therefore inherent in successful state-building.

The reality of sovereign states was reflected in European political thought. The writings of Machiavelli, Bodin, and Hobbes disclose clearly a world of positive sovereignty. *The Prince* (1513) captures the secular, morally unencumbered, and forceful character of statesmen in its leading concepts of *animo, ambizione, appetito, ingegno, prudenza, fortuna*, and *virtù* which Machiavelli believed were necessary for political success and survival in a dangerous world. *Six Books of the Commonwealth* (1576) discloses the leading characteristic of the new state as a sovereign government which 'can secure itself against external enemies or internal disorders'.[6] *Leviathan* (1651) postulates the contractual establishment of such a government as the sole escape from a fearful domestic state of nature but also as the necessary condition of a belligerent international state of nature: 'in all times, kings, and persons of sovereign authority, because of their independency, are in . . . a posture of war'.[7] For these writers the state is an independent reality in the world and for the last two it is the only foundation of order and security.

The starting point of international relations undoubtedly is empirical statehood. The earliest modern states such as France and England or rather Francis I and Henry VIII were palpable political realities internally and in their neighbourhoods. One could try to ignore them or pretend they did not exist but one could not rationally and probably would not prudently deny their existence. The reality consisted in a populated territory under a ruler who claimed the territory as his realm and the population as his subjects and was able to enforce the claim.

51

He possessed a government apparatus that could project royal power and prerogative both internally and externally. However rudimentary that apparatus might be it was sufficiently credible to sustain the ruler both domestically and internationally and, if it was not, he and also possibly his realm might be replaced by another. Since European states were in close geographical proximity and since the devices and techniques of empirical statehood were means of success and survival they were quickly adopted by rulers throughout Europe. Proximity and power meant there was always a strong possibility of war: the classical problem of a states-system. Deterrence, alliance, and the balance of power are responses to it. But competition was also a spur to state-building and one of the main reasons for the eventual global hegemony of Europe.

The starting point of international law is the same: the reality of multiple sovereign powers each possessed of pride and capable of doing or suffering harm. Classical international law is the analogue of common moral and legal rules: a *societas* or civil society. On an empirical view morality arises out of the facts of human existence. And the facts are that humans are endowed with brains and limbs, have desires, can move about in the pursuit of their desires and in the course of doing so can collide. This human reality lays the groundwork of common morality and law which seeks to regulate the uses of power and to reduce collisions and therefore harm. Classical international legitimacy and law operate the same way. One original element was acknowledgement of not only the reality but also the dignity of sovereigns: according to Samuel Pufendorf 'just as a king owes his sovereignty and majesty to no one outside his realm, so he need not obtain the consent and approval of other kings or states, before he may carry himself like a king and be regarded as such'.[8] It is a small step to consider him the legitimate bearer of rights and duties which belong properly to all who are kings. The balance of power and classical international law evolved in conjunction. From the seventeenth century to the twentieth statesmen have developed international law, not to prevent war, but to regulate the conduct of states in war and in peace.

International law presupposes empirical statehood whether it is conceived as natural law or as positive law. The law of nature is the law of things or facts as revealed by man's reason without the assistance of revelation. Pufendorf insists that states, as Hinsley puts it, 'must do as they would be done by': the golden rule of reciprocity.[9] Grotius derives positive international law from the freedom, will, and agency of statesmen. States and only states in virtue of controlling large populated territories and being organized realities in the vicinity of other states are in a position to participate in the making of international law by signing treaties, sending and receiving ambassadors, attending international conferences and giving their consent in various other conventional ways. The following statement by Georg Schwarzenberger and E. D. Brown is typical of empirical statehood in international law:

> Before recognising an entity as an independent State, the existing subjects of international law usually require a minimum of three conditions to be fulfilled. The State in quest of recognition must have a stable government, which does not recognise any outside superior authority; it must rule supreme within a territory – with more or less settled frontiers – and it must exercise control over a certain number of people. These features have come to be taken as the essential characteristics of independent States.[10]

And J. L. Brierly remarks: 'Whether or not a new state has actually begun to exist is a pure question of fact.'[11] Classical international law is therefore the child and not the parent of states.

The conventional answer to the questions posed at the beginning is that sovereign states have a double dual dimension: they face inward and outward, and they have an empirical and a normative aspect. Sovereign states declare normative supremacy over all domestic authorities and moral and legal equality to all other states: juridical statehood. Under ordinary circumstances short of major warfare they also disclose the ability to enforce both claims. The definitive statement of positive sovereignty remains that of John Austin: 'If a *determinate* human superior, *not* in a habit of obedience to a like superior, receive *habitual* obedience from the *bulk* of a given society, that determinate superior is sovereign in that society and the society (including the superior) is a society political and independent.'[12] Of course there has always been and indeed there must in the nature of political things always be a gap between the absolute authority and the relative power of states: like all other human organizations states are conditional on leadership, cooperation, knowledge, resources, fortune, and much else. Absolute power is an impossibility. In major cities of the greatest power on earth today, including the capital, there is in some districts at night a state of nature rather than a state.

In law states are only *deemed* to be substantial and capable. This has been a reasonable working assumption historically, however. 'An independent political community which merely claims a right to sovereignty (or is judged by others to have such a right), but cannot assert this right in practice, is not a state properly so-called.'[13] Under the forgiving conditions of the contemporary collaborative states-system, however, it is sovereign nevertheless. In a leading study of international law published in 1968 the following statement is made: 'The international legal order does not provide foundation for the State; it presupposes the State's existence. Recognizing the appearance on a territory of a political entity showing the characteristics generally attributed to the State, it merely invests it with personality in the law of nations.'[14] However, the international legal order centred on the UN is attempting to provide precisely such a foundation for many Third World states. Contemporary international legitimacy and law are not only the parents but also the continuing benefactors of such states. If their existence were a matter exclusively of power or the balance of power rather than birthright many might not have been born.

THE DUAL ASPECT OF THE STATES-SYSTEM

According to Martin Wight, 'the dual aspect of the states-system' was conceived originally, if tentatively, by Grotius. 'There is an outer circle that embraces all mankind, under natural law, and an inner circle, the *corpus Christianorum*, bound by the law of Christ.'[15] Dualism in different forms has persisted in international relations ever since. It is a big subject, of course, and there exists as yet no comprehensive account of which I am aware.[16] However, it is possible to review the history of international dualism to gain some background perspective on the dualism which exists today and the place of negative sovereignty in it.

Three 'stages' are discernible. The first was an inner circle of positive international law among Christian–European nations and an outer or universal circle of natural law governing the conduct of mankind. Relations between the two spheres (which in practice were Europe and the rest of the world) were nevertheless pragmatic politically, uncertain morally, and untidy legally. They were conducted on a basis of rough equality notwithstanding the historically accelerating inequality of power in favour of Europe, and they expressed a fair measure of toleration. There was not yet anything resembling a global international regime under common rules. Before the nineteenth century, little emphasis was placed by Europeans on the legal criteria of statehood in their encounter with non-Europeans. The two spheres were simply different and the main problem facing European states was still that of regulating their own relationships. Non-European rulers were not under challenge and dealt with Europeans the same as other foreigners. It was not yet an ordering of global relations in terms of the power and beliefs of Europe.

The projection of European state power far beyond the confines of

Europe and even more so the increasingly successful territorialization of that power in other continents eventually brought forth such an order in the nineteenth century. Occupation had to be justified to other European powers and consequently it invoked international law and particularly the rules of *terra nullius*, conquest and cession. A new form of international dualism appeared which was connected with European colonial expansion in Asia and Africa: rough equality and diversity was replaced by precise hierarchy and uniformity in the relations between European and non-European countries, with the former in a position of superiority. (The same dualism existed in North and South America and Russian Asia, but it was internal rather than external colonialism and consequently was never subjected to eventual decolonization.) The determination of sovereignty throughout the world now demanded that certain criteria be satisfied which derived from a Western and specifically liberal concept of a capable and constitutional state. For the first time the entire globe was organized in terms of European positive international law: there was a single regime of world politics in which colonialism was an integral institution. Dualism now consisted of a superior inner circle of sovereign states and an inferior outer circle of their dependencies in Asia, Africa, and Oceania. The inner circle was composed almost entirely of European countries and their offspring in the Americas – apart from noteworthy exceptions, such as Turkey and Japan. By 1900 the number of sovereign states was at its lowest and the extent of their territorial control was at its greatest, enclosing the entire globe.

The latest stage of international dualism was first intimated by Wilsonian liberalism and specifically the League of Nations' belief in 'the virtue of small states' and 'the juridical equality of all states'.[17] The League did not abandon empirical statehood, however, as indicated by the mandates system. That was the result of decolonization after the second world war and particularly 1960 which granted membership in the community of states and specifically the UN to all dependencies which desired it regardless of any other considerations and according to the principle of self-determination. This international change was essentially normative and basically entailed abolishing international legal disabilities previously imposed on non-Western peoples.

A NATURAL LAW REGIME?

The hierarchical states-system based on European hegemony which reached its zenith during the heyday of colonialism in the late nineteenth and early twentieth centuries was the culmination of Western commercial, military, and political expansion to the four corners of the globe over several previous centuries. During most of this period relations between European and non-European states were casual and intermittent and characterized by equality and diffidence more than hegemony and arrogance. Most of the contacts were made by private European traders who may or may not have been representatives of states. Before the nineteenth century the power advantage was not consistently with the intruders.

The Americas were a major exception where Europeans established their dominion at an early stage. The initial division of the hemisphere between Spain and Portugal was based on a fifteenth-century Papal Bull: a remnant of the medieval concept of an *imperium mundi*. The Spaniards and the Portuguese at first and the French, English, and Americans later destroyed indigenous civilizations, which were weak, and marginalized their populations, whose numbers were particularly small in North America. They also imported millions of slaves from Africa to develop plantation agriculture in their vast new territories. The Spanish and Portuguese in the new world 'might find it expedient to make agreements with savage tribes, but did not regard them as moral equals with a legitimate right to territory'.[18] Some natural lawyers, such as Vitoria, defended their status under the law of nature. However, European hegemony was thoroughly imposed throughout the region in the name of Christian religion or commercial civilization. In short, the Americas were an object of European conquest and an extension of European sovereignty. When European jurisdiction ended in the eighteenth and nineteenth centuries sovereignty did not revert to the native peoples but was inherited by settlers or their descendants.

In Asia where ancient civilizations and significant indigenous powers existed relationships were very different. Here the European competition from the sixteenth to the eighteenth centuries was for overseas trade and not territories. This required permission from local rulers who controlled the entrepôts. European trading companies subjected themselves to these rulers to secure access to prized commodities. Trading contacts settled into practices which were useful to both parties. Watson says that in dealing with non-European civilizations at this time, 'European traders and representatives took account of the particular stipulations laid down by individual Asian rulers as well as European rules and precepts.'[19] These international relationships eventually extended from Western Europe and particularly Holland and England to the greater part of maritime Asia including the Indian Ocean littoral. Among the Asian states involved at one time or another were the Maratha State, the Mogul Empire, the Kingdoms of

Ceylon and Burma, the Indonesian States, and Madagascar. Persia and Siam also 'were linked with a number of European Powers by treaty and diplomatic relations in the seventeenth and eighteenth centuries'.[20] The Dutch contributed more to this expansion of international society than any other Western trading state. After largely displacing the Portuguese they were deeply involved with Asian rulers and middlemen for several centuries and carried their international outlook to Asia along with goods for trade.

If Holland's prosperity derived significantly from overseas trade her liberty was owed not only to the balance of power in Europe but also to international law. It is perhaps no accident that the first great theorist of international society was Dutch: Hugo Grotius. His primary aim in *De Jure Belli ac Pacis Libri Tres* (1625) was to establish rules of war and peace that were immune to theological and political controversy and depended only on the faculty of reason – like mathematics – and could therefore secure acceptance from all statesmen. Natural law was the only certain foundation for such rules: it was the voice of human reason and would exist even if God did not (*etiamsi daremus non esse Deum*).[21] International legal thought, building on Grotius, presupposed a 'Family of Nations' that was not limited to the European continent because it was based on a human faculty common to all mankind. Non-Western states therefore possessed sovereignty. The natural law of nations, according to Charles Alexandrowicz, postulated principles not only of just war but also universality, non-discrimination on grounds of religion, civilization or race, and prohibition of genocide, slave trade, and piracy.[22]

Whether or not something resembling Grotius's law of nations was observed routinely in relations between European merchants and non-European rulers is still debated and therefore open to question.[23] Vast geographical and cultural distances lodged ultimately in the minds of men separated Europe and other regions of the world. Commercial relationships were conducted slowly and tenuously at very great distance in an age of sail. Even to speak of a global 'economy' and much less a family of trading nations is questionable: 'Links across the oceans were built up over three centuries . . . but to refer to the international commerce of that mercantile age as a "world economy" is to misapply a contemporary concept which . . . has relevance only for our times. Throughout the pre-industrial era connections between economies (even within states) remained weak, tenuous, and liable to interruption.'[24] The conventions of free passage and safe domicile upon which long distance commerce depended rested as much on instrumental and personal considerations as on moral understandings and political agreements. For isolated traders in search of valuable goods far away from home it was prudent to respect local customs and curry favour with those in authority. This can be read without cynicism as the usual expediency that would be expected by visitors to places where fortunes could be made but one's own state could not enforce contracts. European powers were not yet able to dispatch fast gunboats to cow uncooperative local rulers. The law of nature may have been practised but whether it was international law is open to reasonable doubt.

The world before the industrial age was far more loosely connected than it would later be. It was also marked by extreme diversity not only of societies and cultures – as is still the case today – but also of fundamentally different human cosmologies. There was no overarching system of rules which could be even recognized let alone observed by Confucianists, Buddhists, Hindus, Moslems, and Christians. The globe was home to various self-centred and mutually incomprehending civilizations which were as yet only in the most superficial contact: islands in an ocean of non-jurisdiction. Grotius' description of the sea as 'so great' as not to have any 'definite limits' and therefore subject to no political will conveys the idea.[25] The seas and also the enormous Asian and African land masses divided the world into separate orbits: a civilizations-system rather than a states-system consisting of great empires or suzerain-state systems such as the Chinese or the Moguls or the Ottomans, self-isolating feudal systems such as Japan, scattered tribal cultures in sub-Saharan Africa, tropical South America, north-western North America and parts of Oceania, European colonists in the Americas, South Africa, and, at the end of the period, Australia, and of course European sovereign states gradually projecting their power and rivalries at increasing distances from home.

European or rather Christian rulers never dealt with non-Christian rulers the way they dealt with each other: as equal members of a single diplomatic republic which consisted of independent states 'resembling each other in their manners, religion and degree of social improvement'.[26] There were obvious 'family resemblances' in religion, government, philosophy, science, architecture, literature, art, and much else among European states. Burke still spoke of Europe in the late eighteenth century as 'virtually one great state having the same basis of general law, with some diversity of provincial customs and local establishments' and remarked that 'no citizen of Europe could be altogether an exile in any part of it' where the traveller 'never felt himself quite abroad'.[27] Little if any of this commonwealth extended beyond Europe except in places where substantial settlements of Europeans existed, as in the Americas. Even the Turks who were half-European although not

Christian and for centuries occupied large parts of southeastern Europe disclosed few family resemblances. In Constantinople the European traveller was no longer not abroad. There was still no coherent theory of recognition which could define insiders and outsiders beyond the obvious recognition that European states naturally and customarily gave to each other and later to their rebellious offspring in the Americas. Their commonwealth could not be distinguished from their common culture.

If there was a family of nations that extended beyond Europe it lacked the customs and conventions by which European states recognized family members and it seems scarcely distinguishable from ordinary prudence and common courtesy. And if such a family of nations existed then it was because Europeans abroad yet had little choice in the matter. When they did acquire such a choice in the nineteenth century which derived from unprecedented technological and industrial developments in Europe they did not subscribe to natural law tenets but insisted on more demanding positive standards which they alone could easily recognize and subscribe to. And when this began to happen European trading companies abandoned diffidence towards local rulers and started to act and look like states.

THE CLASSICAL POSITIVE SOVEREIGNTY REGIME

By the nineteenth century the leading European powers were deeply involved in territorial expansion in Asia: the Russian land empire extended to the Pacific Ocean, and the Dutch East Indies and British India were solidly established. (Americans and later Canadians were similarly involved in North America.) Traditional political systems could not compete with intruding states which could now project their power into every ocean and continent. Those that survived were difficult to penetrate – such as Afghanistan and Persia which became buffer states between the Russian and British Empires – or they were powers in their own right, like Japan. Far less competitive were the lightly organized, preliterate and in many cases small-scale tribal societies of tropical Africa and Oceania which historically were protected from intruders more by forbidding geography and climate than by indigenous power. European expansion in Africa was confined largely to the coastal fringe until late in the century. Once natural barriers could be overcome by technology, however, territorial aggrandizement became possible and the entire continent – with the exception of Ethiopia and more equivocally Liberia – rapidly came under European colonial jurisdiction.

I cannot go into the numerous and varied historical causes of European expansion which are a subject of continuing controversy. What is beyond dispute, however, is the timing of expansion which coincided with the development of the technological and industrial means (and the novel ideas behind them) that finally gave European states a decisive advantage over most non-European societies. If earlier eras of European expansion were based on the armed sailing ship and the discipline of professional soldiers, nineteenth-century imperialism was owing to steam transport both on water and on land, rapid firing weapons, high explosives, and new medical knowledge.[28] Modern technology and industry also gave some European states a marked competitive advantage over others – as indicated by the ease with which the United States achieved victory in the Spanish–American war (1898). Moreover, the new means of state power were not magically restricted to Western civilization. Japan demonstrated this in the defeat of Russia in 1904–5 which confirmed not only equal membership in international society but also emergent great power status.

The superior power which European intrusion demonstrated could not be exercised without some justification, however. In a legally articulated international society it is not sufficient that power alone occupy territorial spaces: legitimacy is necessary also. Most of the leading states of Western Europe had been justifying political power for centuries. Despotism was a term of abuse for Montesquieu and Burke and something hostile to Western European civilization although far from absent. Constitutionalism was a criterion by which many nineteenth-century Europeans judged governments both inside Europe and outside. It was an international as well as a domestic standard. Perhaps the clearest expression of international constitutionalism was the recurrent congresses and conferences of powers held throughout the nineteenth century and into the twentieth which enacted general treaties on important questions of mutual concern.

The European notion of the state and of international legitimacy current throughout most of the century therefore presupposed not only capable but also civil government. It was by this time no longer important whether a country was a monarchy or a republic as long as it was reliable and responsible. Capability was first in importance because the balance of power depended on it. Civility was not far behind, however, because international relations required forbearance and reciprocity in the exercise of power. It was taken for granted that European states and also the United States disclosed these characteristics. This positive sovereignty outlook was consistent with the theory of progress which captured the nineteenth-century European mind. It was compatible with a morality of paternalism which not only John

Stuart Mill but many nineteenth-century Europeans believed should guide advanced civilizations in their dealings with backward societies.[29] It took for granted the civilization of European states or their offspring in other continents. In short, positive sovereignty doctrine expressed a presumption of superiority based not simply on ethnocentrism but also on demonstrated achievements of Europeans in science, technology, warfare, government, political economy, architecture, literature, and the rest. This presumption was not yet perplexed – as it later would be – by contrary ideals of international legitimacy.

This outlook of Europeans at the historical moment of their greatest power and hubris was formalized in positive international law which recognized empirical criteria of sovereign statehood: a delimited territory, a stable population, and most importantly, a reliable government with the will and capacity to carry out international obligations. It was widely believed that non-Western societies did not meet such criteria. W. E. Hall, an English legal positivist, even claimed that modern international law 'cannot be supposed to be understood or recognized by countries differently civilized'.[30] This is the doctrine of 'constitutive recognition' which as Bull comments 'is widely viewed as having been simply an instrument of European dominance'.[31] According to Alexandrowicz 'no such constitutive theory of recognition existed in the pre-positivist world'.[32] Arguably it did not exist because it could not be enforced. By the nineteenth century, however, Europe had the power and the will to impose its international system on the rest of the world. Even highly credible non-Western states which were never colonized, such as Japan, now had to assert their statehood in positivist terms. The result was the first universal international society based on a selective membership principle which discriminated between a superior class of sovereign states and an inferior class of various dependencies. Application of the principle resulted in the incorporation of some political systems into the exclusive club of independent states by constitutive recognition, and the subordination of the rest within a dependent framework of colonialism.

The initial expansion of international society beyond Europe and the United States was achieved either by compulsion or invitation. The former was evident in the enforced recruitment of Turkey, China, and Japan – which historically operated according to their own rules of superiority and enclosure – into European international law, which was based on reciprocity. These states were forced to be free. The latter was evident in the incorporation of the Latin American states, the independent states of the British Empire, and the new states of Eastern

Europe all of which previously had been under the jurisdiction of European sovereigns. These states merely split off from European empires and still retained the essential characteristics of European states. Recognition of the former states consequently required more explicit standards of empirical statehood than the latter which were presumed – rightly or wrongly – to be capable and responsible, whereas the non-European states had to demonstrate it. Some Latin American and East European states might very well have failed the test had it been applied to them. There was if not a double standard at least a divergent one.

The legal tools for bringing about the observation of Western norms by non-European states were capitulation treaties of various kinds which Western powers were now in a position to enforce. Increased movements of Europeans around the world in the nineteenth century brought demands for guarantees of personal liberty and freedom of commerce wherever they went. European governments were inclined to provide such guarantees. This led to impositions of extraterritoriality which gave Europeans exemption from the jurisdiction of non-European governments. Rulers in India or in China had traditionally exempted settlements of foreign merchants from local jurisdiction as a matter of courtesy. Nineteenth-century positive international law turned this into an 'unequal treaty' obligation. The resort to extraterritoriality was now considered evidence of inferior civilization. 'The next step', as Alexandrowicz puts it, 'was to argue that non-civilized nations had to be admitted into the Family of Nations by the civilized nations which constituted its superior inner club. Some were admitted and some were not.'[33]

Turkey was involved in relations with Europe for centuries, but as the leading representative of Islamic civilization the Sublime Porte historically had refused to observe European international law and was sufficiently powerful not to be made to do so. Indeed, Europeans seeking relationships with the Ottoman Empire were required to defer to its rules which were inspired by Islamic tradition. Although still a power to reckon with, by the nineteenth century the empire was in decline. Leading European states were now in a position to enforce compliance with their international usages by means of capitulations and they had a strong diplomatic and economic interest to do so. In accepting reluctantly over the period of a century such principles as equal sovereignty, reciprocity, and freedom of commerce and in finally being formally inducted into European international society by treaty in 1840 and 1856, Turkey repudiated its Islamic traditions in external relations and thereby contributed to the universalization of the states-system.[34] In Article VII of the Treaty of Paris (1856) the signatory states solemnly 'declare the Sublime Porte admitted to participate in the advantages of the Public Law and System of Europe'.

China was the centre of another political cosmology to which European 'barbarians' and others previously had to kowtow. When Chinese power in East Asia was overturned in the nineteenth century by these same barbarians the middle kingdom was itself forced to submit to a very different European cosmology and was gradually incorporated into international society although under terms which were coordinated to a greater extent among encroaching powers. Western impositions aimed at securing resident diplomatic representation at Peking and opening the vast Chinese market to external commerce. The principal means again were 'unequal treaties' and similar capitulations which, among other things, enforced the European 'standard of civilization' for the benefit of traders, missionaries, and other foreign residents and travellers in China.[35] Important parts of Chinese jurisdiction fell under Western direction from the mid nineteenth century: treaty ports and particularly the international community at Shanghai, extraterritorial courts for foreign residents, combined military intervention and river patrols by foreign navies, and coordinated diplomatic interference in the Chinese imperial government. Although never formally colonized by the West, China was gradually obliged over an extended period to abandon its historical self-image as the 'Middle Kingdom' and conform to Western diplomatic norms. The last capitulations were not terminated formally until 1943 when China's support was required by the allies in the war against Japan. China finally emerged as a great power in 1945 when it acquired permanent membership on the UN Security Council.

Although initially subjected to enforced opening to foreign ships and commerce by the United States, Japan entered international society by successfully imitating Western states in government, law, industry, technology and, indeed, even in art, dress, architecture, and whatever was considered necessary to retain independence. Japan was in many ways already on a par with European powers in economic development, centralized self-government, military credibility, and literacy and was therefore in a position to satisfy Western standards. She not only accepted international law and diplomacy and adopted Western-style parliamentary government but also achieved military success in wars against China (1894–5) and, as indicated, Russia (1904–5). Japan also participated in the capitulations imposed on China. By the turn of the twentieth century she had already emerged as the leading sovereign power of Asia.[36]

Solicited incorporation involved new jurisdictions such as the republics of Latin America, the gradually emerging British dominions (Canada, Australia, New Zealand, South Africa and, more ambiguously, Ireland), and the mostly small states of Central and Eastern Europe. The United States falls into the same category, although it had been a peripheral participant in European diplomacy since the late eighteenth century and by the end of the nineteenth was a reluctant great power. Except for the dominions, all these states entered international society following the collapse or defeat of European empires as a result of major war. Virtually all were either European states or the offspring of Europe and enjoyed privileged membership as a consequence of this kinship – some would say racial – principle.

The emergence of the Latin American states derived from the beheading of the Spanish and Portuguese empires by Napoleon's armies during the Peninsular War (1807–14). Following successful rebellions against Spanish colonial rule – or independence under the Portuguese crown in the case of Brazil – the first steps towards incorporation into the states-system were initiated by American and British diplomatic recognition in the early decades of the nineteenth century. The Latin American states were plagued by post-colonial wars and began to use European international law to order their own relationships when still politically isolated from the European system. They also became involved with the global capitalist economy before they entered overseas international society. After 1870 the region experienced unprecedented expansion in its socioeconomic relations with Europe by means of trade, foreign investment and immigration – the latter going mainly to Argentina, Brazil, Uruguay, and Chile.[37] Although considered to possess full international legal personality, the Latin American states did not begin to participate in the European diplomatic system until the turn of the twentieth century when they were invited to the First Hague Peace Conference in 1899. Mexico was the only Latin American state in attendance. However, at the second in 1907 all the South American countries were represented. The Hague conferences are usually considered to mark the formal extension of the club of sovereign states beyond Europe and the United States.

Unlike the Spanish-speaking republics of Latin America and also of course the United States, the British dominions acquired sovereign statehood in accordance with evolving colonial practice. These states possessed domestic self-government for some time before asserting a right to participate in international society as equal sovereign states which was not acknowledged by Britain until the Imperial Conference of 1926. Canada and Australia considered their substantial contributions to the allied victory in the first world war as valid grounds for their claims. Canadian governments pointed to the battle of Vimy Ridge and Australians to Gallipoli. South Africa also earned military honour on the battlefields of the first world war. The dominions' international credibility was reflected by the Treaty of Versailles which they signed as British but also as independent states becoming members in their own right of the League of Nations. In 1926 they acquired independent status which was formally acknowledged in the (British) Statute of Westminster (1931) and judiciously if not indeed brilliantly described in the Balfour Report as 'autonomous Communities within the British Empire, equal in status, in no way subordinate one to another in any aspect of their domestic or external affairs, though united by a common allegiance to the Crown, and freely associated as members of the British Commonwealth of Nations'.[38] These countries were forerunners of the British practice of evolutionary decolonization.[39]

Although modern Greece emerged in 1830 from the first major retreat of the Ottoman Empire in the Balkan Peninsula, all of the remaining new states of central and eastern Europe gained independence between the 1870s and 1920. During this period the Ottoman territories in the Balkans began to splinter and finally that empire along with the Habsburg, Hohenzollern, and Romanoff dynasties in central and eastern Europe shattered as a consequence of the first world war. The political map of Europe was fundamentally redrawn as a result. Romania, Bulgaria, and Albania emerged before the war (as did Serbia and Montenegro which were later incorporated into Yugoslavia); Poland reappeared in 1916. The remaining territories were parcelled out among seven additional states in the immediate postwar period.

Some of these states had independent ancestors and could perhaps be seen as reverting to sovereignty, but most could not. Consequently this region became pre-eminently one of new states even if its nationalities had ancient histories as oppressed minorities. Hungary had an immediate previous existence as the Austro-Hungarian Empire and earlier independent existences. Poland was newly resurrected after having been drawn, quartered, and buried in the late eighteenth century. Three states could claim tenuous kinship with a sovereign of quasi-sovereign ancestor: Czechoslovakia's relation to the Kingdom of Bohemia, and Finland and Lithuania's connection with earlier Grand Duchies of the same names. Estonia, Latvia, Yugoslavia, Bulgaria, Romania, and Albania, however, were novel formations. And although a major goal of the Paris Peace Conference was to create

65

nation–states by plebiscites and where necessary the resettlement of populations, many of these new states still contained significant minorities. The most extreme case was Yugoslavia which encapsulated recently independent Serbia (1878) and Montenegro (1878) as well as several distinctive nationalities – Croats, Slovenes, Albanians, Macedonians – and religions – Orthodox, Catholic, Moslem, Jewish.

These states consequently harbour potentially and sometimes actively divisive minority groups possessed by strong and frequently intransigent nationalist sentiments. The new constitutional frameworks promoted by the League often could not accommodate these divisions. The nationalities wanted to live apart, and were not particularly devoted to mastering the political arts of living together. Later, when these states fell into the Soviet orbit, communist parties only succeeded in papering over the nationality 'problem'. It is no surprise, therefore, that the term 'balkanized' has become synonymous with recurrent instability rooted in ethnicity. Peter Lyon asks: 'What did being a new state mean in eastern Europe in 1919?' and answers 'For the most part it meant being a beneficiary of the Versailles settlement.'[40] Here is a foreshadowing of what was later to become the fast track to sovereign statehood: self-determination by right.

Elements of the positive sovereignty game were nevertheless evident in central and eastern Europe. Rights of self-determination obviously did not prevent Soviet imperialist absorption of Latvia, Lithuania, and Estonia in 1940 – one of the last instances either inside Europe or outside of coerced territorial acquisition by a European power which was still operating according to nineteenth-century norms. Finland retained its independence the hard way by going to war with the Russians and making 'Finlandization' – independence as a buffer state – an easier choice for Moscow than military conquest. The other states (excluding Yugoslavia) were sufficiently significant to be part of the Warsaw Pact and thereby involved at the centre of the East–West conflict. Soviet imperialism obviously did not concede complete independence to its East European vassals, but neither did it absorb them constitutionally nor could it without undermining its cohesiveness as a power. And in remaining aloof Yugoslavia did not evidently place its independence at risk. Even if Eastern Europe for most of the time since the second world war and before the Gorbachev era of *glasnost* and *perestroika* is most aptly conceived as a suzerain-state system, the fact remains that the non-suzerain parts of the system figured in the balance of power between East and West.

Yet, in considering membership by invitation in the club of sovereign states one cannot fail to notice anomalies. At the turn of the twentieth century a few quasi-states were in existence which bore virtually no resemblance to the historic states of Western Europe and some were receiving invitations to attend international conferences. Haiti had long existed as an independent although neglected land which nobody evidently desired to recolonize. Liberia and Ethiopia were beginning to appear on the political map of Africa alongside recently established European colonies and protectorates. Persia and Siam were present at the first Hague Conference. When Liberia acceded to the Act of the Brussels Conference (1890) and more significantly to the Hague Declarations and Convention of 1907 additional irregularities were created. In short, precedents were being set that were at variance with current rules and practices of positive sovereignty. And in the world of law precedent is important.

In 1904 an eminent British legal theorist argued that the architects of international law consisted of all European states and their offspring plus Japan. The Christian African states of Ethiopia and Liberia were also international legal persons as was the Congo Free State since its sovereign was the King of Belgium. A number of states including Turkey, Morocco, Muscat, Siam, Persia, and China were partial but not full members of international society.[41] As for the rest of the world's political systems, their status was that of colonial subjects of one kind or another.

The second path in the globalization of positive sovereignty consequently involved the acquisition of jurisdiction and control by certain European powers over extensive populated territories in Asia, Africa, and Oceania which owing to their 'backwardness' were considered unqualified for recognition as sovereign states.[42] The episode was a kind of international enclosure movement. Colonialism resurrected a dynastic practice killed by the rise of nationalism in Europe whereby sovereigns acquired and held various non-contingent lands as parts of their states or empires. The most obvious new example was the Congo Free State which literally was the personal property of King Leopold before its cession to Belgium in 1908.[43] The clearest and most significant instance of this path was undoubtedly the partition of Africa in the last decades of the nineteenth century. And it is this case I examine.

The political character of Africa at that time gave little indication of either states or a states-system as defined by the positive sovereignty criteria of the day. Africa was a continental archipelago of loosely defined political systems: a world of societies rather than states and far more recognizable to anthropology than to international relations. The European-style territorial state with its legal order, institutionalized government, and defined boundaries was largely unknown. Even

African 'states' in the looser anthropological definition exercised uncertain control: 'the authority and power of the central government
faded away more and more the further one went from the centre
toward the boundary. Thus boundaries between the states were
vague, sometimes overlapping.'[44] Many African societies lacked centralized authority structures and consisted essentially of segmentary
lineage systems. Some societies were so small as to be 'coterminous
with kinship relations'.[45] Government based on written laws and impersonal administration was virtually unknown throughout most of
the continent. Traditional African states had noteworthy features of
transitory and personal rule. Even the Islamic states which historically
appeared and disappeared in the region between the Sahara Desert
and the equatorial forests are described as 'the hastily assembled
empires of Muslim adventurers'.[46] Personal rule remains a characteristic of many African states today which are fixed territorial entities
primarily in their juridical statehood. International boundaries are
defined not by the extent of government authority and power – which
in some cases still fades as distance from the capital city increases – but
externally by the post-colonial international community.

Before the advent of colonialism there was no 'Africa' in any international sense and of course no political map of the vast continent.
African geography was not known accurately before the second half of
the nineteenth century when Western explorers finally completed
mapping the interior. The first continental political maps were of
colonial Africa. The political map of traditional Africa was also drawn
only during the colonial era after completion of anthropological field-
work which could not be carried out before that time. It revealed a
complicated lacework of more than a thousand variously defined political societies – some isolated and some interdependent, some free
and others slave, some entangled in imperial relations, others in feudal
ties, and so on. Traditional Africa was a world of limited political scale
somewhat reminiscent of the localized feudal societies of Europe
during the Middle Ages. Africa of course lacked entirely the overarching equivalent of *societas christiana* (or of the Chinese Empire in
East Asia or the Mogul Empire in South Asia). The political technologies which historically enabled large-scale political orders to be
built and sustained in Europe and Asia – organized armies and navies,
means of transport, universal religion, literacy, coinage, bureaucracy,
extensive division of labour, communications – were absent in most
parts of the continent. These technologies and the territorial state
along with it were introduced only at the end of the nineteenth century
by European colonialists.

Without fixed territorial bases under central governments there could of course not develop the usual marks of statehood which presuppose defined borders, domestic jurisdiction, civil peace within the jurisdiction enforced by a government with the sole right to exercise force, and the administrative ability to mobilize public revenue. Traditional Africa was marked instead by the ebb and flow of continuous warfare and violent feuding at all levels of society, often ritualized and organized in terms of kinship. The absence of money in most places obstructed public finance. Territorial states also make possible orderly and lawful international relations between juridically equal, mutually recognized and therefore independent governments. Old Africa more closely resembled a world of suzerain-state systems which operate on the principle of dependency and tribute between unequals. There often were no firm borders at the periphery and tribute could be paid to more than one suzerain at the same time.

The absence of defined territorial states meant that international relations in the conventional meaning were absent also. 'One cannot speak convincingly of an African system of states on the analogy of, for example, the modern European states-system, or the city states-systems of ancient Mesopotamia and classical Greece . . . African states were fluid and *ad hoc* creations that did not require a fixed human or territorial base.'[47] Although various particular customs regulated intercourse among contiguous political systems, there was no international society extending over large regions and much less the continent as a whole and consequently no general diplomatic practices or international law. Europeans and Africans for centuries engaged in treaty-making along the coasts, but whether it had the same meaning and significance for both parties is open to doubt. Europeans signed treaties with an eye on other Europeans and with the aim of acquiring trading rights or territorial claims which conformed with international law. Africans probably made them to gain commercial and political advantage over local rivals. They could hardly have realized the European international legal implications of what they were doing. This in outline was the political character of Africa a century ago when European governments partitioned the continent and incorporated the parts into the international system as their dependencies.

The partition of Africa, it should be emphasized, was not only a scramble for territories by European powers but was also a joint take-over based on an international agreement made at the Berlin Conference (1884–5) which established basic rules of partition intended to prevent conflict between these powers. And it succeeded by and large. Therefore, while the conference itself did not partition Africa it did institutionalize the process in the aim of creating a *pax Europaea* in the continent. European states occupied territories by signing bilateral treaties with African rulers in accordance with rules set down by the conference. It should be emphasised that these rules concerned only the relations of the European powers *inter se* and did not apply to African rulers who were not present at the Berlin Conference and were excluded entirely from this sovereignty game. Their exclusive role was to sign a treaty. If they refused they could be forced in accordance with international law. In the circumstances of powerful intruding mechanized states and weak undeveloped African societies, cession can easily be imagined as the lesser of two evils from the African point of view.

International title to all but very few African territories was transferred to European states usually by cession and occasionally by conquest – although rarely if at all by the occupation of *terra nullius*.[48] Although conquest was not common in Africa it was of course legitimate in nineteenth-century international law. Current legal analysis sees cession as evidence that African rulers were sovereigns. Hence, Alexandrowicz's description of the colonizing process as a competition for title deeds.[49] If the European successor's title was valid, the former holder's title also had to be valid and for this he had to be sovereign. This interpretation usually claims the authority of M. F. Lindley. However, he makes the crucial point that cession did not imply equal sovereignty, hence his distinction between an 'advanced sovereign' and a 'native sovereign.'[50] The very notion of 'backward' territory denoted an absence of equal sovereignty. This is crucial because it clearly signifies a pre-existing dual system of superior and inferior states. Martin Wight has more accurately captured the character of these treaties in referring in this case to 'protected states' which of all dependencies had the greatest residual sovereignty: 'it is probable that such treaties are domestic matters and have validity in international law only in that they are internationally recognized as establishing a dependent relationship between the protected state and the British Crown which precludes other states from interfering'.[51] A. C. McEwen likewise uses the equivocal term 'quasi-treaty' in referring to the formal acquisition of territory by Europeans in East Africa.[52]

The Berlin Conference resulted in an international framework of large-scale jurisdictions imposed by European powers on Africans with only the most tenuous indication of their consent. Most explanations stop at this point. By the positive international law of the day, however, Africans had no consent to give: they were not considered to be capable of consenting. The colonies were the first territorial states with fixed boundaries recognized by international law that Africa possessed. These were the jurisdictions from which African membership in international society would eventually spring. The colonialists likewise were the first modern state-builders. They expanded enormously the political scale of the continent by reducing many hundreds of traditional political systems to some fifty new and usually arbitrary jurisdictions which were painted on the map in the colours of occupying European states. In brief, the partition amounted to an international enclosure movement in which the vast continent was divided among several European powers and its populations were subjected to their jurisdiction with little if any regard to African values or institutions. The entire episode was authorized and guided by international law which was still a European institution.

THE 'SACRED TRUST' OF CIVILIZATION

By the time of African partition in the late nineteenth century it was necessary for European governments to justify their control of foreign populated territories considered not 'fit' for self-government. A doctrine of 'the sacred trust of civilization' was elaborated for this purpose at a succession of international conferences. It paralleled domestic guardianship of aboriginal peoples in North America by continentalizing settler states.[53]

'Trusteeship' was a codeword for paternalism which is a moral practice that arises whenever significant gaps in capability exist between agents, such as those between parents and children, the able and the disabled, rich and poor, and so forth. As indicated, such a gap opened between Europe and many parts of Asia, Africa and Oceania in the nineteenth century. Europeans were now in unchallenged control of millions of square miles of territory and hundreds of millions of people outside Europe which they had to justify to themselves if not yet to those people. They were in a position to extend the blessings and benefits of their civilization to the rest of the world which hitherto had not been able to enjoy them. This became their 'civilizing mission' or the 'white man's burden'. The African, according to Sir Frederick (later Lord) Lugard, 'holds the position of a late-born child in the family of nations, and must as yet be schooled in the discipline of the nursery'.[54] The self-identification of European states as 'civilized parents' and of many non-European societies as 'backward children' and the consequent practice of paternalism acquired moral and legal standing in international relations. 'Wardship' entailed, according to Lindley, both 'the duties which the advanced peoples collectively owe to back-

71

ward races in general' and 'the duties which a particular Power owes to backward races under its immediate control'.[55]

This doctrine was a significant change of international legitimacy. Prior to the nineteenth century there was no such thing as an explicit 'standard of civilization' and no need for one. It was natural for Europeans to assume the superiority of their civilization but not its hegemony. Outsiders were still a threat. The ascendancy of nineteenth-century mechanized statehood was marked by a shift in international legitimacy from fearing barbarians to patronizing them. International trusteeship also reflected prevailing ideologies of the day. And Europe and America were strongly influenced by various 'positivistic' and 'evolutionary' theories of progress which sought to explain and justify the remarkable ascendancy of Western civilization over all others. Natural law was no longer a law of morality and justice but of success and survival. It accounted for the obvious fact that whites were far in advance of other races which was construed as evidence of superiority. Racial paternalism was often expressed explicitly, as in the 1923 comment of an American on the League of Nations mandates system: 'The negro race has hitherto shown no capacity for progressive development except when under the tutelage of other peoples.'[56]

Positive sovereignty doctrine tended to equate 'civilization' with the ability of states to defend themselves and to protect civil conditions. 'Civilization' became a scale for defining the international standing of countries, including their legal capacity and rights. The standard of civilization emerged in response to two problems: protecting the lives, liberty, and property of Europeans abroad, and determining which countries deserved recognition as sovereign states. As regards the former, the standard demanded effective legal protection of foreign nationals by the government of whatever country they happened to be in. Either the constitutive recognition of a non-Western state as sovereign or its reduction to a European dependency can be understood in terms of this requirement. As regards the latter, the standard addressed the subsequent problem of dependencies whose populations were living in 'barbarous conditions' and required, among other actions of the colonial power, suppression of slavery and the slave trade (and also offensive customs such as polygamy and suttee), physical protection of 'backward peoples', and promotion of their 'improvement'.[57]

A new body of international law to advance the civilization of dependent peoples was enunciated at successive international conferences during the heyday of Western colonialism. The Final Act of the Congress of Vienna (1815) had already provided for the suppression of the slave trade which was accomplished on the high seas by the middle of the century. The General Act of the Berlin Conference (1885) sought in addition the abolition of slavery which was then widespread in Africa and the Middle East. These were restraints laid on colonial subjects. The signatory powers themselves undertook an international obligation to improve the 'moral and material well-being' of Africans and 'to protect and favour all religious, scientific, or charitable institutions' which aim at 'bringing home to them the blessings of civilization' (Article 6). The Conference agreed that although native populations were unable to defend their own interests they were nevertheless entitled to protection by international law which 'demanded the observation of a certain level of conduct on the part of the powerful nations in dealing with defenceless backward peoples'.[58] The efficacy of these requirements are questionable, of course, as disclosed for example by the outrageous abuses of plantation capitalism in King Leopold's Congo. The fact that it was a public scandal in Europe, however, is indicative of the paternalist international morality of the day. In commenting recently on the historical significance of the Berlin Conference, Lewis Gann concludes that it 'helped to set up a new international opinion and a new international standard whereby the colonizers – at least in theory – judged themselves and their competitors' and it 'helped to write a new chapter in the history of international obligations'.[59]

The 'sacred trust of civilization' was institutionalized after the first world war in the League of Nations' Permanent Mandates Commission which was superseded after the second by the United Nations' International Trusteeship System. Article 22 of the Covenant declared that for territories 'inhabited by peoples not yet able to stand by themselves under the strenuous conditions of the modern world' there 'should be applied the principle that the well-being and development of such peoples form a sacred trust of civilisation'. 'Tutelage' of such peoples was 'entrusted' to certain 'advanced nations' and 'exercised by them as Mandatories on behalf of the League'.[60] Three classes of Mandates were recognized based on 'the stage of development' of the populations involved: 'A' Mandates for peoples of the Middle East who soon would be capable of exercising sovereign statehood, 'B' Mandates for most peoples of sub-Saharan Africa who still required an indefinite period of European tutelage before this stage was reached, and finally 'C' Mandates for the 'primitive' peoples of South West Africa and the Pacific who very likely would remain wards of the states-system for centuries, if not forever.

The standard of civilization was still in evidence at the founding of the UN. Although 'development' was by now displacing the more value-loaded 'civilization', the doctrine of trusteeship was institution-alized in the UN Charter. Article 73 declared that UN members with foreign territories 'whose peoples have not yet attained a full measure of self-government . . . accept as a sacred trust the obligation to promote to the utmost . . . the well-being of the inhabitants of these territories'. A Trusteeship Council was established to administer international dependencies inherited from the defunct League and additional territories detached from Japan and Italy by their defeat in the second world war or voluntarily placed in trusteeship by a colonial power.

Although the war set in motion changes which eventually contributed to the illegitimacy of colonialism, in 1945 this radically different international society was not yet a reality. International trusteeship only became controversial following the war. A division opened at the UN between the Trusteeship Council – which was identified with colonialism – and the emergent Third World minority in the General Assembly, which if decolonization were to continue would eventually be in the majority. At the first session in 1946 it was evident that some delegations considered the Declaration Regarding Non-Self-Govern-ing Territories (Chapter 11 of the Charter) as a warrant for the UN to supervise colonialism in general. The distinction between ordinary dependencies and trust territories became blurred and paternalism was placed on the defensive. In an age of equality it was difficult to justify a practice grounded in hierarchy – even if it was benevolent or the people it affected were as yet not sufficiently equipped or prepared to operate a modern state.

THE CONSTITUTION OF NEGATIVE SOVEREIGNTY

About the mid-1950s a reversal of classical positive sovereignty in international relations concerning the dependency system began to occur. The change was extremely rapid in historical terms: by the early 1960s it was virtually complete. And it was general: almost the entire colonial and trusteeship system was dismantled. It paralleled a domestic revolution in the United States in which formal racial discrimination was abolished within a ten-year period between the 1954 Supreme Court judgement against school segregation in Brown versus Board of Education and the 1964 Civil Rights Act. Domestic and international anti-discrimination doctrines were undoubtedly related. Both focused on racial minorities. Both involved claims for equality and dignity. Both met eventually if not at first with widespread public

74

acceptance to the point where nobody but a few diehards were prepared to defend the old regime. Both were instituted by law. Sovereign rights for colonial peoples in the community of states was the equivalent of civil and political rights for members of racial minorities in Western democracies.

Renunciation of the standard of civilization was – according to Georg Schwarzenberger – part of the 'secularization of international law': a shift from law between 'civilized states' to law between 'sovereign states'.[61] Secularization excluded not only Christian definitions of 'civilized' customs or even liberal values such as constitutional government and the rule of law but also nationality as criteria of membership in international society. Sovereignty was now to be based on a universal doctrine of categorical self-determination which did not presuppose underlying nationhood but only subject colonial status. The doctrine stopped at the independence of all pre-existing colonial entities and did not extend to nationalities or ethnic communities which were not colonial jurisdictions.

Self-determination originally postulated peoples rather than princes as the only grounds of international legitimacy: that is, *national* self-determination. The 'self' was a nation which was assumed to be a substantial entity based on either political tradition or ethnic distinctiveness. Britain and Switzerland were instances of the former, Germany and Italy of the latter. Nineteenth-century nationalism in Germany and Italy involved the formation of nation-states by the unification or absorption of various principalities or city states which shared a common language. 'Determination' presupposed not only the existence but also the capacity of peoples to establish their own constitutional life and to govern themselves as independent states. This implied both personal and national freedom as the ultimate grounds of sovereign statehood. The spirit of the doctrine is disclosed by the following assertion of John Stuart Mill: 'Free institutions are next to impossible in a country made up of different nationalities.'[62] Mill was thinking of the multinational Austro-Hungarian Empire which denied not only individual but also national liberty to its subject peoples.

The principle of national self-determination first received quasi-official recognition at the 1919 Paris Peace Conference under the influence of American President Woodrow Wilson and, to a lesser extent, British Prime Minister David Lloyd George. Although it was considered a political rather than a legal principle and was not acknowledged by the League Covenant, it nevertheless fostered a plebiscitarian method of determining sovereign statehood in Central and Eastern Europe based on nationalities and the protection of minorities. It acknowledged the international legitimacy of small states and reversed the course of nineteenth-century nationalism by dividing rather than uniting historical states. It also combined the principle of self-determination with treaties guaranteeing the rights of ethnic minorities.

Under the League, however, national self-determination was restricted to Europeans. Non-Europeans were subject, as noted, to the mandates system. Mandates and Trust Territories were therefore a denial and not a grant of self-determination. The UN Charter invokes 'the principle of equal rights and self-determination of peoples' (Article 1) and reiterates it in connection with 'international economic and social co-operation' (Article 55). However, as noted, the Charter still recognized unequal capacities of different peoples for self-government and the necessity of trusteeship. Article 73 acknowledges the obligation 'to develop self-government ... according to the particular circumstances of each territory and its peoples and their varying stages of advancement', and Article 76 speaks of 'self-government or independence as may be appropriate'.

Although trusteeship is an 'obligation' under the Charter whereas self-determination is only a 'principle', one cannot but agree that it has nevertheless 'clearly proved to be a principle of the utmost importance in international relations'.[63] For lawyers the main issue is whether self-determination has the force of law.[64] For political scientists the issue is the efficacy of self-determination in international relations. And international developments since 1950 suggest that it became completely effective as an anti-colonial injunction. The principle did not appear fully formed in the Charter but was brought into existence by international politics following the war. Third World nationalists used the rhetoric of self-determination to capture the moral high-ground in international relations, and the older argument of trusteeship proved utterly inadequate to counter it. The negative sovereignty ideal of self-determination as a categorical right of all colonial peoples was asserted by a succession of UN General Assembly Resolutions which eventually shaped international legitimacy on the issue. Among the most significant were Resolution 421 (1950) which called for a study of the ways and means 'which would ensure the right of peoples and nations to self-determination', Resolution 637 (1952) which declared that the right to self-determination 'is a prerequisite to the full enjoyment of all fundamental human rights', and Resolution 1188 (1957) which held that self-determination was a right deserving due respect from member states.

The victory of categorical self-determination was signalled by the celebrated 1960 Declaration on the Granting of Independence to Colonial Countries and Peoples (Resolution 1514) which proclaimed that 'all peoples have the right to self-determination' and 'inadequacy of political, economic, social or educational preparedness should never serve as a pretext for delaying independence'. It was passed in the General Assembly by a vote of 89 to 0, with 9 abstentions. Even the colonial powers were unwilling to reject it. The Declaration is considered by Third World states and by many others as a 'second Charter' of the UN promulgated to liberate all remaining dependent peoples. From this time empirical statehood as a valid ground for determining the right to sovereignty in the Third World went into eclipse. Having previously condemned Portuguese colonialism and South African apartheid as 'crimes against humanity', in 1970 the General Assembly in Resolution 2621 declared: 'The further continuation of colonialism in all its forms and manifestations is a crime which constitutes a violation of the Charter of the United Nations, the Declaration on the Granting of Independence to Colonial Countries and Peoples and the principles of international law.' It also declared that the struggle for self-determination in colonial territories where it was being resisted, such as Portuguese Africa, was legitimate as was foreign intervention to support it, and any attempt to suppress the struggle was contary to the UN Charter. We now live in a world virtually devoid of formal colonial jurisdiction and its reinstatement seems impossible.

The new doctrine changed the definition of both the collective 'self' and political 'determination'. The self was no longer either historical or ethnic 'nations' but artificial ex-colonial 'jurisdictions' which were multi-ethnic entities in most cases and ironically reminiscent of the old multinational empires of Europe. The 'nation' was now merely all who had been subjects of a particular colonial government and were of different race from their alien rulers. Indigenous successors to those rulers were by definition legitimate whether or not they expressed the popular will. Their rights as sovereigns and the human rights of their subjects to self-determination were one and the same. The self was not determined by plebiscites and virtually no concern was shown for minorities. Determination came down to the eviction of alien European rulers and the assertion of majority rule based on a racial definition of the majority. Since colonialism was essentially 'a violation of racial sovereignty', self-determination was decolonization.[65]

Self-determination no longer means the same as previously and almost means the opposite. The new sovereign states are not usually based on nationalities either ethnic or historical. Ethnonations only rarely coincided with colonial jurisdictions and most colonies never developed into authentic political nationalities. The new doctrine explicitly denies self-determination to ethnonationalities since if it were granted most existing ex-colonial states would be broken up just as the Austro-Hungarian empire was broken up by granting self-determination to the nationalities of Central Europe. Resolution 1514 declares emphatically that 'any attempt aimed at the partial or total disruption of the national unity and the territorial integrity of a country is incompatible with the purposes and principles of the Charter of the United Nations'. Consequently, ethnonational self-determination is now illegitimate and the prospects of independence for the numerous ethnonationalities of the Third World are bleak. And since most of the new states also do not provide minority rights and internal autonomies to compensate ethnonationalities and indeed often deliberately withhold them, they tend to provoke civil discord along ethnic lines as did the old multinational empires of Europe. Martin Wight commented at the time of decolonization: 'with national self-determination being applied in conditions so different from those in which it originated that the word "nation" has lost any distinct meaning, heterogeneity has returned. The states represented at the United Nations are more various in origin, size and structure than were the states represented at the Congress of Westphalia.'[66]

EVOLUTION, RESTORATION, OR INNOVATION?

How can we understand the change of international legitimacy and legality which accompanied the demise of Western overseas colonialism and the appearance of numerous sovereign states in the Third World? How should we characterize the contemporary international regime and how does it compare to those outlined above which existed previously? The orthodox positivist argument is that the rise of self-determination is consistent with an historically expanding international society that finally assimilated all of the world's political systems to its institutions which have been decontaminated of Western values and are now authentically secular and universal. In other words, the club of states has been opened to all regardless of religion, race, culture, or geography. Since overseas colonialism has been abolished no further admissions are possible without upsetting existing jurisdictions.

New statehood therefore springs from international recognition including the formal transfer of sovereignty from a European power to an indigenous government. New states are legally 'posited' by formal actions of international society and 'the will of states already established'.[67] This implies that they reflect conventional criteria of sovereign statehood. Although these criteria have evolved over time, it is possible to say that the contemporary global system of 'sovereign' states has emerged out of an earlier Eurocentric system of 'civilized' and before that 'Christian' states. There is institutional continuity, therefore, between the old European states which formed the original community of states in the mid seventeenth century and the admission of new states such as India or Ghana or Fiji into the United Nations in the mid twentieth. The globalization of the sovereign states-system therefore discloses an unbroken history. Although its normative structure has become far more complex than previously 'the basic principles of the international society have remained the same, as have the motives and many of the modes of behaviour of its member-states'.[68] This is because the underlying imperatives of independence are still the same.

A contrary argument associated with natural law doctrine and the work of Charles Alexandrowicz holds that post-colonial international norms are a return to the practices of a more tolerant family of nations era which existed prior to the rise of Western hegemony and hubris in international relations. The old natural law regime was destroyed in the nineteenth century by European states who instituted contrary positivist doctrines to justify their territorial expansion overseas. A key change was the rejection of declaratory recognition – which acknowledged the existence, dignity, and equality of non-Western governments – and the adoption of constitutive recognition – which justified the imposition of Western values on non-Western societies. Traditional international society, which had been open and embraced Asian as well as European states who engaged in reciprocal relations, 'shrank into a Eurocentric system which imposed on extra-European countries its own ideas'.[69] These ideas included capacity for self-defence and the standard of civilization as criteria of constitutive recognition. A few non-Western states were recognized, but most were reduced to dependencies.

Independence of Third World states is therefore a 'reversion to sovereignty' based on traditional natural law precepts.[70] By 'reversion' Alexandrowicz means that states are having restored to them an independence that was taken away during the age of European domination and is their natural right. Just as Poland had its international status restored during the first world war after more than a century of deprivation, so also have India, Burma, Sri Lanka, Indonesia, Malagasy, Algeria, Morocco, and other traditional states had their sovereignty returned. They consequently are not new states at all but are as old if not indeed older than most Western states. And although Alexandrowicz concedes in the case of Africa that most of the ex-colonial entities 'are new states in the present day meaning of the word' he nevertheless argues that the African continent as a whole has reverted to sovereignty after an interlude of protectorate status under the terms of the Berlin Conference the main point of which always was to restore the continent's independence.[71] The result is a global community with more of the characteristics of the old natural law regime than of the hierarchical positivist structure of the more recent past.

A third explanation spelled out in the following chapters accepts parts of these arguments but also detects novel postulates and precepts in the normative framework of contemporary international society as it applies to the ex-colonial states. It agrees with the positivists that the large majority of Third World states have been 'posited' by international society and never existed previously even in remotely similar geographical or constitutional shape. Not only the sovereignty but also in most cases the territorial jurisdictions and bureaucracies of these states are creatures of colonialism or trusteeship. Likewise, the third view subscribes to the natural law thesis that non-discrimination is a reversal of positive sovereignty doctrine. But it cannot agree that current international society is a restoration of the old loosely connected natural law regime. The pre-imperial and post-colonial worlds are different in fundamentals. Most fundamental is the contemporary emphasis on actively reinforcing the fragile integrity of the ex-colonial states by nonintervention and international development assistance. This is a doctrine not only of nondiscrimination but also of positive discrimination, international aid, and state-building.

Today the international community does not merely tolerate diversity but also seeks to supply a 'safety-net' for numerous insubstantial countries which are unable to provide very much in the way of civil or socioeconomic goods for their populations. If the post-1960 international regime were merely a restoration of traditional norms of non-discrimination the emphasis on Third World development would not be there. There would not be this emphasis because it would be assumed that states different in form or substance are nevertheless equal in value to their inhabitants. The old natural law regime was a *laissez-faire* world. There were no international standards of empirical statehood, of developed and underdeveloped countries. The new post-colonial regime is an activitist and constructivist mode of international relations. Negative sovereignty is a twentieth-century institution which was unknown in traditional international relations. It was unknown because the problem it has been arranged to deal with – the emergence and development of numerous precarious states – was not perceived prior to the decolonization of the non-Western world in the mid twentieth century. The problem of international development was not apparent because the states-system was not as deeply divided as it is today between developed and underdeveloped states.

In brief, we are witnessing the emergence of a community of states with a normative, legal, and organizational superstructure that is far more elaborate than anything which existed previously. This brings us back to the controversy identified at the beginning. Many Third World states are scarcely self-standing realities but nevertheless are completely sovereign jurisdictions recognized by international legitimacy and law. Rugged individualism in international relations hardly applies to these entities which for the most part are creatures of a novel international protectionism.

4 INDEPENDENCE BY RIGHT

The historical change from positive to negative sovereignty is most specifically and concretely evident in European political disengagement from Asia, Africa, and Oceania.[1] As indicated in the last chapter, the right to independence and the corresponding duty to decolonize was installed as an international categorical imperative following the second world war and by 1960 it was the unchallenged and unchallengeable declaration of the United Nations. There is no better place to look for changing norms and assumptions about sovereign statehood, therefore, than in the sphere of decolonization. It is one of the momentous international reversals of the twentieth century whose consequences – material and moral, intended and unintended – continue to reverberate and will for decades to come. We live in a post-colonial world which has undoubted significance for international relations. The termination of colonialism has necessitated and called into existence alternative international arrangements and practices to deal with the special circumstances and problems of post-colonial states, as we shall see in chapters 5 and 6.

Decolonization is often understood as a successful revolt against the West and there is evidence to recommend this positive sovereignty view.[2] The usual image is of a decline of European primacy by the devastation and demoralization of two global wars and the rise of powers on the peripheries of Europe (United States, Russia) and beyond (Japan) which 'ultimately displaced the European system'.[3] It is indicated by vigorous anti-colonialism during and following the second world war which made it impossible to reestablish Dutch rule in the East Indies and French colonialism in Indochina. British decolonization in the subcontinent in reaction to credible nationalist movements, such as the long established Indian Congress, is a further instance. The successful anti-colonial war of liberation against the French in Algeria is yet another. These episodes are consistent with positive sovereignty: new statehood is primarily a question of fact.

In many other parts of the Third World, however, forceful and credible anti-colonial nationalism capable of inheriting sovereignty in rough conformity with positive international law usually did not develop. This is evident from British revisionist colonial historiography based on the post-1945 imperial archives.[4] According to one historian: 'Western Europe's status and capacity relative to the United States was clearly on the wane for most of the twentieth century, and violently so after 1945, but whether that status and capacity fell in relation to Upper Volta or the Gold Coast/Ghana is very doubtful.'[5] According to another: 'whatever persuaded the British empire in1947 to plan its own demise in tropical Africa, it was not fear of black African freedom fighters'.[6] And in government discussion papers of the day 'there was little sense . . . of Britain being too impoverished for the task of colonial rule, or of her retreating in the face of nationalist hostility'.[7] Nor was there any conviction that Africans were now adequately trained and equipped for self-government.

The pressures for transferring sovereignty were to an increasing extent international and principled. The postwar era witnessed an anti-colonial ideology expressed with growing conviction by the annually enlarging number of newly enfranchised states who, as Peter Calvocoressi wrote at the time, 'are weak but not meek'.[8] Anti-colonialism in retrospect looks more and more like a sea change in international legitimacy. Although decolonization in Asia was provoked by forcible Japanese occupation of colonial territories during the war, afterwards when Japan was defeated and the colonial powers regained their stature and capabilities they could not successfully reassert colonialism in moral and legal terms. Their claims of domestic jurisdiction in the colonies and of the lack of indigenous capacity for self-government fell increasingly on deaf ears – especially at the UN. By the late 1950s international opinion had turned fundamentally against colonialism.

The image of a massive and violent revolt against the West is most apt as regards the breakup of the Dutch East Indies and French Indochina. The successful invasions of these territories and others by Japan during the second world war are unambiguous instances of the decline of European power in that part of the world. At the time, however, it was far from certain that colonialism would not be restored when Japan was defeated. In 1942, according to Lord Hailey, the Netherlands government contemplated granting 'autonomy' to the East Indies but within the framework of a continuing union with Holland.[9]

Japanese occupation provoked Indonesian nationalism, however, which during and after the war was engineered by Sukarno and other nationalists into a force to be reckoned with. Athough an Indonesian Republic was proclaimed in Jakarta (Batavia) in August 1945, the Dutch (with initial British assistance) nevertheless attempted to reassert their colonial rule. By 1947 they had 150,000 troops in the colony. They did not become reconciled to an independent Indonesia until 1949 by which time the UN was already a platform of vocal anti-colonialism and the cost of persevering in their enterprise was high.[10] Holland by then was also involved in the emerging Western alliance against the Soviet Union. Pressures from the United States including a threat to suspend Marshall Aid obliged the Dutch government to cut its losses in the East Indies and concentrate its limited armed forces on the defence of Western Europe.

The French were even more determined to reestablish colonial rule in Asia after the defeat of Japan. The war likewise aroused anticolonial nationalism in Japanese occupied Indochina. An indigenous government under the communist Viet Minh with effective control over important territories in northern Vietnam established itself in 1945 following the Japanese withdrawal. Ho Chi Minh read a 'Declaration of Independence of the Democratic Republic of Vietnam' which contained Thomas Jefferson's immortal words 'all men are created equal'. The return of the French to South Vietnam in the spring of 1946 consequently set off a bloody anticolonial war in which the Viet Minh forces were able to secure material support from communist China after 1949. In 1954 the French were forced to concede independence. Although a Republic of Vietnam briefly existed and elections were planned throughout north and south Vietnam, they were never held. Instead two independent Vietnamese states emerged (which later became the scene of another war involving the United States). The entangled decolonization of Laos and Cambodia occurred in 1949 and 1953. Although France never applied its full military might and the conflict was confused by the issue of communism and the cold war, the transfer of power in French Indochina is one of the least ambiguous instances of positive sovereignty in postwar decolonization. Had it not been for this issue the United States would have been hard pressed to deny Ho Chi Minh's claim to be one of Jefferson's successors.

Unlike the Dutch and the French, the British did not endeavour to prolong their colonial rule in South Asia by force. Decolonization was not a new policy. India had been a candidate for independence as a dominion within the British Commonwealth since the late 1920s. Although accelerated by the war, the independence of the subcontinent in 1947 completed a constitutional process which had been underway for two decades. The impact of the war including the fierce campaign of the Indian Army against the Japanese in neighbouring Burma had enormous significance not only for Indian decolonization but also Burmese. These episodes made it impossible to delay the independence of Sri Lanka (Ceylon) even though the island colony was not as advanced as India constitutionally, was deeply scarred by an historic division between the majority Buddhist Sinhalese and the minority Hindu Tamil populations, and had been ruled separately by Britain as part of the dependent empire. Sri Lanka was the first territory under the Colonial Office to gain independence which set an important precedent for other colonies.

European decolonization in these parts of Asia signalled 'the end of empire-as-power'.[11] In most places after the mid-1950s the revolt against the West ceased to be a credible rebellion against colonial power and became instead a worldwide moral campaign against the ideology and institutions of colonialism.[12] The doctrine of negative sovereignty in postwar decolonization is therefore seen most clearly in the international emergence of Black Africa and Oceania. Before this sea change of international legitimacy the complete independence of these areas was rarely contemplated.

Although there is wide agreement about the significance of the episode the underlying causes of decolonization continue to be debated and no consensus among scholars has yet emerged. What is important from the perspective of this study, however, is not only its significance but also its character. Independence became an unqualified right of all colonial peoples: self-determination. Colonialism likewise became an absolute wrong: an injury to the dignity and autonomy of those peoples and of course a vehicle for their economic exploitation and political oppression. This is a noteworthy historical shift in moral reasoning because European overseas colonialism was originally and for a long time justified on legal positivist and paternalist grounds which postulated the unpreparedness of such peoples for self-government and the responsibility of 'civilized' states to govern them until they were prepared. It is difficult to make this point today without seeming to be a colonial apologist. But the fact is that until the second world war and even for some time afterwards this was the predominant doctrine of international legitimacy and law. Decolonization amounted to nothing less than an international revolution on this question in which traditional assumptions about the right to sovereign statehood were turned upside down.

EVOLUTIONARY DECOLONIZATION

British colonialism operated with the idea of trusteeship: colonies were held in trust by Great Britain until such time as they were able to govern themselves in accordance with 'modern ideas of civilized rule', as Lord Hailey once put it. In British political thought this idea was at least as old as Burke. Not every people were yet able to stand alone under the arduous conditions of the modern world. Nor were all indigenous rulers capable of civil government. Just as it was a dereliction of duty for a British colonial ruler to act unconstitutionally – which was the basis of Burke's argument to impeach Warren Hastings – so also would it be a dereliction of duty if, for example, Northern Nigeria were restored 'to the uncontrolled rule of the emirs, or Malay to that of its sultans'.[13] Indeed, the policy of indirect rule or what Lord Lugard called 'The Dual Mandate' – which pursued the goal of transforming traditional authorities into modern local governments – was intended to avoid this.[14] The traditional British idea was expressed in a 1938 speech in the House of Commons by Malcolm MacDonald, Secretary of State for Colonies:

> The great purpose of the British Empire is the gradual spread of freedom among all His Majesty's subjects in whatever part of the world they live. That spread of freedom is a slow, evolutionary process ... In some colonies ... the gaining of freedom has already gone very far. In others it is necessarily a much slower process. It may take generations, or even centuries, for the peoples in some parts of the Colonial empire to achieve self-government.[15]

Moreover, it would be premature to assume that every unit within the British Empire would eventually attain complete sovereignty. Many had populations which were still almost entirely illiterate not only in the strict linguistic sense but also – and perhaps more importantly – in the institutional sense of having little or no understanding of the workings of a modern state and the responsibilities of citizenship. Many were plagued by divisions among their population which were so deeply rooted in religion, language, or custom that democratic self-government without an impartial external referee seemed impossible. Many were too small for independence regardless of their level of development. And furthermore it could not be assumed that every colony would necessarily seek self-government: a policy of categorical independence for all would abandon many against their will. The only practical and responsible course of action was the continuation of colonial development following the distinctive lines of each particular colony under the overall protection, freedom, and justice afforded by the imperial system.

The British had long operated with the apparently contradictory concept of 'colonial self-government'. Since Lord Durham's Report of 1839 which launched responsible government in Canada, decolonization meant achieving self-government within the Empire. Britain, according to John Stuart Mill, had 'always felt under a certain degree of obligation to bestow on such of her outlying populations as were of her own blood and language, and on some who were not, representative institutions formed in imitation of her own'.[16] Britain could not transfer sovereignty to non-constitutional governments and remain faithful to her ideology of developing the civil and political as well as the social and economic conditions of colonies.

The British Empire and Commonwealth was likened to a grand political procession whose members were positioned according to their degree of self-government with Britain and the independent dominions in the vanguard and the least developed African and Pacific colonies bringing up the rear. This Whiggish metaphor of colonial development contrasted sharply with the static image of the old British Empire in which dependencies revolved around the mother country in perpetuity like the solar system and could never develop to equality with it. The constitutional shape of the new Empire was constantly evolving, therefore, and the position of each colonial unit was only a temporary stopping place along the road to eventual self-government.

For those many backward territories at the rear of the procession, however, the road ahead was still long and difficult. The British were operating within a familiar tradition of colonial development which had already led to dominion status for white colonies and, according to Margery Perham, 'there was no reason why it should cease to operate for brown or black ones'.[17] Constitutional development was a far more formidable assignment in Asia, Africa, and Oceania than it had been in the dominions, however, where it occurred more or less naturally within predominant European communities. New Zealanders were as capable of self-government as their first cousins in the British Isles. The same could not be said of Nigerians or Fijians who sprang from entirely different stocks. A 1937 report of the Royal Institute of International Affairs declared unequivocally that 'decolonization proceeds to the goal of independence only in countries which are economically and politically advanced. Over the whole of tropical Africa and the greater part of the Pacific areas this prerequisite has not been attained, and direct advance on Western democratic lines is not feasible'.[18] This was so self-evident that the authors felt no need to give any further explanation.

After the 1941 entry of the United States into the second world war, however, significant new demands were placed on the colonial powers to make plans for decolonization. It was now necessary to explain the practices and institutions of colonialism which were no longer self-justifying as they previously had been – at least within the Eurocentric international community. The British in particular were faced with justifying their longstanding conception of evolutionary decoloniz-ation to suspicious if not outright anticolonial American allies who were now in the driver's seat. The American view of decolonization was almost exactly the opposite: idealist and revolutionary. US Sec-retary of State Cordell Hull considered that the Atlantic Charter ap-plied 'to all nations and to all peoples' and the State Department requested timetables for independence throughout the war.[19] This necessitated official British interpretation which was that the Charter only concerned previously sovereign countries overrun by Axis powers. The British War Cabinet in September 1941 expressed the view that it was not concerned with the British Empire or, for that matter, with relations between the United States and the Philippines which were internal matters subject exclusively to domestic juris-diction. Prime Minister Winston Churchill, replying to a question in Parliament, said:

> At the Atlantic Meeting, we had in mind, primarily, the restoration of the sovereignty, self-government and national life of the States and nations of Europe now under the Nazi yoke, and the principles governing any alterations in the territorial boundaries which may have to be made. So that is quite a separate problem from the pro-gressive evolution of self-governing institutions in the regions and peoples which owe allegiance to the British Crown.[20]

This questioning of the European empires by the superpower at the moment of its ascendancy could not but undermine their international legitimacy to some degree. Although the United States' enthusiasm for universal decolonization declined following the advent of the cold war and its new realities and complexities, from this time the practices and institutions of colonialism had to be supported by an ideology which could communicate to states that were constitutionally unsympathetic to the enterprise and more likely to construe it as exploitation than benevolence and enlightenment. During the war when Britain was heavily dependent on the United States this required diplomacy and careful attention to terminology, as when Lord Hailey, the foremost colonial theorist of the time, noted to his British colleagues that any attempt to draw a distinction between 'self-government and indepen-dence suggests a refinement which will be viewed with a great deal of suspicion in the USA'.[21] Hailey was commissioned by the British government during the war to report on prospects for political development in the colonies. He cautioned against premature and ill-considered changes. In his confidential wartime report *Native Administration and Political Development in British Tropical Africa* he sounded a warning against premature 'constitution-mongering'.[22] And in lectures at Princeton University in February 1943 he noted the quickening demands for self-government but emphasized to his American audience that decolonization had to be consistent with modern ideas of civilization: 'the demand for "liberation" must ... imply the grant of self-government to areas which are already fitted for it, and the active promotion in others of a graded political education which will enable them eventually to manage their own affairs without external control, but on terms consistent with modern ideas of civilized rule'.[23] The difficulties of explanation and justification are obvious.

In defending the empire against criticism, leading British spokesmen felt obliged to point out, repeatedly, that the conditions for granting independence were far from existing in many colonies which still required tutelage and would require it for some time to come. The British government frequently confronted critical opinion within parliament particularly from the Labour Party left wing. Colonial Secretaries or Under-Secretaries had to defend their policies in parliamentary statements – as in a 1942 speech when Harold Macmillan (then Under-Secretary of State for the Colonies) claimed that the governing principle of the Colonial Empire was 'partnership'. An opposition member suggested the correct term was 'subordination' and asked: 'Is it real partnership or just another form of words to delude people?'[24] In 1943 the Colonial Secretary declared in the House of Commons that 'it is no part of our policy to confer political advances which are unjustified by circumstances, or to grant self-government to those who are not yet trained in its use'.[25] A year later a British memorandum prepared for the Dumbarton Oaks Conference observed that 'the development of self-government within the British Commonwealth' must occur 'in forms appropriate to the varying circumstances of Colonial peoples'.[26] And in an influential 1945 *Foreign Affairs* article written for a select American audience Marjory Perham revealed not only the official British mind but also uncanny foresight about the likely consequences of rapid universal decolonization: 'Were they [the colonies] thus cut loose, they would probably be set up as very weak units under an experimental world organization.'[27] Here was the emergent imperial riposte to those who assumed that independence was a categorical good which required no further justification.

The British continued after the war to regard American attitudes to decolonization as a simplistic ideology which – according to the British Ambassador in Washington – disclosed 'wooly sentimentality towards dependent peoples' and an uninformed belief that colonialism was but a mask on simple 'exploitation'.[28] The task was to counter these attitudes with facts about the reality of the colonial situation which varied greatly from one place to the next. However, the idealist outlook in favour of universal decolonization was also reflected by official pronouncements of Soviet bloc countries, many Latin American governments, and the UN General Assembly – whose anticolonial voice strengthened with the admission of every new ex-colonial member. It was also expressed by articulate liberal and left-wing opinion in the imperial countries themselves.

In 1946 it was evident to Margery Perham that the gradual pace of constitutional development in British colonies had to be more rapid than was previously thought desirable or even possible in some cases. However, she felt obliged to identify 'four chief obstacles to the achievement of early and effective self-government': (1) the general populations of many colonies if not most were still 'too unaware' of the operations of modern, large-scale government to be capable of citizenship; (2) most colonies as yet lacked any basis of national unity; (3) a number of colonies were so insubstantial that 'anything more than a limited internal self-government' was impossible; and lastly (4) the level of economic development was still far too low to support a modern state.[29] A 1946 Colonial Office memorandum observed that it was 'clearly impossible in the modern world' for smaller colonies 'to reach full self-government' and it was 'ludicrous' to imagine Barbados or British Honduras 'standing on their own feet'.[30] In a 1948 memorandum for the British Cabinet the Colonial Office could foresee independence only for Nigeria, Gold Coast, and a Federation of Malaya with Singapore. In 1950 colonial officials in Southeast Asia foresaw a transition period of twenty-five years 'before the peoples of Malaya would be ready for complete self-government'.[31]

According to Porter and Stockwell, British colonial policymakers 'were at one in assuming self-government to be generations distant'.[32] Although in public it was becoming impolitic to say so, in private memoranda colonial officials still spoke of political change in terms of generations or longer. Commentators took it for granted that some dependencies were so far removed from the conditions of a modern sovereign state that they would probably have to remain as colonies indefinitely. In the speech quoted above, Harold Macmillan ended by observing that colonies 'are poor because they are just beginning. They are four or five centuries behind . . . they are, as it were, in the Middle Ages.'[33]

There was also a moral issue: the concern that a premature transfer of power would leave many simple, rural folk in the colonies vulnerable to inefficiency, exploitation and even oppression by indigenous governments staffed by inexperienced or inadequately educated or self-serving elites. British commentaries on imperial subjects in the late 1940s therefore reveal a continuing assumption that indigenous peoples must achieve an acceptable level of competence and responsibility before self-government could be granted. In private the point was made with greater candour. A 1946 confidential Colonial Office memorandum stated that 'the standard of African public morality is low . . . if African participation in local or central government is to be successful the Colonial governments must face this problem squarely'.[34] The point was made with less restraint in a 1947 diary entry of Sir Philip Mitchell, then Governor of Kenya, who observed that as yet there was no reason 'to suppose that any African can be cashier of a village council for 3 weeks without stealing the cash'.[35]

DECOLONIZATION AND DEVELOPMENT

Evolutionism was reflected in British decolonization policy by both Conservative and Labour governments, although the former were more inclined to believe that some colonies would never achieve independence whereas the latter felt that it was a question ultimately of colonial development. This idea eventually prevailed. Since 1929 the Labour Party had strongly supported the progressive policy reflected in Colonial Development and Welfare Acts which were renewed in 1940 and 1945. In 1944 the Colonial Office saw 'a dynamic programme of colonial development' as the most effective way of addressing critics who were demanding decolonization.[36] Development would later become an international doctrine, except that independence would no longer depend on it and the international community – including particularly the rich countries – would then be responsible for assisting the development of poor countries.

Before the great depression of the 1930s, however, colonies were not usually conceived in terms of development planning. Instead, they were opportunities for private investment in agriculture or mines or infrastructure, and sometimes for European settlement. The earliest organized expressions of European colonialism were profit seeking companies of private adventurers: the Hudson's Bay, Dutch East Indies, Royal Niger, and British South Africa Companies – among many others. Burke characterized the British East India Company as 'a state disguised as a merchant' but the reverse could equally be said of many colonies.[37] They were commercial enterprises whose native inhabitants were treated as economic instruments: supplies of cheap labour which could be exploited to enhance the profitability of foreign capital. The role of colonial government was limited to that of providing law, order, and perhaps education – if missionaries were not available to take on the latter task. This instrumental and inhumane orientation undoubtedly shaped the current image of colonialism as the institutionalization of exploitation or at least capitalist profit-seeking.

However, as with any significant institution there were other facets of colonialism, including, as indicated, a trusteeship idea that colonies were to be developed at least in part for the benefit of indigenous inhabitants. This was the doctrine which prevailed in international law. It is evident in Article 6 of the General Act of the Berlin Conference (1885) which bound all colonial powers in Africa 'to watch over the preservation of the native tribes, and to care for the improvement of the conditions of their moral and material well-being'.[38] As noted in chapter 3, the idea was expanded in the League Mandates and UN Trusteeship Systems.

British Colonial Development and Welfare Acts also disclosed the ideology. The 1929 Act gave the Treasury and the Colonial Secretary concurrent authority to allocate funds for agricultural and industrial development in the colonies. The object, as Barbu Niculescu comments, was not 'to exploit' the natural resources of the colonies but 'to use' the capital and technology of Britain 'to enable' their development.[39] Likewise, the aim of the 1940 Act – according to Malcolm MacDonald – was to establish 'the duty' of British taxpayers 'to contribute directly and for its own sake' to the development of colonial peoples.[40] In reply to a parliamentary question in the late 1940s concerning the benefit of colonial expenditures to the British taxpayer, Sir Sydney Caine, Deputy Under-Secretary for Colonies, remarked: 'I think it was always understood that the expenditure of money under the Colonial Development and Welfare Act was not expected to result in any direct return or benefit to the United Kingdom Government. It was a deliberate act of assistance to Colonial Governments.'[41] Of course, this did not exclude the desire that colonies be economically self-sustaining or that colonial development contribute to British power and prestige. But it did provide explicitly for the economic welfare of indigenous peoples.

Once the prospect of decolonization began to appear the British believed, as previously indicated, that substantial colonial economic development was necessary before sovereignty could be transferred. Until that time it was a colonial responsibility to promote development. In 1951 the Colonial Secretary, Oliver Lyttelton, submitted a memorandum to the Cabinet which stated in part: 'We are directly responsible for the welfare of the Colonial peoples. We have preached and continue to preach the gospel that they must be developed in order to make adequate contribution to the world's needs and to raise their own standards of living, which are for the most part miserably low.'[42] A succession of Colonial Secretaries made similar statements. Development was evidently the highest stage of colonialism.

In December 1948 the colonial theorist and then Labour Colonial Secretary, Arthur Creech-Jones, told the Commonwealth Affairs Committee that complete independence could be achieved only if a territory was 'economically viable and capable of defending its own interests' which also implied the capability of self-defence.[43] He emphasized that while the policy of self-government was a general one, colonial withdrawal obviously depended on the circumstances of each colony at a given time. Porter and Stockwell speak of his 'brand of constructive colonialism' which 'sought to convert Empire into Commonwealth to the benefit of all concerned'.[44] Empiricism continued to be evident in British policy well into the 1950s, although the egalitarian Labour Party view that every territory was a candidate for eventual self-government began by then to prevail. Oliver Lyttelton, Conservative Secretary of State for Colonies between 1951 and 1954, took pains to emphasize the bipartisan nature of British colonial policy: 'we all aim at helping the Colonial Territories to attain self-government within the British Commonwealth. To that end we are seeking as rapidly as possible to build up in each territory the institutions which its circumstances require.'[45]

But institutions are not impersonal machines which run by themselves. They are human arrangements which require knowledge, cooperation, good will, and above all leadership to work. It was for long widely assumed among colonial officials that responsible self-government in colonies therefore necessitated the formation of an indigenous ruling class with a solid political education. Colonial tutelage was necessary until a level of competence sufficient to manage an independent country had been achieved. Transferring power without providing instruction would – in the words of the Labour Deputy Leader, Herbert Morrison – be 'like giving a child of ten a latch-key, a bank account and a shot-gun'.[46] The most essential element was education and training to enable indigenous people to occupy not only junior but also senior administrative posts in the bureaucracies of the various colonies. The length of time required to institutionalize self-government therefore depended on the creation of a competent and dedicated indigenous elite.

Circumstances were still a consideration as late as 1957. A paper prepared for the British Cabinet recommended that colonies should not be abandoned if they were not yet equipped for self-government or 'capable of sustaining independent status with a reasonable standard of government'.[47] Another Cabinet report in the same year took pains to warn that 'any premature withdrawal of authority by the United Kingdom would seem bound to add to the areas of stress and discontent in the world'.[48] It was now feared, however, that there might no longer be sufficient time to prevent it. In the case of Nigerian decolonization, for example, which still confronted enormous and potentially disintegrative problems of regionalism, it was believed that the accelerated independence of the Gold Coast (Ghana) had 'cost us some fifteen to twenty years'.[49] Nevertheless, even at this date it was still officially assumed at the highest levels of the British government that not every colony could realistically expect to become fully self-governing. Consequently, some intermediate statuses between colonialism and sovereignty would probably be occupied indefinitely. Sierra Leone, for example, was only likely to achieve 'internal self-government'. The Gambia probably could not even 'aspire to independence'.[50] But this traditional reasoning was definitely ending and Britain was about to embark on an acceleration of decolonization which would result in the independence of virtually every colony regardless of its circumstances. Under timetables being shaped increasingly by international politics the time for evolutionary decolonization was running out. The world was becoming horizontal morally and legally if in no other ways.

Although seemingly reasonable and empirical, the theory of colonial development proved to be very vulnerable. Once it was confronted by practical questions and particular cases it was found wanting in the lack of precision of its answers. What level of development was necessary for independent statehood? What criteria were appropriate to make such a determination? And when and where in the past was independence granted on such a basis? The international system had never operated in such a deliberate way: politics which is to say diplomacy or war had always been the final arbiter. It was of course impossible to point to any uncontestable criteria of empirical statehood for determining independence that would satisfy those for whom colonialism was becoming unnecessary and illegitimate. Neither Lord Hailey nor Margery Perham nor anyone else was able to do it. Politicians recognized this reality. In his now famous 1960 speech in Capetown British Prime Minister Harold Macmillan, who once spoke of political change in terms of centuries, now declared categorically: 'The wind of change is blowing through this continent. Whether we like it or not, this growth of national consciousness is a political fact. We must all accept it as a fact. Our national policies must take account of it.'[51]

If nobody could say what amount or type of development was necessary for self-government, then development could not be a justification for granting or denying independence. Nor could small or even micro-states be refused if that was what their indigenous inhabitants desired. Independence was a matter of political choice and not of empirical condition. New Third World heads of government at the 1964 Commonwealth Conference made what by then was already the standard moral argument: the conference should not be discussing decolonization but rather the 'development of all former colonies and the material aid the Commonwealth could provide. The issue, as the new Prime Minister of Trinidad and Tobago (Dr Eric Williams) put it, was no longer independence but 'development needs'.[52] Decolonization would contribute to development by giving governments control over their economies which colonialism denied them. This was the argument of the first UN Conference on Trade and Development (1964).[53] Independence was now necessary for development. But it was an independence without precedent supported by novel international organizations which inherited many responsibilities from colonialism but no powers. Some of the dilemmas that resulted are analysed in the next chapter.

ACCELERATED DECOLONIZATION

When it initially became conceivable that some British colonies would probably move towards self-government more rapidly than was previously thought possible the hitherto unquestioned assumption that the transfer of sovereignty must be contingent on empirical conditions began to be undermined. Decolonization was divorced from the capacity for both self-government and political development in the plans of the Colonial Office. The traditional requirement that independence follow development started to erode and the progressive assumption that it could prepare the way for development began to prevail. A younger generation of colonial officials was coming to the fore – men such as Sir Andrew Cohen – who did not share Hailey's conservatism and came to believe that colonial governments should be working themselves out of business by transferring power to indigenous peoples as rapidly as possible even at the risk of inviting post-independence problems.[54] By the late 1950s this was the new orthodoxy.

In numerous British colonies, therefore, plans were stepped up to engineer the institutional framework of a modern constitutional democracy, complete with legislative, electoral, and judicial institutions which were grafted to what had been primarily although not exclusively a colonial administrative state. In British constitutional logic a colony overseas was the equivalent of a county in Britain: it was subordinate to parliament at Westminster. The principle had to be reversed to achieve responsible self-government. Independence was a graded process, and political education was like any other: one had to pass through the various grades in order to graduate. The following stages of constitutional development were necessary for this to happen: (1) formation of a legislature if one was not already in existence; (2) creation or expansion of an electorate; (3) electoral control of the legislature; (4) legislative control of the executive; and (5) independence from the British government.[55] These stages reflected the constitutional development of Britain, which was a history of evolving independence of parliament from the crown and of increasing dependence of the House of Commons on an electorate eventually based on universal suffrage.

What was distinctively democratic about British decolonization was the requirement that all previous stages be passed before the last stage was completed. Every colony that achieved independence proceeded through all these grades, although at the end of empire after 1960 the passage was made with increasing and even unseemly haste. The British stuck with the process often in difficult circumstances where it was not at all certain that effective legislative and electoral institutions had been formed not only because this was their traditional approach to decolonization but also to demonstrate their long standing claim that the empire existed ultimately to prepare colonial peoples for constitutional self-government. Any act of decolonization which bypassed these stages would be not only irresponsible but an admission of failure also.

The year of Ghanaian independence, 1957, is perhaps the date which marks the time from which British decolonization accelerated. The British Cabinet became more directly involved and the responsibilities of the Colonial Office were reduced to organizing conferences for the transfer of power. In 1957 the Labour Party claimed that all the smaller territories had a right to the constitutional status of a dominion within the British Commonwealth. But as late as 1959, according to

J. M. Lee, the British Conservative Colonial Secretary reportedly contemplated self-government for Tanganyika by 1970 and for Kenya by 1975.[56] Independence for each country and also Uganda arrived in the early 1960s. Britain was now prepared to grant independence to very marginal African dependencies, such as The Gambia, Zanzibar, and the High Commission territories (Lesotho, Botswana, Swaziland). In 1965 the Labour Colonial Secretary, Anthony Greenwood, declared categorically that Britain's main task was 'to liquidate Colonialism either by granting independence to a number of territories or by evolving for the others forms of government which secure basic democratic rights for the people but which involve some degree of association with this country without any stigma of colonialism'.[57] The latter alternative – the last whisper of positive sovereignty – proved to be impossible in all but very few cases and title to independence was duly transferred to virtually every remaining dependency regardless of its capacities or circumstances.

Decolonization had ceased being a substantive enterprise aimed at state-building and had become a formal activity to transfer negative sovereignty. Few of the officials in the Colonial Office legal department 'during the quinquennium of its greatest activity, 1959–64', reportedly thought the new constitutional frameworks 'would have any lasting significance'.[58] Apart from Southern Rhodesia, all of the remaining British colonies in Central and Southern Africa, whatever their substance, achieved independence by 1968. Most of the numerous and tiny British island territories in the Caribbean, Pacific, and Indian oceans acquired sovereignty in the later 1960s and 1970s. Decolonization in its final stages was separated not only from considerations of development and leadership but from almost any empirical considerations whatsoever. Of the Commonwealth's 49 members in 1985, 27 had populations under 1 million and 14 occupied land areas of less than 1,000 square kilometres.

The hierarchical procession of miscellaneous British dependencies of the past had turned into an egalitarian vanguard of uniformly emerging states with almost every remaining dependency now in the front rank impatiently demanding equal independence and receiving it in fairly short order. The extraordinary character of this historical change is captured in the remarks of one of its close observers:

> It is ironical in a post-colonial age – which has in effect virtually elevated the state into being the only widely accepted political standard – to recall that great empires in the past, the British not least, recognized, even encouraged, political diversity: so that within its capacious and variegated jurisdictions were not only colonies but

97

suzerains, tributaries, condominia, protectorates, protected states, etc. Indeed, the well nigh universality of the claim that all erstwhile single colonial administrative units are 'states' in posse if not already in esse, and thus endowed with the potentiality of becoming 'a sovereign state', is one of the most surprising and ironical outcomes of this age of triumphant, tendentious anticolonialism and of the spawning of many small states.[59]

Rapid and general decolonization also had to be accommodated by a reshaped Commonwealth. Most ex-British colonies altered or abandoned their Westminster constitution as rapidly as they acquired it. Many became presidential republics in theory but personal dictatorships in practice. If they were to remain members of the Commonwealth, political expediency stipulated that its received institutional assumptions would have to be given up. Instead of an association of states sharing not only the English language and an affection for the royal family but also an inheritance of British political arrangements and legal practices, by the mid-1960s it was a new orthodoxy to regard the Commonwealth as a convenient and very loose and constitutionally undemanding association: a club of rulers who succeeded the British. The effect was to enhance the liberties of ex-colonial sovereigns who felt under no obligation or pressure to conduct their governments in terms of constitutional democracy and the rule of law as historically understood by older Commonwealth members.

In a prophetic essay on 'The Colonial Dilemma' published in *The Listener* in 1949 which was intended to respond to colonial leaders and new members of the United Nations who were demanding or expecting 'quick results' from colonial development, Margery Perham observed that the colonial peoples least equipped to operate a modern sovereign state were likely to have the shortest apprenticeship in modern statecraft: 'This is because they are reaching it, not as with the older dependencies because of internal growth, but mainly as a result of external influences and pressures which accelerate the movement to self-government.'[60] This was in fact what happened.

PRECIPITOUS DECOLONIZATION

The policy of preparing colonies for self-government so that the colonial mission would be vindicated was most clearly evident in the British Empire. The other colonial powers lacked this tradition and consequently had difficulty seeing and responding to international changes which were beginning to expect decolonization. France, in particular, had long operated with the contrary idea that colonialism was preparation not for independence but for assimilation in the metropolitan community. The British conception was the key to the fate of the European empires, however. If the largest and most significant empire was to embark on constitutional decolonization it would establish a precedent which other democratic imperial powers could not ignore. A small example is the French Trust territory of Togoland which in 1955 was made into an autonomous republic within the French Union as the result of British decolonization in adjoining Gold Coast. 'If little Togoland achieved internal self-government,' as John Hargreaves noted, 'it would be difficult to resist comparable reforms in A.O.F.[French West Africa].'[61] But French and Belgian decolonizations were more precipitous and were undertaken with minimal conviction that successor constitutional governments could be established. They also assumed that after independence some form of close association with their ex-colonies could be maintained which proved to be the case in regards to many former French dependencies. Authoritarian Portugal was the only colonial power that completely ignored international condemnation of colonialism and never became reconciled to decolonization which only took place after the Caetano regime in Lisbon was overthrown by a military coup in 1974.

The historical policy of France, like that of Portugal, was integrative. The French did not officially refer to their 'empire' but instead used the expression *La France d'outre-mer*. Until 1956 the French could scarcely conceive of colonies in the British manner as schools for self-government. On the contrary, French colonialism involved 'assimilation' rather than 'autonomy': the development of overseas France as a whole rather than constituent units within it. Uniformity and not diversity was the French way. The idea was the education of individuals in the language and culture of France and the creation of elites consisting of such individuals who could serve in the colonial administration at the highest level. They could also become citizens of France and even members of the French government – as a few did. French policy, as is frequently pointed out at least by Anglo-Saxon commentators, reflected the Francophone proclivity for universalism: 'When Montesquieu, Voltaire, Rousseau or Diderot set out to establish the laws which should govern human society, they believed that they were discovering universal laws . . . which would apply to all societies. They did not envisage different laws for Frenchmen, Germans, Senegalese or Chinese.'[62] Although he could not foresee the policy of assimilation reaching its logical conclusion by the incorporation of the colonies in the metropole, in 1943 Lord Hailey saw 'no indications' of any definite developments toward self-government in French colonies.[63]

In 1946, as a direct result of the war, France was reconstituted as the Fourth Republic which at the same time changed its relationship to the colonies. The French Union was formed which united metropolitan France and the overseas departments and territories. The distinction between *citoyens* and *sujets* in overseas France as well as other legal disabilities of colonial subjects, such as forced labour (*l'indigenat*), were abolished. Elected assemblies were also established overseas. However, the franchise was based on criteria of civic competence, such as French literacy, and therefore stopped well short of one person, one vote. Colonial citizens nevertheless did elect representatives not only to their own territorial assemblies but also to the French National Assembly – although representation was limited and there was obviously no intention of allowing overseas deputies 'to become so numerous as to make France a colony of her colonies'.[64]

In the African territories of overseas France in 1956 the *Loi-Cadre* (framework law) was instituted which significantly extended representative government. Black African leaders were involved in writing the *Loi-Cadre* and one person, one vote was instituted for the first time. Although the *Loi-Cadre* was a turning point which gave French overseas territories many powers comparable to those granted to British colonies during the terminal colonial period, there was still no clear intention that it would lead inexorably to independence. In 1958 the Fifth French Republic was formed and, as in 1946, the new constitution extended to overseas France. The French Union was replaced by the French Community: a looser framework which gave increased autonomy to overseas territories but not independence. Foreign, defence, and economic policy was still controlled by Paris. The changes therefore built upon the *Loi-Cadre* reforms by differentiating between France and the French overseas African territories which were reconstituted as states within the Community. This equivocal arrangement did not last, however. In a referendum on the proposed Community held throughout overseas France, the West African territory of Guinea, under the leadership of the radical Sékou Touré, voted *non* and became independent almost immediately. In 1959 President Charles de Gaulle acknowledged the right of Franco-African states to become sovereign, and in 1960 every dependency of France in sub-Saharan Africa acquired constitutional independence. Within four years French colonial policy had been completely overturned.

In Dakar, Senegal in 1959 at a meeting of the executive council of the French Community, President de Gaulle acknowledged the independence of Mali formed earlier that year by the union of Senegal and the former French Soudan, and he remarked: 'This state of Mali will take what is called the status of independence, and what I prefer to call that of international sovereignty . . . Independence is a word signifying an intention, but the world being what it is, so small, so narrow, so intertwined with itself, that real independence, total independence belongs in truth to no one.'[65] As if to avoid the stark reality of negative sovereignty significant ties providing for military, economic, and cultural cooperation were retained between Paris and every new Francophone African state – except Guinea. French financial aid in particular was made available and this continuing external dependency was later reinforced by the close association of the Franco-African states and other former French colonies with the European Economic Community under the Lomé Convention. They also became associated in *La Francophonie* – a French-speaking parallel to the Commonwealth – which included Canada as a major new source of foreign aid.

Decolonization of the Belgian Congo (Zaire) was compressed into what not only in retrospect but even at the time was an impossibly short period, with the major steps frantically taken between January 1959 and June 1960. 'It is hardly surprising that it was fraught with disaster', as one historian put it.[66] The episode was completely unforeseen until almost the last moment not only by Europeans but also by Africans. In July 1955 a leading Belgian commentator wrote: 'The Belgian Congo is the most prosperous and tranquil of colonies, the one whose evolution is the most peaceful and normal.' This was, according to Jean Stengers, 'the unanimous judgement of that time'.[67] In 1950 an African intellectual likewise remarked: 'We subjects of Belgium know and understand that it will require sixty or one hundred years, or more, before we shall be ready to be left to ourselves.' Even the man who became the first Prime Minister and martyr of the new African state, Patrice Lumumba, wrote in 1956 that it was too early to say whether the Congo would achieve 'the more advanced degree of civilization and the required political maturity' to enable it to be 'raised to the ranks of self-governing peoples'.[68] These evolutionary assumptions were abruptly abandoned in the late 1950s.

A progressive coalition government which came into office in Belgium in 1954 initiated tentative political changes in the Congo. But it was planning, along the lines of British indirect rule, in terms of developing African local government. In 1957 the first municipal elections were held. Late in 1955 a leading Belgian professor of colonial law, A. A. J. van Bilsen, shocked his countrymen by proposing a plan of decolonization which anticipated Congolese self-government in thirty years upon successful completion of a 'positive' process of creating capable and responsible Congolese elites and gradually transferring control of government to them.[69] He emphasized the changed international situation and the movements for independence elsewhere in Africa, and concluded that Belgium would not be able to ignore them. His prognosis was correct but the timetable proved utterly mistaken. In January 1959, only a year and a half before independence, a Belgian working group still 'considered that decolonization would be a long-term process. Van Bilsen's thirty years certainly seemed to them a minimum'.[70] As late as December 1959, according to Crawford Young, the Belgians conceived of 'independence' as involving 'continued Belgian sovereignty in several key policy fields (defence, foreign affairs, currency, and telecommunications)'.[71]

After the Belgians belatedly awakened to the revolution of international legitimacy which condemned colonialism categorically, they hastily fell in line with the British and the French. Belgium was a democracy and a staunch member of the NATO alliance. When it became clear that the United States and some other democratic NATO allies would not support a prolonged period of gradual decolonization and that Belgium would also be condemned loudly by the UN General Assembly, the government felt it had no alternative but to decolonize as quickly as possible. Events in British and French Africa, especially the independence of Ghana in 1957 and even more so the abrupt decision of France to decolonize – in particular, the 'spectacle . . . of General de Gaulle proclaiming in 1958 at Brazzaville, within earshot of the Congolese capital, that those who wished independence had only to take it' – undoubtedly provoked the Belgians to dramatically alter course.[72] If France was going to accept international demands for immediate decolonization, how could Belgium reject them?

INTERNATIONALIZATION

Following the second world war no colonial power could escape the chorus of international questioning and criticism even if, like Portugal and South Africa, it chose not to listen. As noted in the last chapter, the UN General Assembly played a central role in internationalizing the issue of decolonization and removing it from the sphere of exclusively domestic jurisdiction of the colonial powers. Although the UN Charter (Article 73) was rather conservative on the issue of decolonization by making self-government subject to 'circumstances' and 'stages of advancement', the General Assembly read it differently and sought to legislate on colonial questions. A leading Brazilian diplomat and lawyer considered that Articles 73 and 74 disclose the 'juridical philosophy' inherent in the United Nations since they express 'the ideal of universality' and authorize the organization 'to deal systematically' with 'the interests and aspirations of hundreds of millions in non-self-governing territories'. It would be a distortion of that ideal if they were to be left 'under the exclusive competence of the internal public law of the states holding jurisdiction over them'.[73] At the first UN session in February 1946 it became clear that many noncolonial powers wished to extend UN supervision not merely over trust territories but over all colonies. Morgan speaks of the 'tendency in many quarters to contravene the provisions of the Charter' on colonial issues by seeking to expand its authority.[74]

Initially the leading colonial powers held international meetings among themselves in the attempt to control international politics on colonial questions. But it was not easy for Britain and France – who had a large role in setting up the UN – to ignore international opinion. The democratic colonial powers were accustomed to conducting their own governments according to majority rule and found it difficult to repudiate that democratic practice at the UN concerning colonial issues. International pressure to decolonize increased until by 1960 the emerging Afro-Asian bloc and its supporters in Latin America and elsewhere ensured that anticolonial resolutions could not be defeated in the General Assembly. The overwhelming passage of UN Resolution 1514 marked the victory of a far more expansive reading of the Charter and constituted in effect a major revision. From about this time arguments to delay independence on grounds of circumstance were considered morally inferior to universal claims to self-determination. Although in the past Britain had publicly voiced the empirical argument that many remaining territories were lacking in important requisites of independent statehood, most UN members ignored such arguments or dismissed them as self-serving attempts to delay granting independence which was an unequivocal good. Latter day Burkes could make no headway against the *philosophes* of contemporary international relations. Rationalism had triumphed over empiricism. Thereafter the British pragmatically sought 'to carry international opinion with us' as the Labour Colonial Secretary put it in 1965.[75]

The Commonwealth also became an important vehicle of international pressure for decolonization. By the early 1960s British Colonial Secretaries were reporting on their decolonization plans and policies to the Commonwealth Prime Ministers. Australia and New Zealand, which administered UN Trust Territories in the South Pacific, also engaged in such reporting. At the 1961 Commonwealth Meeting, Prime Minister Nehru of India publicly reminded his colleagues that the 1960 UN Declaration 'was an indication of the weight of world opinion on the need to bring colonialism to a speedy end'.[76] Three

103

sessions of the 1964 meeting of Commonwealth leaders were devoted to decolonization. British Prime Minister Sir Alec Douglas-Home, although reminding his colleagues that decolonization was the constitutional responsibility solely of the British government, acknowledged that it was also a legitimate concern of the Commonwealth. Later that year the new Labour Secretary of State for Colonies said he had been appointed with 'the task of working himself out of a job as soon as possible'.[77]

The egalitarian argument that independence should be granted categorically even if the territory in question was extremely marginal became morally impregnable. According to President Kwame Nkrumah of Ghana, it was now the responsibility not only of Britain but all rich countries to enable his country and all other poor ex-colonies to develop by providing foreign aid. Sovereignty was a right not only to political independence but also to development assistance afterwards because colonialism was not merely political but also social and economic. Decolonization would not be complete until the international economy was reformed to give less developed countries an equal opportunity to become developed. This became Third World orthodoxy on North–South issues. The political difficulty of arguing for the contrary view that a different juridical status should be held by marginal states until they were more developed is indicated by a message sent from Canadian Prime Minister Lester Pearson to British Prime Minister Harold Wilson in 1965. Pearson reportedly expressed 'uneasiness' at the unexpectedly rapid growth of the Commonwealth but 'realized' that to refuse, or suspend, such applications would have been 'difficult'. He suggested that the Commonwealth might reconsider its organization with a view to membership on a different basis for 'smaller dependent territories'.[78] Even this very restrained proposal to consider empirical qualifications in determinations of membership could not get anywhere in the face of the postulated international equality of all peoples.

Pearsons's concerns reflected the lingering idea of international trusteeship. Similarly, at the 1961 Commonwealth meeting Prime Minister Robert Menzies of Australia agreed with the spirit of UN Resolution 1514 but warned against interpreting it too literally. It would be an act of irresponsibility if Australia were to grant immediate independence to Papua New Guinea whose population 'had reached only the most primitive stage of civilization'.[79] And in a 1963 UN debate the United States expressed the view that 'classical independence' might not be suited to small territories.[80] Periodically there were serious discussions in British official circles concerning the desirability of creating the status of 'associated states of the Commonwealth' which would be internally self-governing but not fully independent.[81] It proved impossible, however. The Commonwealth felt it had to accommodate as a full member any ex-British Colony which was a UN member. The UN could deny membership to no former colony which asked for it and actually solicited such requests. The positive sovereignty concept of an 'associate state' implied formal inequality which was utterly unacceptable to a world community that had elevated legal equality to the level of virtually a sacred principle.

The internationalization of the decolonization issue is evident in the ultimately successful attack on the traditional right of domestic jurisdiction over colonial territories.[82] As noted, the colonial powers legally justified their dependencies by reference to Article 2 (7) of the UN Charter which prohibits intervention by the UN or any member state in the domestic jurisdiction of any other member. In the course of the controversy 'domestic jurisdiction' became a contested concept reflecting the view taken of the legitimacy of colonialism. The growing number of ex-colonial members of the UN and their supporters held that colonial territories separated by expanses of sea water from the metropolitan power were not a legitimate part of its domestic jurisdiction. The Soviet Union and China, needless to say, were also strong advocates of such a view which removed their subject territories and peoples from anticolonial criticism. This concept of domestic jurisdiction, in contradiction to classical international law, likewise held that Chapter 11 of the Charter – Declaration Regarding Non-Self-Governing Territories – provided the legal foundation for the claim that the UN was constitutionally authorized to bring about decolonization. The main legal defences against this claim were the French and Portuguese arguments that colonial territories overseas were integral parts of the metropolitan state, and the Belgian thesis that Chapter 11 applied not only to dependent territories overseas but also to those at home. They failed to ward off the attack on the international legitimacy and legality of such possession.

Geography was the fatal vulnerability of the first argument. Looking at a map it was difficult to believe that Angola was an ordinary province of Portugal despite its substantial number of Portuguese settlers. The same could even be said of Algeria which, although on a different continent, was in closer proximity to France and had a larger settler population. In 1960 the emergent anticolonial majority in the UN secured a General Assembly resolution stating that Algeria had a right to self-determination and that the UN had a duty to advance that right. Late in the year President de Gaulle conceded the argument in a speech in Algiers: 'It is vain to pretend that it [Algeria] constitutes a province like our Lorraine . . . It is so vain that it is not worth saying because it is not true. It is something else, it is an Algerian Algeria.'[83] In subsequent resolutions, as I indicated in chapter 3, the UN repudiated the legal ground of colonialism in domestic jurisdiction. This was simultaneously an affirmation of the current doctrine 'that colonial powers have no valid claim to sovereignty over non-self-governing territories beyond their metropolitan bounds, regardless of whether they call them colonies or provinces'.[84] India was successfully able to use this claim to justify its seizure of Portuguese Goa by force in 1961 against Portugal's counterclaim that it was a victim of armed intervention. This legitimation of the international use of force for the liberation of colonized peoples was subsequently affirmed by a series of UN resolutions concerning Portuguese Africa and Rhodesia.

The Belgian thesis is more telling because it disclosed the ambiguities and hypocrisy in the decolonization argument. Numerous independent countries contain non-self-governing territorial groups which may or may not be permitted to participate constitutionally and equally in the political life of the ruling community.[85] Domestic legal and administrative arrangements of a paternalist kind sometimes exist for dealing with them – such as the specialized laws, bureaucracies, and policies by which American, Canadian, and Australian governments have historically ruled aboriginal peoples. In some cases they are victims of political or economic oppression by the dominant community. Legitimate and indeed lawful international concern for the welfare of such groups was established under the Covenant of the League of Nations and some international organizations, including the International Labour Organization (ILO) and the UN Educational, Scientific and Cultural Organization (UNESCO), regard them as 'within the same category as colonial inhabitants'.[86] Canadian aboriginal leaders have from time to time brought their demands for self-determination to the attention of the UN. One is strongly tempted to conclude, therefore, that the Belgian thesis in particular had to be rejected because it probed the 'internal colonialism' of too many existing independent countries, developed and underdeveloped alike. This was of course the appeal of the argument from the Belgian viewpoint but it backfired because the numerous states to which it applied were determined to deny it. To have done otherwise would have opened a Pandora's box. Most new ex-colonial states in particular had to reject an argument which would expose them to demands for self-determination by the usually numerous ethnonationalities they contained.

Internationalization was most dramatically evident in the decolonization of Portuguese African territories (Angola, Mozambique, Guinea-Bissau) and Southern Rhodesia (Rhodesia cum Zimbabwe). Portugal did not become a UN member until 1955 and subsequently argued that Article 73 of the Charter did not apply since, as indicated, her African territories were integral provinces of the metropole. After the 1960 UN Declaration – which in effect passed censure on Portugal – and the successful expropriation of Goa by the Indian army this argument could no longer be sustained. Lisbon's NATO allies deserted her on the issue. During this period Portugal very nearly became another Rhodesia or South Africa in terms of international legitimacy: an outcast under UN censure. In a series of subsequent resolutions the world body mounted a normative assault on Portuguese colonialism which undoubtedly contributed to its eventual demise. Resolution 2184 (1966) condemned Portuguese denial of 'the political rights of the indigenous population' as a 'crime against humanity' and appealed 'to all States to give the peoples of the Territories under Portuguese domination the moral and material support necessary for the restoration of their inalienable rights'. Resolution 3103 (1973) confirmed that colonialism was 'a crime', that armed struggle for self-determination was legitimate and that any attempts to suppress the struggle were contrary to the Charter and 'a threat to international peace and security'.[87] Portuguese resistance to decolonization therefore served as a major opportunity for international society to repudiate colonialism totally and explicitly. From serving as an agency of civilization less than a century before colonialism had become not only morally repugnant but also a crime against humanity.

The universal condemnation of the Ian Smith regime flowed directly and powerfully from this new doctrine of international legitimacy. Rhodesia after its white settlers' Unilateral Declaration of Independence (UDI) from Britain in 1965 is therefore a telling instance of the ascendancy of negative sovereignty in decolonization. Since 1923 it had been a 'self-governing colony' under the control of European settlers during which time British authority was minimal. It was never part of the dependent empire but was a sort of semi-dominion under the Dominions Office. The day after UDI, however, Britain abandoned its earlier argument that intervention was forbidden by Article 2 (7) of the Charter and called upon the UN to intervene on the grounds that an illegal government based on white minority rule was a matter of world concern. The Ian Smith regime was universally denied recognition – even by South Africa – despite the fact that it satisfied criteria of positive sovereignty in the determination of statehood for more than ten years. The Rhodesian courts accordingly held that since the United

Kingdom had lost its efficacy the regime was the sovereign government. Even Britain's high court, the Judicial Committee of the Privy Council, ruled that it was impossible to predict with certainty whether or not Britain would regain its sovereign control.[88] James Crawford remarked at the time: 'There can be no doubt that, if the traditional tests for independence . . . applied, Rhodesia would be an independent state.'[89] Despite the fact that Rhodesia disclosed traditional characteristics of a sovereign state at least for most of its existence, it was universally denied recognition. Instead, the principle of 'no independence before majority African rule' (NIBMAR) prevailed, strongly supported by Britain, the Commonwealth, and the UN. Rhodesia was morally repugnant to the international community of the late twentieth century and in the end that proved decisive in its downfall. Crawford concludes: 'The proposition that statehood must always be equated with effectiveness is not supported by modern practice . . . a new rule has come into existence, prohibiting entities from claiming statehood if their creation is in violation of an applicable right to self-determination.'[90] That rule is negative sovereignty.

5 SOVEREIGNTY AND DEVELOPMENT

THE DESTITUTE IMAGE OF THE THIRD WORLD

The way we think about international relations today is strongly influenced by a picture of the world as sharply divided between a rich and technologically advanced North, and a poor and backward South. The North–South cleavage rivals and increasingly surpasses the East–West conflict as a dominant perception of the contemporary international system.

They are categorically different, however. The latter could be greatly mitigated by agreements between the United States and the Soviet Union to reduce their arms and increase their dialogue and intercourse. Although it is not yet a certainty, the end of the East–West conflict within the foreseeable future is entirely conceivable. If it happens one statesman, Mikhail Gorbachev, can take a large share of the credit. No such statement can be made about underdevelopment which is not a problem of the same kind. It is not a dispute which can be resolved by diplomacy and international agreements. Instead, it is likely to persist indefinitely since it is a condition deeply rooted in economic, social, cultural, and even psychological facts which are exceedingly difficult to alter even with the greatest good will. It is not a question of honouring one's commitments. Even if firm agreements were made between rich and poor states aimed at ameliorating underdevelopment by increased transfers of finance and technology, they presuppose performances on the part of Third World governments which could not be guaranteed. They could not because those governments are themselves underdeveloped and therefore part of the problem. There could be no assurance that the transferred resources would be put to use efficiently and properly because it is not yet within the capacity of such governments to do this. The North–South cleavage consequently is likely to be a predominant feature of the international landscape for decades or even generations to come.

This global socioeconomic division has existed since the time Europe

109

began to outdistance other parts of the world in arms, technology, science, political economy, and related spheres of human endeavour. Later 'the West' was defined by its superiority in these activities. During the colonial era, however, development and underdevelopment was a domestic rather than an international issue, if it was an issue at all. Decolonization therefore did not create the North–South gap which has been in evidence for several centuries. Instead, it internationalized it just as a century ago Western imperialism internalized it. These episodes also disclose the categorical difference noted above: whereas the gap could be colonized and decolonized merely by the will and agreement of states, it cannot be eliminated in this way because it is not a diplomatic or legal problem at all.

Elaborate statistical documentation of the North–South gap is available today in reports of various organizations, international and national, public and private. The World Bank alone publishes various studies which describe and investigate in detail the comparative ranking and performance of all reporting countries according to a wide variety of socioeconomic indicators.[1] These data reveal a continuing and in some cases widening gulf between the industrial market economies of the North and the agricultural or primary commodity economies (mostly) of the South. In 1986, for example, the annual GNP per capita of the world's richest countries of Western Europe, North America, and Japan was approximately $13,000 whereas that of the poorest countries of Africa and Asia was under $300. Even the 'upper middle-income' economies of Latin America and some parts of Asia registered on average only about one-fifth of the per capita income of the rich economies. These data are widely accepted as valid and serve as the empirical foundation of the North–South perception. Although some countries and particularly the so-called Newly Industrializing Countries (NICs) of Asia have achieved very impressive rates of development in the last decade or two and we should not rule out the possibility of similar developments elsewhere, the breadth and depth of the global socioeconomic gap remains more or less as it was at the time of decolonization and is likely to persist indefinitely.

This fundamental division forms the basis of a new understanding of the world. Since some countries are already developed it is usually assumed that all countries at least in principle can reasonably hope to achieve this goal. It is also commonly posited that the knowledge required to bring this about either exists or can be acquired. In the past thirty years enormous efforts and resources have gone into the creation and application of a new developmental statecraft. Today there exists an international knowledge regime focused on problems of underdevelopment that is embodied in numerous and still proliferating technical and socioeconomic agencies, international and national, public and private. Although the results of the global development enterprise in general have been disappointing so far, there is no doubting that a significant body of knowledge has been brought into existence very largely in response to the emergence of numerous underdeveloped countries.

Most studies of development are not merely descriptive accounts of the gap between the rich and the poor or technical-economic proposals for reducing it. They are also prescriptive. Not only are underdeveloped states acknowledged to exist but underdevelopment is generally regarded as unacceptable and even unconscionable. Moreover, underdevelopment is considered to be a problem not merely of the underdeveloped countries themselves but also at least in part of the international community and particularly its richest members. This reasoning upsets the traditional practice and theory of international economic relations. In the past independent states were responsible only for their own wealth and welfare and international law merely acknowledged their freedom to promote it without external hindrance. Of course, governments (sometimes) recognized that certain international rules such as reciprocity and nondiscrimination in matters of trade were generally more favourable to national development than was protectionism or other forms of economic nationalism. This was evident in the General Agreement on Tariffs and Trade (GATT) inaugurated by international society in 1947 which aims at eliminating discrimination in international commerce by reducing tariffs through reciprocal trade agreements. But some sovereign states were not under any obligation to actively and substantially assist others on a *non-reciprocal* basis. Today this is no longer entirely the case. The evolving Law of the GATT now recognizes that all its members 'are not economically equal and that among unequal parties, the principle of reciprocity does not obtain'.[2]

The differentiation of sovereign states in terms of development and underdevelopment has consequently had an impact on the practice and theory of international relations. Sovereignty and development have been divorced largely as a result of decolonization, and development has become an international expectation or goal. Third World states advertise their poverty and demand the international community and particularly its rich members assist them to develop their economies and raise the living standards of their populations. And the latter respond with financial and technical aid or debt relief believing in many cases that they are under a moral if not a legal

111

obligation to do so. Although the resources transferred in this way are still a tiny fraction of global wealth, this is a noteworthy emergent international norm. Sovereignty therefore has a novel character nowadays: every sovereign government possesses negative rights of nonintervention but some assert additional positive rights or at least demands of external material support. This is not only unprecedented in the annals of the states-system but is also a real dilemma in the normative structure of contemporary international relations as I indicate below.

In sum, the North–South division is reflected in an emergent regime of international organization, aid, law, and ethics. There has been a remarkable expansion of international organization to support underdeveloped countries. Moreover, international transfers of finances and technology and reform of the rules of the international economy to aid Third World states to develop is accepted in principle even if there is as yet limited agreement in practice. It has been argued that 'the Third World is the creation of foreign aid: without foreign aid there is no Third World'.[3] This is a partial although distorted truth, for the Third World would exist without foreign aid but its existence has led to the necessity and morality of foreign aid. There have also been efforts to articulate international development law based on positive rights of states, as contrasted to traditional economic law grounded in reciprocity and contract. The existence of destitute states challenges the classical rule of reciprocity in international economic affairs precisely because such states cannot reciprocate and are still in a condition of dependency in economic if no longer in political relations with other states. Some ethic of positive assistance seems necessary. These novel post-colonial arrangements are consequences of the existence of numerous quasi-states.

INTERNATIONAL DEVELOPMENT ASSISTANCE

In recent decades an elaborate international superstructure has been built to cater for the socioeconomic needs of underdeveloped countries. This supportive regime is in spirit with our age of social engineering but it is unprecedented in the history of the modern states-system which hitherto has been concerned only to respect the freedom of credible sovereigns, large or small. It is the unusual if not paradoxical instance, to borrow an image from Marxism, of an international 'superstructure' attempting to shore up national 'substructures' on Third World peripheries of a new egalitarian society of states. Having recognized the sovereignty of ex-colonial peoples the international community is now endeavouring to provide them with the furniture and equipment of statehood.

112

We take this international feature for granted but it was almost unknown before the last world war. Although the League of Nations was concerned about the adverse socioeconomic circumstances of mandates, most underdeveloped territories were still under the domestic jurisdiction of colonial powers who retained exclusive responsibility for them. The international community was not then involved in their development, although some wanted it to be and British Colonial Development and Welfare Acts, as indicated, were responses to the trusteeship idea that mandates and by implication regular colonies should be provided with socioeconomic assistance for the benefit of their inhabitants. Even at the founding of the UN little attention was given to development as an international issue 'which was indeed almost certainly not at that time foreseen'.[4] In 1945 the problem was to restore the world economy and particularly the European economies which had been devastated by war. The Marshall Plan which involved massive transfers of financial and technical aid from the United States to Europe had this aim. But this was reconstruction of already developed economies. The problem of underdevelopment was then still largely an imperial responsibility. By 1960, however, it was beginning to rival war and peace as an international issue. Indeed, it was seen as a major underlying cause of war. 'We have before us now a brand new diplomatic problem of vastly greater dimensions than anything previously, including the Marshall Plan for European economic recovery.'[5] These are the words of a World Bank President writing at the moment of change in 1960. The problem has preoccupied the community of states ever since.

Once that community began to admit a large number of underdeveloped members their predicaments were bound to become internationalized. As imperial operations were wound down, international organizations were expanded or built to take over many of their tasks, although not direct administration, of course. In some ex-imperial states colonial operations were converted into ministries concerned with development problems of former colonies. Today development is a continuous preoccupation of numerous international organizations including virtually all UN bodies, the IMF, the World Bank, the EEC, the Commonwealth, *La Francophonie*, various regional international organizations in Asia, Africa, and Latin America, international development agencies of industrial countries, and countless nongovernment organizations (NGOs). The UN system alone consists of sundry specialized agencies concerned in one way or another with problems of underdevelopment. UN bodies which originally had universal aims have turned their attention to underdeveloped countries: ILO, FAO,

ECOSOC, UNESCO.[6] Additional organizations concerned specifically with North–South issues have been fostered under UN auspices: Asian Development Bank, African Development Bank, UNCTAD, UNDP, UNIDO, ECAFE, ECA, ECLA.[7] The policies of the IMF and the World Bank have become fundamentally involved with the monetary and fiscal problems of Third World countries.

A responsibility once borne almost entirely by colonial powers at a far lower level of material support is carried out today not only by the international community at large but also by every developed country including many which were never imperial powers and bear no historical responsibility for colonialism. Bilateral international development organization has expanded enormously: all developed states including every member of the Organization for Economic Cooperation and Development (OECD), some members of the Organization of Petroleum Exporting Countries (OPEC) and the Soviet Bloc, and also China have established international development agencies or programmes. Although the expansion of positive international organization slowed in the 1980s, it has been faster than the growth of national governments which themselves expanded more rapidly than national economies.[8]

Sovereignty has given Third World states global institutional standing, influence, and support. This was noted by Martin Wight as it was happening: 'The existence of the United Nations has exaggerated the international importance of the have-not powers, enabling them to organize themselves into a pressure group with much greater diplomatic and propaganda weight than they would otherwise have had.'[9] Mohammed Bedjaoui puts it as follows: 'The advantage . . . of being a member of an international organization and profiting from it, is going to prove as important as belonging to a trade union or professional organization within an industrial State.'[10] But this implies an activist form of international organization which is radically different from anything that has existed before.

Third World states have radicalized international society by introducing collectivist ideologies and goals that challenge classical positive sovereignty doctrine particularly in the area of international economics. The 'pressure group' which Wight discerned as it was forming has become a major coalition of Asian, African, Latin American, Oceanic and even a few East European states, such as Yugoslavia. The first UNCTAD (1964) expressed novel global economic demands which postulated positive entitlements of poor states. A new Group of 77 nonindustrial countries, whose membership by 1989 had increased to 128, became the collective expression of the underdeveloped world in international relations. Subsequently at UNCTAD conferences, at special sessions of the UN General Assembly on North–South relations, and at various international gatherings the new doctrine was framed and reiterated in a series of resolutions promoting the creation of a New International Economic Order (NIEO) to provide distributive justice for the Third World.

The comparative poverty of many states and the resultant gap which divides the globe between underdeveloped and developed countries underlines the urgency and legitimacy of international aid which has found expression in the principle that the industrialized countries should annually contribute 0.7 per cent of GNP to the less developed states. Although most developed countries have not met this standard, few if indeed any are prepared to disavow the moral principle involved. Annual official development assistance from OECD countries increased almost sixfold in constant currency value from a total of $6,480 million in 1965 to $36,497 million in 1986.[11] As a percentage of donor GNP this ranged from 0.22 for the United States – still the largest donor contributing $9,395 million – to a high of 1.43 for Norway, with Sweden, Denmark and the Netherlands all exceeding 1.00 per cent GNP and France coming nearest to it among major donors (0.82 per cent). Japan in 1986 was the second largest donor after the US at $5,761 million (0.3 per cent GNP) but as a result of the increased strength of the yen and a changing international policy by 1989 was emerging as the leading foreign aid benefactor.

Although the supply of international aid disbursed is a small fraction of the budgets of rich countries, it nevertheless is a significant transfer of resources for the smallest and poorest economies of Third World peripheries, such as those in parts of South Asia, most of sub-Saharan Africa and much of Oceania. More than half the members of the UN receive socioeconomic aid. Virtually all economies classified by the World Bank as low-income and some lower middle income as well (about forty countries in all) are major recipients of public and publicly guaranteed external capital.[12] Many of the poorest economies especially in sub-Saharan Africa are unable to attract substantial private investment which diminished almost to nothing in the 1980s. If international development assistance were not forthcoming they would have no external sources of finance whatsoever. This prospect is morally unacceptable in today's interdependent world.

Aid dependency is evident in the debt predicament of many Third World states. According to the World Bank the external public debt of underdeveloped countries as a percentage of GNP increased sharply between 1970 and 1986. Some underdeveloped countries have external debts that exceed their GNP. During British decolonization it had been assumed or at least hoped that by the time of independence an ex-colonial state would be able to borrow on Western capital markets in London or New York. However, this proved impossible when many colonies became independent before they were financially viable. If private foreign investment is not forthcoming presumably there are no investment opportunities, no real 'economies' properly so-called. Public international aid, both grants and loans, becomes necessary if such countries are to enjoy any investment at all. Here is a novel kind of state whose prospects of development are determined significantly by international handouts and bailouts. This indicates a partly welfare world rather than a purely business world and the necessity of a new system of international finance resting on assumptions which differ from those of classical capitalism.

The reverse of this picture of international aid deserves comment. For the 1980s there was a net outflow of public and private capital from many Third World states to the industrial countries and this will continue in the 1990s unless the rules of international financial obligation are changed. Payments on loans, repatriated capital, royalties and the like constitute transfers that can exceed foreign aid disbursements moving in the opposite direction. One can even speak of the 'decapitalization' of countries that are suffering a continuing long-term net loss of capital in these ways. This often results from the fact that past loans were used for consumption or unproductive investments and now have to be repaid with no gain in production to finance it. Since such capital movements between states are consistent with the logic of international capitalism this phenomenon would seem to contradict any argument about the significance of international welfare. What it really indicates, however, is the extreme socioeconomic dependency of some states and usually the economic mismanagement of their governments also. The concept of 'decapitalization' is normative as well as descriptive: it is an evaluation of financial relations between countries of highly unequal capacities and resources which are deemed unfair to the weaker. This rests on the assumption that poor states should not be expected to play by the same rules as rich states. Such reasoning has been disclosed in demands for debt relief (as discussed below p. 127). This thinking seeks at a minimum to make underdeveloped states exceptions to some rules of the liberal economic order and at a maximum to devise new rules and perhaps a new order with their circumstances and predicaments explicitly in mind.

Financial transfers between countries amounting to many billions of dollars annually which cannot be justified by commercial prospects must be justified in some other way. The 1969 Report of the Commission on International Development set up by the World Bank and chaired by Lester Pearson saw the desirable relationship between developed and developing countries as 'expressing the reciprocal rights and obligations of donors and recipients'. Donor governments should be consulted in matters of policy and be assured that their funds will be allocated according to economic criteria. In return, recipients should be entitled to a prompt and steady flow of aid which would 'survive changes of government, short of extreme tyranny or financial irresponsibility'.[13] There is evidence in these remarks of positive sovereignty thinking based on traditional norms of reciprocity. Pearson was a Liberal Prime Minister and also a liberal. But there is also an assumption of international obligation to give and entitlement to receive aid. For the Pearson Commission the justification of international development assistance was moral as well as economic, and the morality was new.

The 1980 Report of the Independent Commission on International Development Issues under the chairmanship of Willy Brandt – a Social Democratic Chancellor and also probably a socialist – went much farther: developed states should not make their external assistance depend on traditional liberal values of merit or desert.[14] The moral issue was larger than merely the efficiency and responsibility of individual southern governments. A reformed if not a new international economic order was urgently needed to accommodate both North and South on an equitable basis. 'The international debate on development, at the threshold of the 1980s, deals not just with "assistance" and "aid" but with new structures . . . Such a process of restructuring and renewal has to be guided by the principle of equal rights and opportunities.'[15] Behind Brandt's remarks about structures is an assumption that states enjoy not only traditional rights of sovereignty but in addition socioeconomic entitlements to an equitable share of global resources and opportunities. The existence of legal equality seems to imply not only the desirability but also the right of eventual socioeconomic equality. Here is the implicit if not indeed explicit image of an emergent world economy with a single organization of production and distribution not unlike the usual macroeconomic image of a national economy in which transfer payments from rich to poor are both necessary and justifiable. This is a normative shift from classical liberal ideas of commutative justice based on reciprocity towards distributive justice necessitated by the gross material inequalities of states.

The traditional positive sovereignty assumption that all states ought

117

to be subject to the same performance criteria regardless of development or any other disabilities has become deeply controversial. The principle of reciprocity was challenged by the NIEO in the early 1970s. It is at the centre of debate concerning international development law and Third World debt.[16] The Charter of Economic Rights and Duties of States adopted by the UN General Assembly in 1974 is an explicit affirmation of social justice in international economic relations affecting the Third World. In calling for a reduction of global inequalities and claiming that it is the responsibility of the international community to provide the means of Third World development, the states-system is being conceived in a different way that raises many questions about the traditional rules of international relations.

INTERNATIONAL DEVELOPMENT LAW

The birth of one hundred sovereign states has unsettled international law. 'All is in flux. Even the sources of international law are changing.'[17] Recent decades have seen unprecedented legal activity among developed and underdeveloped states involving numerous 'Declarations', 'Final Acts', 'Joint Communiqués', 'Memoranda of Understanding', 'Codes of Conduct', 'Guidelines', 'Gentlemen's Agreements', 'Arrangements' (such as IMF 'Stand-by Arrangements'), and much else. Although the strict legality of these enactments is debated, they would not command the effort and attention they do 'if they were nothing but mere scraps of paper, which they are certainly not'.[18] The Third World, as one Moroccan scholar puts it, is 'the bearer of a democratizing tendency in international relations and will exercise an influence on the evolution of international law in the direction of a greater equality of opportunity and of a better protection of underprivileged countries'.[19] One result is a formative and controversial 'international law of development'.

As indicated, the law of nations continues to disclose an age-old preoccupation with moderating and regulating the relations of independent states. The proliferation of new sovereignties has not altered this reality. Third World governments assert the traditional liberties of sovereign states. They are vocal and passionate advocates of nonintervention and have no desire to repudiate the classical law which upholds their sovereign immunity. However, as they see it, strict adherence to universality and reciprocity in economic relations neglects their special overriding problem of underdevelopment. They are in no position to bargain with developed states on a basis of reciprocity. (This is an inversion of the traditional European claim that non-Western rulers would not reciprocate and should therefore be subjected to colonial domination.) They believe it is necessary to establish new norms of preferential treatment which compensate for their disadvantaged position in the international economy. (This is an inversion of imperialism and colonialism.) They consequently make unprecedented claims to socioeconomic entitlements: 'cette nouvelle réalité juridique qu'est l'inégalité economique des Etats'.[20] Just as minorities in the United States and other Western democracies have made use of domestic law to advance themselves, the Third World has resorted to international law in its pursuit of socioeconomic development and justice: 'never before have so many treaties been adopted, never have such precise international legal rules been agreed upon . . . and never has international law been more frequently invoked than it is nowadays'.[21] New international norms of development have been articulated which confound the positive sovereignty assumptions of the past.

Classical international law consists in universal rules of reciprocity among sovereign states deemed to be capable and responsible agencies. These rules, according to Georg Schwarzenberger, include recognition, consent, good faith, international reliability, freedom of the seas, and self-defence.[22] These are good conduct requirements which do not require international assistance of any material kind. As noted previously, they are 'negative' because they forbid intervention and discrimination in relations between sovereign states. They posit states as viable entities and are indifferent to their socioeconomic conditions. They do not therefore have to be positive and constructive themselves. 'International relations did not purport to penetrate beyond the shell of diplomatic intercourse into the economic and social aspects of the polities that dealt with each other as units.'[23] This is the negative logic of international *laissez-faire* or *free trade*.

The characteristic feature of international development law is the limitation of reciprocity and extension of preferential treatment for a select category of underdeveloped countries. It posits countries which are not in a position to reciprocate on an equal basis with developed countries. Indeed, they require international rules that enjoin developed states to assist them materially. This is the positive logic of *fair trade* which distinguishes between the strong and the weak in international economic relations and gives preferential treatment to the latter. According to a recent observer: 'what strikes one as special . . . about the law of development is that it imposes on the duty-bound States positive obligations to do, *facere,* and not merely to abstain from doing'.[24] The reason for such constructivist international obligation is the emergence of a new class of states which cannot compete under classical *laissez-faire* rules.

B.V.A. Roling and Wolfgang Friedmann were perhaps the first to theorize this emergent structure of nonreciprocal international law. Already in 1960 Roling discerned a movement from an old 'international law of liberty' to a new 'international law of welfare'. The former is consistent with a liberal economic order which makes provision for mutual adjustments amongst more or less equally developed states. The latter, however, by active intervention in international trade and finance and by international economic redistribution seeks to assist states to enhance the welfare of their populations. Roling concludes: 'The world community is bound to become a welfare community, just as the nation-state became a welfare state.'[25] Friedmann in 1964 likewise detected a shift in international legal norms 'from an essentially negative code of rules of abstention to positive rules of cooperation' which 'is an evolution of immense significance for the principles and structure of international law'.[26] International development law draws an explicit distinction between negative and positive sovereignty. According to one Third World commentator: 'The principle of sovereignty . . . in relation to international development norms is not equated with mere political independence, but incorporates substantive economic sovereignty . . . Similarly the principle of self-determination has an economic content.'[27] In other words, independence cannot be complete until all states have acquired positive sovereignty and that can only be made possible by reform of international relations and law along these lines.

Some legal scholars locate the sources of international development law in the UN Charter, including Article 1 which speaks of international cooperation to solve economic problems, Article 55 which refers to the promotion of 'higher standards of living, full employment, and conditions of economic and social progress and development', and Article 56 by which 'all Members pledge themselves to take joint and separate action in cooperation with the Organization' to achieve these standards. General Assembly Resolutions such as the obligation of rich countries to transfer 0.7 per cent of their GNP to poor countries in the form of public financial aid are additional sources. The International Covenant on Economic, Social and Cultural Rights, the UN Declaration on the Establishment of a New International Economic Order, and the Charter of the Economic Rights and Duties of States are also identified as foundations of international development law. On this view the UN system has a far wider working conception of international peace than all preceding systems since it is preoccupied not only with preventing war but also with removing the attributed underlying sources of international conflict, such as colonialism and underdevelopment.[28]

A different and more compelling argument has been advanced by Mohammed Bedjaoui, a Tunisian legal theorist and member of the International Court of Justice.[29] Bedjaoui rejects the view that international development law is derived primarily from the UN Charter because international development was still a nascent idea in 1945. The authentic source is the principle of self-determination which he considers to be the legal foundation of an entirely new post-colonial international society that has resulted from the anti-colonial revolution of the Third World:

> The 'open' community of today, which has replaced the 'closed' community of yesterday, owes this distinguishing feature to the self-determination of peoples . . . Without self-determination there is no contemporary international community . . . Thus self-determination belongs to the *jus cogens*. The 'right to development' flows from this right to self-determination and is of *the same kind*. For it is pointless to acknowledge self-determination as an overriding and preemptory principle, if we do not simultaneously acknowledge a 'right to development' for the people which has determined its own future. This right to development cannot be other than an absolute inherent, 'built-in' right, inextricably enshrined in the right to self-determination.[30]

In other words, the sovereignty of the Third World presupposes a new kind of international community in which self-determination and development are entailed primary legal norms. A Third World state has a right not only to political but also to economic sovereignty: to be 'master in its own house'. Here is the international equivalent of positive liberty. The right to permanent sovereignty over natural resources proclaimed repeatedly in UN Declarations and Resolutions is considered by Bedjaoui (and many Third World legal scholars) to be the paradigm entitlement of international development law linked directly to the *jus cogens* of self-determination (whereas some scholars consider it merely to be *in statu nascendi*). Consequently, international proclamations which embody this right such as the UN General Assembly Declaration on the Establishment of a New International Economic Order are endowed with special legitimacy and legality and are therefore authentic manifestations of international law. The controversy among lawyers which this view of international legality provokes is not my concern. The assumption that Third World states claim special rights to development which derive from self-determination is of crucial interest, however.

Perhaps the clearest expression of this assumption is the Charter of the Economic Rights and Duties of States which defines international entitlements at the centre of the NIEO.[31] Among its key provisions are the following: Article 10 which observes that all states are 'juridically equal' and therefore possess 'the right to participate fully and effectively in the international decisionmaking process in the solution of world economic, financial and monetary problems ... and to share equitably in the benefits resulting therefrom'; Article 14 which acknowledges the duty of 'every State' to promote the welfare and living standards of all peoples and 'in particular those of developing countries'; Article 18 which calls upon 'developed countries' to extend an improved and enlarged 'system of generalized nonreciprocal and nondiscriminatory tariff preferences to the developing countries' and to 'give serious consideration to the adoption of other differential measures ... to meet ... development needs of the developing countries'; and finally Article 22 which urges all states to promote 'increased net flows of real resources to the developing countries' and to expand 'the net amount of financial flows from official sources to developing countries and to improve the terms and conditions thereof'. This activist doctrine is fundamentally at odds with the *laissez-faire* postulates of classical international law.

Lawyers continue to debate the justiciability of international development law. Whether it is law or only morality, law *in esse* or merely *in posse*, is less important, however, than its significance as a normative feature of international relations. And the fact is that development norms command widespread regard not only in the Third World but elsewhere. Although their legal basis is still controversial they cannot be ignored. Even more significant, for the purposes of this study, is the dilemma between positive and negative sovereignty that this normative feature has provoked. Writing at an early stage Roling and Friedmann foresaw the new structure of positive cooperation gradually displacing the old regime of abstention and liberty and therefore resulting in a totally changed international moral and legal order. Instead, what appears to have happened is the formation of a *dual* system of international legitimacy and legality. This is revealed in the *concurrent* practice of acknowledging the special claims of marginal Third World governments to preferential and nonreciprocal assistance while respecting their universal and reciprocal rights of nonintervention. It is expressed explicitly in Article 17 of the Charter of the

Economic Rights and Duties of States which invokes 'international cooperation for development' as 'the shared goal and common duty of all States' but declares in no uncertain terms that every state should extend 'active assistance' to developing countries 'with strict respect for the sovereign equality of States and free of any conditions derogating from their sovereignty'.[32]

The perplexities which result are evident in the rules of the GATT since membership in that international trade regime was extended to Third World states. Under the GATT, as originally established, there are no distinctions between member states in terms of their ability to reciprocate. All members are assumed to possess roughly equal bargaining positions in international trade and therefore to benefit in similar proportion from 'reciprocal and mutually advantageous' tariff reductions. Although significant international economic inequality of course existed before the GATT expanded and the United States was undoubtedly a major beneficiary, other national economies – large and small – could and did profit from the GATT rules of free trade. However, the GATT's original assumptions 'began to be falsified', as Kabir Khan puts it, 'as the membership expanded to include developing, the least-developed and the landlocked countries'.[33] A GATT which includes a large majority of underdeveloped members must operate with different assumptions if they also are to benefit from the regime. New rules which acknowledge their special problems are necessary. Third World states have succeeded in getting preferential tariff arrangements built into the GATT as a matter of principle. However, the GATT evidently regards these concessions, for example, the Generalised Scheme of Preferences, as merely 'exceptions' to its general rules (such as the Most Favoured Nation principle) which still aim at non-discrimination in international trade.[34]

Khan argues, like Roling and Friedmann, that this emerging anomaly in the GATT rules is moving it incrementally away from the classical Bretton Woods system towards the International Law of Development based on the principle of nonreciprocity.[35] This forecast seems unlikely to materialize. But there is a deeper conflict here between assumptions of negative and positive sovereignty. The GATT would no longer exist if it were transformed into an international development regime based on nonreciprocity: its original *raison d'être* of growth in the world economy founded on free or at least freer trade would have been replaced by that of redistribution or justice based on fair trade as expressed, for example, in Article 28 of the Charter of the Economic Rights and Duties of States which declares that 'all States have the duty ... to promote just and equitable terms of trade'. Freedom of states to pursue their own economic advantage within a general framework of free trade, and social justice between states based on rules of economic redistribution are conflicting if not contradictory ideals. The same conflict is also evident in the Third World debt crisis as we shall see in the following section.

To sum up. The developmental concern of Third World states is frequently directed at classical rules concerning trade, finance, banking, and other international economic relations. They see these rules not as impartial norms of equal advantage to all but as legal instruments by which the developed states continue to exploit the underdeveloped after decolonization. What the former consider to be a 'level playing field' the latter see as steeply inclined against them. The rules under attack are those of the traditional liberal economic order which encourage free international exchange of commodities and capital in response to market prices, the comparative vitality of economies and ultimately the economic competence and responsibility of sovereign governments. The rules advocated are those which regulate world commodity prices, interest rates, debt obligations and so forth in such a way as to remove the current bias in favour of the developed economies and render the playing field more level for the less developed. Although Third World states have not yet succeeded in changing the rules of the global economy in the direction and to the extent they desire, their efforts have disclosed a constitutional dilemma of international economic relations which has no historical counterpart and is a direct consequence of the coexistence within the same international society of substantial states and quasi-states.

THIRD WORLD DEBT CRISIS

International responses to the Third World debt crisis are indicative of the dilemma. Can all states be held to the same rules of international financial obligation based on the traditional banking principle of paying one's debts on time, or must extenuating circumstances be taken into account in hardship cases? Should there be easier rules or exemptions for the weak? In provoking questions such as these the debt crisis reveals another facet of international relations involving quasi-states. Only a summary analysis is possible.

The Third World debt league is organized into divisions: a first division consisting of a few countries with heavy external debts which pose a threat to the international financial order, and second and third divisions comprising many countries with far smaller debts which present no such threat but which suffer greater burdens in relation to national wealth. Commercial debt owed to Western banks by a clutch of important countries including Brazil, Mexico, Argentina, Venezuela, Indonesia, and Poland was of sufficient weight to provoke a global debt crisis in the 1980s. The most individually burdensome debt, however, is bilateral and multilateral public loans owed to Western governments or the IMF and the World Bank by a far larger number of poorer countries officially classified as lower or lower-middle income.[36] Many Third World states have been unable to service their external debt by regularly paying interest. A growing number are unlikely ever to repay the principal completely.

Statistics on the creditworthiness of states indicate similar divisions.[37] In the period from 1981 to 1984 when the debt crisis arose the credit rating of a developed economy such as West Germany was consistently over 90 points out of a maximum 100, as compared to underdeveloped Zaire at under 10. Brazil declined from 70 to 36 and Mexico from 50 to 30 in this period. In 1984 the highest rating in Asia was 78 (Singapore) and the lowest 12 (Bangladesh), whereas the corresponding figures in the Middle East were 72 (Saudi Arabia) and 14 (Lebanon), in Latin America 50 (Trinidad and Tobago) and 5 (Nicaragua) and in sub-Saharan Africa 35 (Cameroon) and 4 (Uganda). These figures give an approximate indication of the division between states and quasi-states in the unsentimental risk-assessment view of international investors. It is obvious that Cameroon (not to mention Uganda) will find it difficult to play by the same international financial rules as Singapore (not to mention West Germany). Some kind of compensation would be necessary to level the playing field but it is not clear what this should involve.

Western creditors, public and private alike, have tried to enforce traditional rules by making their lending to Third World countries conditional on the IMF's 'good housekeeping seal of approval'. Conditionality basically involves meeting performance targets agreed between a debtor government and IMF representatives. Many Third World states have adopted IMF negotiated economic restructuring programmes designed to discipline governments deemed unable to discipline themselves. These involve the usual macroeconomic restraints: devaluation of national currencies which are vastly overvalued officially, reduction of inflation by sharply slowing the printing of money, major cuts in government spending and subsidies for such commodites as food or fuel, 'downsizing' of unproductive state or parastatal enterprises which do not cover their costs and consequently are a drain on the economy, elimination of price controls particularly in the agricultural sector which act as disincentives to production and encourage smuggling, and generally opening the economy to international market forces. These measures aim at economic growth by reducing if not eliminating noneconomic considerations in national economic decisionmaking which often result in the consumption of scarce resources by politically privileged urban elites and classes. Governments which fail to live up to their debt restructuring agreements by refusing to take the IMF medicine can be declared ineligible for new loans.

IMF restructuring focuses strictly on national economic indicators and ignores extenuating sociopolitical circumstances – such as the institutional fragility of the state or the dubious legitimacy of rulers or the culture of corruption which may be the roots of government indiscipline and indebtedness in many Third World countries. For example, the IMF has insisted that state enterprises pay their way. Naturally there has been strenuous objection to this policy by rulers who are only too aware that their political base would be undermined and possibly even destroyed if government organizations were scaled down or closed and redundant government employees dismissed. The IMF replies that it also is subject to economic disciplines: its credibility in the international financial community and consequent ability to continue lending to developing countries will be damaged if it does not obey them. In 1987 David Rockefeller, Chairman of Chase Manhattan Bank's International Advisory Committee and representative of that community, described the IMF as the 'convenient whipping boy' of Third World states and defended IMF policies for requiring merely what governments know they ought to do.[38] This is classical positive sovereignty doctrine: incompetent or self-indulgent governments are required on pain of losing their credit ratings to conform to disciplines which exist to uphold traditional banking rules and ultimately the world capitalist economy.

There is little doubt, however, that instability caused by politically crucial urban populations rebelling against declining wages and rising prices has been an important byproduct of IMF restraint programmes. When Sudan devalued its currency by 44 per cent and raised fuel and sugar prices in compliance with an IMF agreement it aroused protests that left six people dead and resulted in the government abandoning the programme and consequently being declared ineligible for new loans. In 1986 anti-government demonstrations in Zambia against the elimination of food subsidies involved the death of at least fifteen people. In 1989 riots in which some 300 people were killed broke out in Caracas, Venezuela, following the imposition of an austerity programme supported by the IMF. Many other examples could be cited. Abolishing subsidies on food harms the urban proletariat; raising fuel

126

prices hurts the urban bourgeoisie. Eliminating government patronage often undercuts the only basis of 'legitimacy' that exists in many Third World states. If people riot shaky regimes can fall.

Many Third World leaders therefore bridle at IMF discipline which they usually see as intervention. In 1987 the President of Zambia accused the IMF of 'blackmailing' African states by insisting on compliance with its policies in exchange for new loans. Botswana's Finance Minister reportedly told the 1987 IMF annual meeting that the institution had pushed its conditionality far beyond the limit of 'social tolerance'. President Carlos Andres Perez of Venezuela placed the blame for the Caracas riots on the 'inflexibility' of industrial states which, through the IMF, forced his government to impose a severe programme of economic austerity which provoked instability and violence. It should be noted that the IMF does not dictate specific policies but only seeks agreement on macroeconomic restraints, such as those outlined above, which are designed to reduce waste and increase productivity. However, such restraints often leave little room for choice by the governments involved. Moreover, they do not address the problem of depressed commodity prices and high interest rates which reduce choice even further. (Of course, these are general market conditions which all countries are subject to and not merely the less developed. They fall far more heavily on the latter, however, which again underlines the distinction between states and quasi-states.)

Does responsibility lie with the sovereign government involved, as the IMF assumes, or does it rest, as President Perez claims, with the industrial powers who have the greatest influence on IMF policies? Is the Venezuelan government a free agent and therefore accountable for its actions, or do the international financial and economic constraints it faces remove that responsibility and locate it elsewhere – presumably among the developed countries? If a country such as Venezuela which enjoyed enormous oil revenues in the 1970s is not fully accountable how much less accountable are the more numerous and less fortunate Third World states which do not have oil wealth? The answer depends on the facts, of course. But it also depends on one's theory of sovereignty: are sovereign states in such circumstances responsible agents, or are they victims of socioeconomic forces beyond their control? Can all states be obliged to play by the traditional nondiscriminatory rules of laissez-faire or can some legitimately claim positive discrimination on grounds of special circumstances or needs?

African governments have vociferously opposed conditionality and called for reform of the international public lending regime. Western sympathizers have charged that the First World has betrayed the trust of poor countries by not substantially increasing concessional aid and otherwise easing their debt obligations by relaxing or abandoning rules which only make sense between developed economies. A special 1987 summit of OAU states called for all African external debt to be re-scheduled over fifty years, without interest, and for sharply increased external financial assistance from developed countries. Debt payments should be suspended without penalizing eligibility for new credits in cases where it was impossible to make them without major social sacrifices. African governments demand concessionality and non-reciprocity in financial transfers between wealthy and impoverished states. UN bodies such as UNCTAD have argued that external debt is a crisis not of some individual states but of international society as a whole. They emphasize the *system* vulnerabilities of the weaker member states as compared to the stronger. Some development economists make the same point: 'The poorest people and poorest countries are always peculiarly vulnerable to economic shocks not of their own making ... the errors and problems of the past are a joint responsibility of African governments and the international community.'[39] This 'collectivist' theory obviously rejects the traditional 'individualist' equation of sovereignty and responsibility and attributes it to the system as a whole.

Globalist proposals have even come from Western bankers. In 1988 James Robinson, Chairman of American Express Company, called for shared sacrifices and rewards by Western banks, the developed countries and the less-developed countries and proposed an Institute for International Debt and Development: the debt crisis is 'more than a banking problem ... It is also a business problem, a geopolitical problem and a world peace problem.'[40] Mr Robinson presumably wanted Western governments and ultimately their taxpayers to pick up his unserviceable Third World loans. This is a convergence of ideology one normally would not expect but it reveals the extent to which at least some Western banks are entangled in the financial difficulties of certain Third World states. They want their money back but they know many debtors cannot repay without additional external financial assistance which both the banks and the debtors would like the developed countries to provide.

The IMF has been operating with classical liberal doctrine in both economics and international law. If governments wish to borrow they must meet the terms of the lender who himself is subject to similar disciplines which extend up and down the line of credit, all of which is consistent with free market economics and international law based on contract. The ultimate aim is to integrate Third World economies into

128

the international economy on a basis of reciprocity rather than singling them out for special treatment. Conditionality has provoked a storm of criticism, however, owing to its seeming intrusiveness into the sovereignty of debtor states which because of poor credit ratings usually have little if any alternative to dealing with the IMF for new loans. The IMF seeks to improve those ratings through its macroeconomic disciplines. But the IMF role has been characterized as that of 'de facto receiver to African governments'[41] and even as amounting to nothing less than a 'recolonization' of the Third World by 'international bureaucracies'.[42] Criticisms such as these assume that Third World debtors are in no position to be held accountable in such ways. The IMF evidently considers Third World sovereignty at least in principle to be the same as sovereignty everywhere else: namely to postulate freedom and responsibility of governments. But IMF critics assume positive freedom to be lacking and exemptions from traditional banking rules and financial assistance on a different basis to be both necessary and justified until such freedom is achieved.

The severe hardship of states which patently cannot meet conditionality has caused concern among Western governments in the so-called Paris Club. In 1987 the Nordic countries began to write off their soft loans to the poorest states. Canada in that year forgave more than half a billion dollars of debt owed by the most destitute members of the Commonwealth and Francophonie. In 1988 Britain converted over 400 million dollars owed by fourteen African countries into grants. Other Western states and the EEC have taken similar actions. The 1988 summit meeting in Toronto of the seven leading Western industrialized countries accepted the principle that debt relief must be granted to the most impoverished African states. In 1989, shortly after the Caracas riots, the new Bush administration in the United States reversed previous Reagan administration policy by advocating debt forgiveness on commercial loans to major Third World borrowers, particularly the Latin American states. Private Western banks would grant at least temporary waivers of the repayment of principal or reduce interest rates. The United States, Japan, and other major OECD countries would underwrite the IMF and the World Bank in the event that debtor countries still faltered on the repayment of loans written down by commercial banks. The Bush proposal did not abandon restructuring, however, which was still a key to future lines of commercial credit in countries granted debt forgiveness. And there was no indication that Western governments (that is, taxpayers) would become involved in financing Third World debt reduction.

The debt crisis has nevertheless brought to light a predicament of international finance in which the traditional doctrine of repaying loans according to one's agreements has been subjected to certain qualification. Those parts of the Third World, mainly sub-Saharan Africa, which are least able to meet their external financial obligations are considered to have a legitimate claim to the largest relief from traditional financial requirements – in some cases outright debt cancellation. Other parts, particularly Latin America, with stronger although not yet developed economies are considered to have a legitimate claim only to some debt forgiveness. In a capitalist regime at least the major debtors must be held to some account otherwise the system itself could be threatened. The former therefore qualify for 'soft loans' administered by international public lending agencies at concessional rates of interest, whereas the latter must be satisfied with commercial rates although these may be written down by the private banks with IMF and World Bank support underwritten by the major OECD countries. The former can only demand relief, but the latter can also threaten default. This is the debt threat presented by major Latin American borrowers. Debt forgiveness for the latter must therefore be handled carefully so as not to erode the rules which are those of borrowers paying off their loans in accordance with agreed rates and terms: the basis of a banking system.

There are different normative assumptions and expectations about sovereign statehood disclosed by the debate on Third World debt. Should all debtor states be held to the same rules regardless of their circumstances? Or should easier terms and conditions be available to hardship cases? There is a division of international opinion on this question. Some are inclined to apply classical commercial obligations as widely as possible. They evidently believe that sovereign members of international society, like adults in domestic society, are legally independent and must be held accountable for their debts. This is the international morality of *pacta sunt servanda*: keep your promises. Such a regime cannot operate permanently on a basis either of debt forgiveness or debt repudiation which 'destroy the obligations between borrower and lender on which any enduring system of international credit has to be based'.[43] Debt forgiveness such as the Bush administration recommends is conceived to be only temporary and therefore not a basic change in the regime. But it would be a precedent. If some Third World states receive forgiveness it should not be unexpected that all such states would claim the same rights and it would be easy for them to consider these rights as something less than temporary. Even on a temporary basis, such a tiered regime of international financial obligation could be read as a retreat from classical positive sovereignty doctrine. Of course, it is also possible to view it as a new realism involving prudential considerations of international financial managers and therefore as a departure from classical doctrine only to save the system in the longer term – an international parallel to President Roosevelt's domestic New Deal during the depression of the 1930s. This undoubtedly is the view of some Western banks and major OECD states including now for the first time the United States.

Others are inclined to go farther because they have a view of international obligation which is fundamentally different from the doctrine of *pacta sunt servanda*. Poor states in the international economy, like poor people in domestic economies, are vulnerable to forces and events beyond their control: they cannot control the high interest rates or low commodity prices in whose jaws they are caught. This is the moral logic of the NIEO and its supporters who reject the principle of strict reciprocity in economic relations and argue that the adverse material circumstances of most Third World states call for a fundamental change of international obligation away from free trade and commutative justice towards economic democracy and distributive justice. But this is far too radical to be acceptable to those with prevailing economic power in international society and particularly the United States. The NIEO therefore remains little more than a pipe dream. This does not mean, however, that a doctrine of positive assistance and discrimination has not found a legitimate place in international relations which major economic powers can accept.

INTERNATIONAL AFFIRMATIVE ACTION?

Today the duties of statesmen evidently are not only to respect the jurisdictions of other statesmen but *in addition* to materially assist underdeveloped countries, especially those in difficult circumstances. The deep poverty and backwardness of many naturally gives rise to a sense of need – basic needs – which in turn are equated with qualifications for material aid: poor countries feel entitled to receive and rich countries constrained to provide developmental assistance or debt relief. If these and similar kinds of positive socioeconomic support do not yet reflect a legal obligation they nevertheless reveal a moral injunction of some kind. It is impossible to deny the impoverished conditions of many states and the obvious ability of other states to help in alleviating them. At the very least providing aid or relief is a decent thing and refusing to do so is worthy of condemnation.

J. R. Lucas points out that moral practice commonly and quite rightly distinguishes 'fair bargains' from 'hard bargains': 'If I take advantage of a man's temporary need, he may have no reasonable alternative except to agree to my terms, but I am exploiting him none the less. He is, in effect, agreeing under duress.'[44] Although Lucas is referring to individuals and not states, this could perhaps be said of IMF restructuring agreements. Indeed, critics of the doctrine that contracted international debts should be repaid in full frequently resort to the moral language of 'hard bargaining' in their condemnations of developed countries and Western banks. International obligation so conceived obviously is different from that postulated by classical positive international law: it is about what is decent and just in the circumstances and not merely contractual or legal. That 'hard bargains' do not have the same moral standing as 'fair bargains' is easier to recognize, of course, than respond to with appropriate rules and practices. However, the willingness of major OECD states to consider debt relief for certain countries in the belief that they cannot repay owing to forces and circumstances largely beyond their control gives some intimations of norms which depart from classical liberal doctrine even if they stop far short of the Charter of the Economic Rights and Duties of States. This seems to be the emergent practice of states but how can we characterize it?

A domestic analogy may be suggestive. Within some Western countries, as indicated, extra socioeconomic entitlements and assistance are provided to certain people who qualify for 'affirmative action' programmes. This is a form of preferential treatment by the state targeted at citizens who are members of particular 'disadvantaged' categories, such as blacks or women. In Canada it has constitutional standing under the 'equality rights' section of the *Charter of Rights and Freedoms* which declares the legality of 'any law, programme or activity that has as its object the amelioration of conditions of . . . those that are disadvantaged because of race, national or ethnic origins, colour, religion, sex, age or mental or physical disability'.[45] The crucial idea is that of extending a special opportunity or benefit to some individual or group who otherwise would not qualify for it in compensation for disadvantages attributed to unchosen membership in such categories. This is usually justified on the grounds of repairing injustice or disadvantage brought about by such membership in the past and in the expectation of thereby enabling the beneficiary to exercise greater self-determination in the future.[46] Affirmative action therefore justifies preferential treatment policies according to either backward-looking principles or forward-looking principles or both.

Affirmative action programmes were instituted in the United States when it became clear that racial integration could not be achieved merely by the repeal of segregation laws and the extension of the franchise and other generally available legal rights to blacks. Although they were now first class citizens by law they nevertheless remained entangled in adverse economic, social, and cultural circumstances which severely limited their freedom of opportunity and over which they were considered to exercise little or no control. In our terminology, negative rights were not sufficient to overcome the adverse consequences of past discrimination. In addition, it was necessary to discriminate positively in education or employment or housing to enable certain people to take advantage of their newly won rights. Regional development programmes such as exist in Canada by which the Federal Government provides special financial assistance to poor provinces might be thought of as affirmative action for territorial communities.[47] Affirmative action is therefore a kind of citizenship plus: temporary dependency in the form of preferential treatment for the sake of future positive freedom.

Affirmative action is a practical policy in countries like the United States or Canada where those actually receiving benefits on such grounds are a comparatively small minority in an otherwise wealthy society.[48] Since it presupposes support only until such time as the beneficiary is able to stand on his own it is not fundamentally inconsistent with a liberal political order. Perhaps this is why it has proved acceptable to the majority of Americans and Canadians and their political representatives at least to date. It is not by any means without controversy, however. Its ethical base is widely questioned and its status is by no means secure. It is a form of discrimination which in favouring some penalizes those who would otherwise qualify for the benefit or opportunity and therefore violates the principle of merit or desert. Another criticism casts doubt on the claim that it will in due course enable its beneficiaries to stand on their own. If it fails to produce the desired results or if it reinforces rather than reduces dependency it could come under criticism sufficient to bring about its abandonment. In which case the traditional practice of negative liberty would presumably be reverted to, as some critics of affirmative action advocate.[49]

A cognate idea can be detected in contemporary international relations. Third World states which have experienced colonialism are the international equivalent of racial minorities whose ancestors suffered under slavery or other legal or economic disabilities. Both represent victims of past institutionalized discrimination or disadvantage and therefore merit special consideration and assistance. Although negative sovereignty was necessary to remove colonialism, it is not sufficient to complete self-determination. Third World states therefore have a legitimate claim to international socioeconomic assistance, compensation, and relief not only on the backward-looking grounds that they suffered from past exploitation by colonial powers and the world capitalist economy but also in the forward-looking expectation that they will thereby develop the capabilities of positive sovereignty. The point is not that such exploitation necessarily took place or must be 'proved' but only that it serves as moral grounds for present actions and institutions of positive discrimination between otherwise equally sovereign states.

International affirmative action, unlike the NIEO, is a moral practice that attempts to fit into a liberal world order. Just as domestic affirmative action in the United States and Canada goes beyond – although not too far beyond – the franchise and other legal rights available to everyone so also does international affirmative action reach a modest distance beyond negative sovereignty. And just as domestic programmes of affirmative action anticipate the day when they will be unnecessary, international programmes look forward to the time when recipient states can stand by themselves. Finally, just as positive discrimination in favour of disadvantaged minorities is only possible within states because of the existence of wealthy majorities, corresponding discrimination between states likewise is consistent or at least not inconsistent with the present division of international society between an underdeveloped periphery in need and a developed centre with resources to address those needs.

International affirmative action therefore presupposes that the global economic playing field is not level for all states and to be made level certain rules and actions of positive discrimination in favour of the currently disadvantaged is required until such time as they are in a position to play the great game of international economics by the classical rules. Something along these lines appears to be happening in international financial and trading relations as my previous remarks indicate. Of course, 'international affirmative action' is not explicitly referred to as such by the actors involved. The idea is present, however, even if the term is not. Those less developed states which are not yet in a position to take full advantage of the traditional rules can legitimately claim exemption from (some of) them or special rules for themselves until such time as they are in that position. The various proposals of debt relief for certain Third World states are consistent with the affirmative action notion of temporary exemption from the general rules of international financial obligation. And modifications to the GATT designed for less developed countries and in particular the suspension of reciprocity and the Most Favoured Nation principle and the adoption of nonreciprocity and the Generalised Scheme of Preferences are consistent with the idea of special rules. Both aim at making the playing field of international economics if not level for such countries at least less steeply inclined against them.

Further, these special positive arrangements are considered to be only temporary. The general rules of reciprocity and nondiscrimination are expected to be applied once the disadvantages are overcome and countries are able to stand on their own. This could be rather long in coming, however, and in many cases such special arrangements could last indefinitely if the beneficiaries are unable to respond positively and the community of states continues to support them. Even those which do respond might still be reluctant to give up their special entitlements which they could very easily come to regard as permanent international rights. In 1987 several countries were considered too rich for concessionary financial assistance from the inter-American Development Bank and other international lending institutions. Some were also 'graduated' from the US preferential tariff regime which previously gave them privileged access to the American market. Graduation day was a moment not of celebration but of bitter complaint by Singapore and Barbados who objected openly at henceforth being required to compete according to the more disciplining rules of reciprocity.[50]

THE DILEMMA OF QUASI-STATES

Perhaps the threads of these remarks can be drawn together. International development doctrine runs up against traditional normative assumptions underlying economic relations between sovereign states. The reality is not that the law of welfare – nonreciprocity – has replaced the law of liberty – reciprocity, as Friedmann predicted. Nor is it likely. Rather, it is that poor states today assert both negative and positive norms at one and the same time, as indicated by Article 17 of the Charter of Economic Rights and Duties of States. And contemporary international society is trying to operate with both. But the two norms may not always be compatible. Indeed, they may be contradictory at some points and the contradiction may not be capable of a resolution without sacrificing one or the other. We arrive at the North–South dilemma because the deprivation of independence for the underdeveloped and the perpetuation of underdevelopment for the independent are both morally objectionable in the contemporary international community. In practice, of course, the dilemma is resolved in the latter way.

This normative conflict was unknown to classical international relations which assumed that all sovereign states were more or less capable of benefiting from a liberal international economic order based on reciprocity. There was not a significant and acknowledged division between some states which were developed and others which were underdeveloped. States required temporary economic assistance from time to time, such as IMF loans to overcome balance of payments difficulties. But no states were in more or less permanent need of positive assistance or compensation which was not expected to be reciprocated in kind. Political independence and socioeconomic well-being were all of a piece: sovereignty was indivisible in this doctrine.

These positive sovereignty assumptions run into difficulty in an international society comprising numerous quasi-states. IMF restructuring is a case in point: it cannot really deal with the fact that most smaller and weaker debtors suffer from far more than merely temporary financial or technical difficulties. They cannot respond to IMF disciplines in the same way as developed countries with balance of payments problems. They have a deeper problem: underdevelopment. Conditionality is often thwarted because not only economies or societies but also governments are underdeveloped: 'Efforts at stabilization and structural adjustment are routinely stymied by domestic political forces.'[51] 'The ability of Third World regimes to frustrate external control and restructuring efforts remains one of the largest lacunae of the growing literature on international debt.'[52] The IMF cannot infringe upon the sovereignty of the borrower by managing the restructuring itself. All it can do is withhold future loans if a government fails to perform according to the terms of its agreement. But withholding cannot resolve the problem of underdevelopment. Similar difficulties were encountered in expecting quasi-states to benefit equally from GATT rules or to repay their debts in accordance with traditional banking rules. These may be viable norms for developed countries but they are stretched to the point of breaking when it comes to underdeveloped ones.

As indicated, some of the requirements of the international economic game have therefore been changed to accommodate quasi-states – although this is usually considered to be only temporary. One can read international development assistance, the GATT preferences, debt relief and other instances of international affirmative action in this light: they amount to a specialized although still rather minimal regime of positive and nonreciprocal assistance or compensation which caters for a new class of sovereign states that are underdeveloped. Institutional arrangements such as these do not and cannot avoid the normative dilemma outlined above, however. In fact they create it and the consequences which follow from it.

The dilemma of quasi-states is rooted in the difference between a state and an individual and therefore discloses one of the limitations of the domestic analogy in international relations. Who is ultimately responsible for human welfare: the individual or society? What is just: rules equal for all or rules that compensate the weak or unfortunate? These are questions which divide Western domestic societies between Right and Left and turn on conflicting conceptions of freedom, responsibility, and equality. A similar debate divides international society roughly between North and South. Classical international relations assumes that sovereign governments are generally capable and responsible, although they can face brief periods of economic difficulty when they may require assistance from the international community or other states. A government receiving assistance today, however, will be obliged by the rule of reciprocity to extend the same to someone else tomorrow. It therefore precludes the dilemma. However, by assuming that international society has the responsibility of providing assistance to underdeveloped countries until such time as they can exercise positive sovereignty the doctrine of international affirmative action encounters the dilemma and is impaled on its horns.

Providing financial assistance or relief to a sovereign member of international society is ethically more ambiguous than providing it to a citizen within domestic society because we cannot be certain that it will get to those who can best use it or most need it. In giving aid to a citizen it is clear who the beneficiary is. But in giving assistance to a country (or other collectivity) it is not as clear. Aid transferred from a rich to a poor country may or may not involve a transfer of income from a rich to a poor person. Citizens of average means in rich state A cannot directly provide financial aid to persons of far lower average means in poor state B because the transaction crosses international boundaries and therefore involves sovereign states. This can only happen if the sovereign government of state B authorizes it and is able to enforce its authorization. A government may invest international assistance productively or redistribute it in accordance with need but there is no lawful international way of guaranteeing this once the foreign resources are on its soil. It depends on the ability and willingness of its officials to do so. If they are prone to mismanagement, corruption or other kinds of incompetence or indiscipline foreign grants or loans may end up feeding the system of waste and abuse. Debt forgiveness can have the same result if past loans were in the hands of such governments. This should not be taken to imply that capable and responsible government is a sufficient condition for development or social justice in Third World states. But it probably is a necessary condition.

In transacting development assistance or relief across international borders the independence of recipients and the principle of nonreciprocity probably undermines the confidence of donors. Although it would be taboo for governments of developed countries to admit it publicly uncertainty on this issue may be one reason why international development assistance is inadequate to the need. In other words, the asymmetrical relationship or divorce of entitlement and responsibility which international development entails may limit severely the effectiveness and justice that such transactions can achieve. Here is perhaps the root of the dilemma in Third World demands for both distributive and commutative justice, development support, and sovereign independence, nonreciprocity and reciprocity. In short, in the real world of international relations one cannot have one's cake and eat it.

6 SOVEREIGN RIGHTS VERSUS HUMAN RIGHTS

THE UNCIVIL IMAGE OF THE THIRD WORLD

In recent decades a clearer picture of political incivility around the world has emerged. Reports of international humanitarian organizations annually catalogue arbitrary detentions, beatings, political killings, torture, terror, political prisoners, disappearances, refugees, death squads, destruction of livelihood, and various other human rights violations which fill the pages of substantial volumes.[1] There would be more were it not for the fact that many governments conceal them. A 1986 study estimated that the world's refugee population was in excess of 13 million and that 'the number of people displaced within their own countries is probably even greater'.[2] Political killings either by governments or by agents which they cannot control have occurred in Guatemala, Indonesia, Cambodia, Uganda, Haiti, Argentina, India, and Libya.[3] Political massacres with genocidal tendencies have been committed in Burundi, Rwanda, Uganda, Cambodia, and Bangladesh.[4] Political abduction and disappearances carried out either by government agents or their opponents in 1985 alone are 'known to have occurred' in Angola, Argentina, Bolivia, Brazil, Central African Republic, Chile, Columbia, Cyprus, Dominican Republic, El Salvador, Ethiopia, Guatemala, Guinea, Haiti, Honduras, Indoniesia, Iran, Iraq, Lebanon, Mexico, Morocco, Nepal, Nicaragua, Paraguay, Peru, Philippines, Seychelles, South Africa, Sri Lanka, Syria, Togo, Uganda, Uruguay, Vietnam, and Zaire.[5] The use of torture as part of state-controlled machinery to suppress dissent has been documented recently in sixty-six countries: twenty-three African (including South Africa), fifteen Latin American, ten Middle Eastern, ten Asian, and eight European.[6] Spain was the only Western democracy included among the offenders. The list goes on and the picture changes only slightly from one year to the next.

These occurrences are not happening outside sovereign states or in wars between them. They are not inflicted on foreigners or colonial subjects. They are occurring inside independent states. Although anti-government rebels are also responsible and foreign intervention can be involved, the principal violators are sovereign governments. The victims are their own citizens. This 'paradox of the state' in which governments are a source of threat rather than security is a general phenomenon by no means restricted to the Third World.[7] The political history of Europe can be read without distortion as a long record of political incivility. Postwar Eastern Europe continued the malpractice. Today, however, it is particularly evident outside the West where citizenship often is scarcely more than a nominal status with little or no real purchasing power. This is because the Third World state is usually the possession and instrument of elites who often act as if sovereignty is their licence to exploit people.)

In the past quarter century the image of the Third World accordingly has become one not only of poverty and underdevelopment but also of incivility and repression. This regrettable reality is in marked contrast to the time of independence when the Third World was 'a vital new force in international affairs'.[8] The revolution of the new states was progressive. Decolonization was an act of liberation. The future was one of promise now that colonial peoples possessed sovereignty and could take their destiny into their own hands. But if we are to believe these reports – and the only ones who dispute them are the sovereign governments involved and their allies – the expansion of the community of states brought about by decolonization has not resulted in a corresponding extension of human rights protection as was originally expected when independence was in the offing. Instead, it increased the opportunity for human rights violations. More than four decades after the Universal Declaration of Human Rights the violation of basic standards of human decency is more universal than the protection.

CIVILIZATION AND HUMAN RIGHTS

How should we interpret international human rights violations? Have humanitarian standards been raised? Or has the incidence of human rights abuses increased? In an imperfect world consisting of men rather than angels, the elevation of human standards will, if other things remain equal, be followed by increased human rights violations even if behaviour is unchanged. International standards of human rights undoubtedly are higher today than at any time in modern history. The elaborate framework of humanitarian law is extensive testimony. Perceptions of human rights abuses are also probably more acute than ever – at least in the West. The comparative civility of Western states and the corresponding expectations of their

140

populations have undoubtedly created heightened awareness of inhumanity everywhere.

The perception of international human rights violations presupposes general standards and expectations of humanitarian conduct. If there were different standards from one place to the next similarities and differences would be all that was noticed: a world of cultural relativism. If standards were low or non-existent such behaviour also would not attract attention because it would be a commonplace everywhere. In an uncivil world nobody but saints would notice incivility. Likewise, if the world's states were in the habit of protecting the civil and political liberties of their populations there would be little or no interest in international human rights. The spread of sovereignty around the world and the protection of human rights would be one and the same. There would be no tension between sovereign rights and human rights. And there would be no international law of human rights and no international humanitarianism because they would be unnecessary. Today, however, human rights violations in most parts of the world are well documented and widely criticized by a growing international humanitarian movement.

Although the term 'civilization' is controversial the concept is necessary in international studies if we are to understand issues involved in the protection of human rights. Most informed people and virtually all students of human relations recognize that the particular rules, institutions, practices, and customs of which societies consist vary enormously from one time or place to the next. Social scientists are professionally inclined to be agnostic about different cultures and to suspend any judgements which might involve ethnocentrism. This is particularly the case as regards differences between Western and non-Western cultures.

The student of international relations is confronted with a special problem, however. His subject is a single global society of states to which all other societies and cultures are connected, directly or indirectly, by means of sovereignty. One cannot conceive of a universal international society otherwise. Moreover, since states consist of humans one must assume some common humanity: perhaps a 'minimal content of natural law' which acknowledges universal human vulnerability and responds by a general rule of nonviolence.[9] Finally, it would be impossible to operate across cultures without not only a shared discourse and framework of communication – including international law and diplomacy – but also common standards which make comparative appraisals and equitable treatment possible. Not only legal and scientific language but also moral, political, and economic discourse require terminology which is not merely relative but also comparative; that is, it involves reference to standards and particularly standards of conduct.

The concept of 'civilization' implied by these remarks was examined at length by the English philosopher R. G. Collingwood in response to the Nazi atrocities of the second world war.[10] According to Collingwood, 'civilization' primarily signifies refraining from the arbitrary use of force and obeying the rule of law which forbids it. 'Civilization is not civilization but barbarity unless it insists that you shall treat every member of your community as civilly as possible.' Acting 'civilly' towards someone means respecting his feelings, dignity, and autonomy. The rule of law is a public standard of conduct which precludes arbitrariness and establishes due process based on formal equality. Both 'civility' and 'the rule of law' presuppose the capacity not only to obey but also to enforce the law. Collingwood points out that the process of civilization involves bringing others, including foreigners, into one's community which is a sphere of human relations governed by the civilities and the rule of law. The expansion of international society is an instance of the civilization process in the broadest sense.

'Civilization' also signifies a corresponding process whereby the comforts and enjoyments of human life are enlarged by the application of science and industry to natural resources. This is the civilization associated with technological and economic development. However, there is no civilization if in the rational exploitation of nature human beings are treated as part of the natural world rather than the human world.[11] Development without the rule of law is barbarism. This is the great temptation when extreme inequalities of technology exist between societies, as in the historical encounter between the Western and the non-Western worlds. Technological prowess unfortunately invites a dangerous kind of hubris which is a real threat to civilization because it reinforces the built-in hubris of the state which has troubled many international theorists and not least Burke: 'I must fairly say, I dread our *own* power, and our *own* ambition; I dread our being too much dreaded'.[12] Today, owing to continuing scientific and technological innovation, that menace is greater than ever. A government which has mastered technology but not the rule of law is the most dangerous of all organizations – as twentieth-century high-tech totalitarianism graphically indicates. It is a regrettable fact that diffusion of technology and particularly the means of violence is easier and more rapid than enlargement of political civility. Many of these means and particularly the means of violence have been spread by the expansion of the states-system. The huge international arms bazaar feeds the insatiable appetite for such means of many Third World governments which could not possess them otherwise.

The secondary process of civilization consequently is *always* subject to the first process and particularly the rule of law which forbids the arbitrary use of force. Collingwood is therefore at pains to emphasize the most important thing of all about 'civilization', namely that it requires self-discipline. *'Law and order mean strength.* Men who respect the rule of law are by daily exercise building up the strength of their own wills.'[13] Civilized men and civilized governments alike exercise forbearance. The concept of civilization clearly has extensive applicability in both domestic and international politics in spite of the fact that the word is avoided today.

A characteristic feature of international law in the late nineteenth and early twentieth centuries, as we saw in chapter 3, was the 'standard of civilization' used in determinations of membership in the society of states. The standard was established not only to eradicate barbarous practices such as slavery but also to regulate the technological power of intruding Western mechanized states. The standard was embedded in colonialism. Today, however, it is of historical interest only. It has been categorically rejected by the Third World as a form of Western imperialism: an expression of contempt for their cultures and a pretext for denying self-government. The expressions 'sacred trust of civilization' and 'civilized state' have been erased from current international law and the dialogue between states carefully avoids these terms.

Even though 'sovereign state' has replaced 'civilized state' the idea of 'civilization' has not been and cannot be abandoned. Without such a distinction it would be impossible to render certain international legal and moral judgements. Immediately following the second world war surviving leaders and high officials of defeated Axis powers were tried for crimes of war and crimes against humanity by the Nuremberg and Tokyo tribunals and many were convicted. The prerogatives of sovereignty were not considered a valid excuse for acts of inhumanity.[14] Legal positivism offers no escape from civilized standards.

The old 'standard of civilization' still exists, but is expressed differently today. Gerrit Gong suggests that these expressions are, firstly, 'human rights' and 'non-discrimination', and, secondly, 'modernity' or 'development'.[15] This is not only similar but virtually identical to Collingwood's twofold concept of 'civilization' already discussed. The ideas of a 'standard of civilization' and a 'standard of human rights' share a common preoccupation with life, liberty, dignity, security, and other fundamental rights which regard human beings as ends rather than means. These are natural rights or human rights properly so-called because to be realized they only require forbearance which is within the capacity of everyone; they are negative rather than positive. The idea of a 'standard of non-discrimination' also resembles Collingwood's concept of civilization as a process of bringing outsiders into one's community. Likewise, the idea of civilization and the idea of development both seek mastery of nature by the application of science, technology, and industry to the material circumstances of humanity. Both invoke comparative standards of wealth and welfare. In short, although it is expressed by a different vocabulary 'civilization' still operates as a standard of international conduct and there really is no avoiding it if states exist for the good of people and not the reverse.

Modern international human rights law is an important acknowledgement that sovereign states cannot automatically be considered civilized. Otherwise there would be no need for such law. 'Today, for the first time in history, how a sovereign state treats its own citizens is no longer a matter for its own exclusive determination, but a matter of *legitimate* concern for all other states, and for their inhabitants.'[16] This postwar development reiterates a central argument of the classical natural lawyers which was lost sight of with the advent of positive international law, namely that human beings are the ultimate members of the society of states. Some lawyers argue that important human rights injunctions, such as the prohibition of genocide, slavery and the slave trade, now have the character of *jus cogens*: that is, overriding principles which cannot be set aside by the independent actions of sovereign states but only by 'the formation of a subsequent customary rule of contrary effect'.[17]

The Kantian image of a cosmopolitan world society consisting of individuals with natural rights immune to political intervention has made considerable headway in recent decades. An elaborate body of international law pertaining to human rights has been developed by the UN, including a Universal Declaration of Human Rights (1948) and an International Covenant on Civil and Political Rights (opened for signatures in 1966 and entered into force ten years later). There have also been special conventions against particular humanitarian offences, such as slavery, genocide, racial discrimination, and torture. In addition, regional human rights instruments have been established in Western Europe, the Americas, and Africa. The most significant is the European Convention on Human Rights which provides for a Commission and a Court each independent of signatory states and authorized to receive complaints and adjudicate cases brought not only by states but individuals also. According to Paul Sieghart, 'this amounts to a substantial retreat from the previously sacred principle of national sovereignty'.[18]

Although the effectiveness of most international human rights law is debatable and enforcement difficult, it nevertheless provides a moral and legal justification for practical humanitarian actions aimed at reducing human rights violations by sovereign states. Even if the common law of mankind cannot be enforced without the cooperation of the states involved in human rights violations, which is obviously difficult to secure, it nevertheless constitutes not merely a moral but a legal standard for attempting to bring them to some accountability. It therefore has utility. When Amnesty International was founded in 1961 there was no single universal treaty establishing the right to fair trials or prohibiting torture as an infringement on the right to life. By 1985 more than eighty countries had ratified the International Covenant on Civil and Political Rights and more than forty had signed a UN convention on torture which went into effect in 1987. Numerous countries to date have elected to remain outside these conventions, however.

A revolution of human rights is also evident in the proliferation of humanitarian organizations since the end of the war and particularly in the past quarter century. The humanitarian movement in the West is, of course, far older with historical roots reaching back to the successful campaign of William Wilberforce which secured abolition of the slave trade by the British parliament in 1807. Today there are more than a thousand private human rights groups in the world, most but by no means all of them based in Western democracies. This is in addition to public humanitarian organizations, whether national, regional, or universal. The interest in international human rights is also evident in rapidly expanding and already extensive literatures on the subject, including not only articles and books but also journals and other periodicals, both popular and academic.[19] Humanitarian awareness is propelled by the mass media and especially television which enables offences against basic human rights committed in one place to be graphically known immediately in other places, particularly the West where most television news images are broadcast. Many more people than ever before apprehend Immanual Kant's concept of a public law of mankind in which 'a violation of rights in one part of the world is felt everywhere'.[20] Undoubtedly the uncivil image of the Third World is a reflection at least in part of heightened humanitarian awareness and legally more explicit international standards of human rights.

The incidence of human rights violations has increased in rough proportion to the expansion of international society. It is not difficult to see why. There are more than three times as many sovereigns today than in 1945. Variation in government conduct has also increased because of decolonization. Before that time most governments of the non-Western world were under the authority of a few Western constitutional democracies. Independence freed colonies not only from imperial direction but also from metropolitan protection under the rule of law. Decolonization multiplied the number of independent governments with responsibility to safeguard civil standards but also with power to violate them. These governments had the sovereign right to abandon the rule of law or do almost anything else in their jurisdictions. Since most came under the control of people who were preoccupied with power and lacked attachment to constitutionalism (and in many cases equated it with colonialism), their decisions were often at odds with civil liberties.

International humanitarianism is a response to developments such as these. But it cannot really make up for shortages of civility or vulnerability of the rule of law in states which are sovereign. Humanitarian organizations point out that human rights problems are frequently institutional as well as behavioural. They can only be addressed by developing a sovereign government's organized capacity and resolve to protect human rights. This is Collingwood's point about the crucial importance of self-discipline and self-restraint. According to Amnesty International, this requires 'a comprehensive programme' including independent institutions and procedures for controlling police, military personnel, prison officials, and other agents of the state. 'But who is to guard the guards themselves?'[21] Who will institute and defend such procedures? Amnesty replies that 'citizens themselves must be made aware of their rights and know how to complain when these are infringed'.[22] But if they live in authoritarian states, standing up for one's rights can be a risky business. Amnesty urges that international aid be allocated to promote such programmes. But why should such aid be accepted and if accepted be properly used? Quiet and persistent human rights diplomacy and even open condemnation of gross violations is possible. Under current international law, however, the efficacy of international humanitarianism is strictly limited by sovereign rights. It is therefore difficult to see how the vicious circle can be broken if a government is determined to act in contempt of civilized standards. Yet the action clearly stands condemned and this is the crucial even if limited role of such norms.

DECOLONIZATION, AUTHORITARIANISM, AND REFUGEES

As noted, the key to civilization according to Collingwood is the rule of law and the forbearance and self-discipline it entails. Neither colonialism by democratic powers nor international trusteeship under the League and the UN were fundamentally inconsistent with the rule of law. For example, although the Secretary of State for Colonies had no formal constitutional obligations to colonial peoples he was responsible to parliament and ultimately the British electorate. David Goldsworthy's study of this topic clearly indicates that members of parliament enforced this responsibility. 'Their devotion to this duty, as they variously interpreted it, deserves to be remembered with admiration.'[23] Various cause groups such as the Fabian Colonial Bureau also enforced it by voicing concerns on behalf of colonial peoples. And international law, according to C. Wilfred Jenks, 'played for generations a significant part in the liberalization of colonial policy'.[24] Britain and other powers with trust territories were also internationally responsible to the League Mandates Commission and later the UN Trusteeship Council. J. L. Brierly points out that the mandates system was one of the few noteworthy successes of the League.[25] In short, although it was far from perfect and serious abuses did most certainly occur there nevertheless was an institutional framework to discourage offences against the human rights of colonial subjects.

Colonial government by the democratic powers was, of course, not democratic. It was paternalistic. There was a double standard between the metropolis and the various colonies. Racial discrimination was more likely to be condoned either officially or unofficially in the colonies. Force was sanctioned and used beyond the limits which would have been tolerated in Europe. Colonial subjects were deprived of important civil liberties. Most colonies of democratic powers nevertheless were in their own terms peaceful, orderly, and lawful places by and large. Inter-tribal warfare was abolished. Slavery was suppressed if not eliminated. The imperial powers created far larger domains than existed previously for the growth of unhindered migration, travel, trade, and commerce. In West Africa 'colonial administrations in varying degrees established the institutions of lawful government within which commercial agriculture could flourish'.[26] The author of these words is not a diehard colonial apologist but an academic commentator on the political economies of contemporary West Africa most of which he compared unfavourably with their colonial predecessors.

Perhaps it is true, as Sir W. Ivor Jennings once argued, that colonialism and self-government were never completely at odds because colonial authorities had to take some account of the interests and desires of their subjects.[27] Until the period following the second world war, however, most colonial peoples were denied the usual rights of democratic citizenship in all but a few exceptional cases. Decolonization therefore necessitated democratic institution-building prior to the transfer of sovereignty. In numerous dependencies, as indicated in chapter 4, steps were taken not only to replace European administrative personnel with indigenous officials but also to create the institutional framework of a modern constitutional democracy to transform colonial subjects into citizens of new states. In British territories sovereignty was only transferred *after* the constitutional process in each colony had been completed and democratic elections held to determine the new indigenous government.

Attempts to institute constitutionalism and the rule of law proved unsuccessful more often than not, however. After independence, government and opposition could not be constrained by an imperial referee which had departed. Constitutions were often replaced by political frameworks which legalized authoritarianism frequently on the model of the one party state. Judges and courts in many cases were reduced from independent institutions which enforce the rule of law to instruments of political rule. The legal category of political crime was enlarged by many post-colonial governments and the number of people detained for political offences consequently increased. Laws of treason, sedition, subversion, and other political crimes characteristic of absolutism and rarely resorted to any longer in most Western democracies are frequently relied upon by many Third World governments.

Parliamentary bodies were deprived of authority and state power was gathered in the hands of narrow oligarchies, usually under the sway of a strong personal ruler. In many countries elections were manipulated by the party in power, abused by the opposition, avoided or abandoned. Not infrequently they were also violent which discredited them further. Opposition parties were often suppressed in the name of one party states. Their leaders faced the choice of joining the ruling monopoly or going underground or into exile. Prime ministers became presidents who were kings in all but name, with life tenure either in law or in fact. The lives of more than a few proved to be quite short once it became clear that the only way to achieve power was to seize it by force. Politics were often reduced to succession struggles.[28] In many African and Asian countries, repeating the historical experience of Latin America, the military coup replaced democratic elections as the usual method of changing governments.

148

The state apparatus of coercion was usually expanded following independence to deter or defeat domestic opposition. Armed forces often increased many times beyond the small establishments that colonial governments relied on. Zambia's army became ten times as large as Northern Rhodesia's. Nigeria's federal armed forces were built up dramatically with external military aid during the civil war between 1967 and 1970 but were never substantially reduced afterwards. The firepower of most post-independent states is many times greater than that of their colonial predecessors. These are but a few instances of the praetorianization of the Third World state which is a general phenomenon aimed not at defending countries from external attack but at maintaining governments in power.[29]

Governments in multiethnic states were often dominated by particular ethnic groups with the frequent result of inflaming rather than dampening the built-in conflicts of divided societies. Members of some groups often would not extend toleration to members of others. Certain communities were beyond the pale, so to speak, and in relations with them anything could be tolerated – including not only discrimination but also intimidation, violence, and in a few extreme cases massacres. Serious civil discord between governments and their ethnic or regional opponents has consequently become a marked feature of the post-colonial state. In some cases it involved violence on a large scale: Iraq, India, Pakistan, Sri Lanka, the Philippines, Indonesia, Zaire, Burundi, Rwanda, Uganda, Ethiopia, Sudan, Nigeria, Sierra Leone, Angola, Mozambique, and Zimbabwe – among others.[30] Countries such as Chad and Uganda amounted to little more than violent arenas where rival ethnic warlords preyed upon innocent bystanders and laid waste to the countryside in a perennial struggle to seize control of a nominal state represented by the capital city. Many ex-colonial states therefore have serious difficulty in establishing what Collingwood terms the 'essence' of civilization where men outside one's community come to be considered 'as human beings and therefore as much entitled to civility as if they had been members of the community'.[31]

Humanitarian reports in effect have documented the consequences of the failure to institute constitutionalism and the rule of law in many Third World states. The most important point about the weakening or collapse of the rule of law, however, is that it did not undermine or even impinge on the sovereignty of the states involved. Although there were moments of uncertainty at first – as when coups began to occur in Africa in the early 1960s and the question arose as to whether or not military usurpers should be recognized – they were short.[32] The new soldier rulers had to be recognized. Otherwise African international society very likely would have been undermined because the dialogue between states would have been interrupted. The alternative possibility that nonrecognition would have prevented the subsequent epidemic of military coups seems far less likely given the weakness of domestic civil and political institutions. Even extreme instances of incivility involving ethnic massacres did not affect the international legitimacy of the governments involved.[33]

That independence was followed all too often by incivility is indicated by the Third World refugee problem. Western Asia and Sub-Saharan Africa had the largest number of political refugees in the 1980s. There were also substantial numbers in Southeast Asia, Central America and Eastern Europe. People have been uprooted and driven into exile in all ages, of course. Political refugees are an integral component of the states-system produced by its recurrent military, religious, and ideological conflicts. But whereas the old despotisms of Europe when borders were comparatively open usually fostered refugees in thousands and occasionally hundreds of thousands, the new authoritarian states of Asia, Africa, and Latin America where borders are far more closed produce them in millions.[34] 'What is unique at the present time is the massive scale of such movements.'[35] The persecution of minorities by totalitarian governments created unprecedented flows of refugees following the Russian Revolution in the 1920s, during the era of Nazi Germany in the 1930s, and throughout the second world war. In the past two decades these movements have been imitated and even exceeded by Third World governments which in the mid-1980s denied safe domicile to more than 13 million people. This trend is not likely to be reversed very soon because repressive governments or anarchical states, which manufacture refugees in large numbers, give no sign of disappearing.

Connections between negative sovereignty and political refugees are not difficult to discern. Colonialism in Africa and elsewhere manufactured numerous economic migrants but comparatively few political refugees. Decolonization inceased not only the salience of boundaries as lines of political control but also their length due to the fact that many previously were merely intra-imperial borders – such as those separating the constituent parts of French West Africa which are now eleven sovereign countries. Other things remaining equal the more the globe is crosshatched with independent jurisdictions in which human populations are confined the greater the necessity of crossing international borders to secure release from oppression or destitution. Independent rulers depend on borders more than colonial governors and as a rule

150

devote more effort and resources to controlling them. Furthermore, as already noted, ex-colonial frontiers deny self-determination to nationalities in many parts of the Third World where cultural borders and state boundaries are at odds. In many countries minorities are not protected constitutionally or accommodated politically. Some nationalities are politically privileged while others are targets of discrimination, intoleration, and even repression which is perhaps not surprising in countries which resemble empires more than anything else. Sometimes the victimized individual (or group) has little choice but to flee and become a refugee. Political, social, and economic conditions common to many Third World countries reinforce this state of affairs: the nationalizing imperative of autocratic governments, militarization of the state, political rebellion, widespread ethnic or racial prejudice, and sharp inequalities of wealth, among others.

In short, decolonization ironically was not only a liberation movement but also an enclosure movement: it confined populations within ex-colonial frontiers and subjected them to indigenous governments which often were not only untried and inexperienced but also unable or unwilling to operate in accordance with humanitarian standards. Canadian authorities who deal with refugees speak of 'unsafe' countries, and legislation before the Canadian parliament in 1988 contained a requirement that unsuccessful refugee claimants be returned only to 'safe third countries'.[36] The rules of the negative sovereignty game uphold safe and unsafe jurisdictions alike, however.

SELF-DETERMINATION AS SOVEREIGN RIGHTS

The principle of 'self-determination of peoples' is enshrined in Articles 1 and 55 of the UN Charter and reiterated in the 1960 Declaration on the Granting of Independence to Colonial Countries and Peoples and the 1966 Covenant on Civil and Political Rights. It is without doubt one of the most significant political doctrines of the twentieth century. As indicated, Ian Brownlie considers it to be part of the *jus cogens* of the law of nations.[37] These UN pronouncements are silent, however, on what counts as 'peoples'. The principle of self-determination has also consequently proved to be one of the more ambiguous and political of all the rights that have preoccupied the twentieth century. Is it a human right or a sovereign right?

According to Martin Wight, it is a combination of majority rule – which excludes racial minority governments – and territorial vicinage – which prohibits the rule of aliens and specifically Europeans or people of European descent in non-Western international neighbourhoods.[38] Only indigenous peoples can govern ex-colonial states and there can

151

be no European immigrant states in Asia and Africa to repeat the experience of the Americas and Australia. The distinctive illegitimacy of Rhodesia and South Africa is disclosed by this logic. The principle has been aptly named 'racial sovereignty' by Ali Mazrui.[39] Self-determination in the Third World also contains an exogenous element, however. The new state is the successor of an identical pre-existing European colony and is legitimate by right of succession regardless of the different ethnonationalities enclosed by it: 'Thus the principle which broke up the Central Empires of Europe in 1918 is invoked for a contrary effect outside Europe. The principle *cujus regio ejus religio* is restored in secular form. The elite who hold state power decide the political allegiance of all within their frontiers; the recusant individual may (if he is fortunate) be permitted to emigrate.'[40] This new doctrine is most clearly evident in sub-Saharan Africa. For example, all Africans who reside within the ex-colonial frontiers of Kenya are Kenyans. Those who are Somalis by language and religion and by an accident of colonial mapmaking are separated from their brothers in neighbouring Somalia have the choice of emigrating. Ironically, therefore, it is the colonial state under new indigenous management which is the embodiment of self-determination in the Third World. The population within its jurisdiction is formally the 'people' regardless of substantive differences of tradition, language, religion, or opinion.

The principle consequently lost important original features and acquired rather different ones in its migration beyond Europe. It was no longer anything remotely resembling *national* self-determination: it was not the positive right to have a state and government which coincided with historical or cultural nationality or was subject to popular consent – the meaning until this time. It was only the negative right not to be ruled by members of a different race. Moreover, self-determination is not a continuing process but was dealt to populations under colonial rule only once at the time of independence. The deck cannot be reshuffled and dealt out again afterwards without the consent of affected sovereign parties which is very unlikely. There are, of course, compelling practical reasons for this change. A weakening of the concept was necessary to incorporate all ex-colonies in the global community of states. If the older democratic concept had been retained it would have been more difficult to recognize the sovereignty of numerous ex-colonies in the Third World. And if it were a continuing possibility rather than a once and for all event it would threaten the geographical integrity of numerous ex-colonial states.

Racial sovereignty and ex-colonial boundaries in many cases have effectively transformed self-determination into a right of sovereigns.

152

We see the primacy of sovereign rights clearly in the 1963 Charter of the Organization of African Unity.[41] The core principles of the OAU embodied in Article III of the Charter are concerned entirely with the rights of member states, including: (1) equal sovereignty of members; (2) nonintervention in their internal affairs; and (3) mutual respect of the sovereignty and territorial integrity of each member and its inalienable right to independence. Moreover, the fifth principle condemns 'without reservation' political assassination and subversion directed against member states. The usual targets of political assassination, of course, are rulers.

These principles disclose the mutual vulnerability of African statesmen and their efforts to reduce it by means of international law upholding absolute sovereignty within inherited ex-colonial frontiers. In a Resolution passed by the first regular OAU meeting in July 1964 those boundaries were declared to be 'a tangible reality' that all members were pledged to respect.[42] Comments of individual African statesmen reiterate the same point. The President of the Malagasy Republic observed that although the colonialists set boundaries which too often ignored the indigenous nationalities it was neither possible nor desirable to modify them. 'Indeed, should we take race, religion or language as criteria for setting our boundaries, a few States in Africa would be blotted out from the map.' The point was made with greater accuracy by the President of Mali: 'African unity demands . . . complete respect for the legacy that we received from the colonial system . . . If we desire that our nations should be ethnic entities, speaking the same language and having the same psychology, then we shall find no single veritable nation in Africa.'[43] The ex-colonial state was the only practical basis for sovereignty and if that basis were rejected it would result in chaos. This has been the prevailing international reasoning in Africa ever since.

The OAU has been resolved to deny self-determination to traditional African nationalities. Only Morocco, an historic kingdom, and Somalia, a nation-state, consistently express contrary views. The resort to international law by African sovereigns to preserve ex-colonial boundaries has been remarkably successful. Although nearly all territorial populations are deeply divided along ethnic lines, not one state jurisdiction has disintegrated. Rebels can gain *de facto* control of territories, of course, but this is insufficient to capture sovereignty. They must first be recognized, but the OAU, the UN, and the leading world powers will only do this if they have received prior recognition from the sovereign governments involved. Eritrean separatists have never achieved sovereignty despite having controlled substantial parts of

153

northern Ethiopia for more than a quarter century. And they will achieve it only when Addis Ababa consents.

Ex-colonial boundaries remain in effect as international frontiers throughout the Third World with very few exceptions. Even where *de facto* borders have effectively supplanted such boundaries, as in Israel, they are still morally and legally insecure. International legitimacy and law is revealed, perhaps surprisingly, as a normative framework capable of withstanding the pressures of armed force and indigenous culture. This is certainly not owing to any shortage of groups that seek to redefine existing territorial jurisdictions. One need mention only the most obvious: Ibos in Nigeria, the southern Sudanese, Baganda in Uganda, Sikhs in India, Berbers in Algeria, Baluba in Zaire, Tamils in Sri Lanka, Karens in Burma, Kurds in Turkey, Iran and Iraq, Somalis in Kenya, Moslems in Chad, Baluchis in Pakistan, Moslems in the Philippines, and various ethnonational dissidents in Mozambique and Ethiopia.

Self-determination of ex-colonial jurisdictions has therefore provoked serious discord in many Third World states. Arnold Wolfers once characterized the political history of Western constitutional states as that of domestic order and international violence.[44] Civility, in the form of constitutional government, was far more in evidence domestically than internationally. Positive sovereignty was conducive to international disorder frequently marked by warfare. Today in many parts of the Third World the opposite is more often the case: statesmen are civil in their international relations but abusive and coercive in their domestic conduct which not infrequently is provocative of internal disorder and violence. The warfare characteristic of negative sovereignty is internal and not international.

THE AFRICAN CHARTER ON HUMAN AND PEOPLES' RIGHTS

⌈One recent proclamation of a regional human rights regime in the Third World is the Banjul Charter on Human and Peoples' Rights adopted in 1981 by the Assembly of OAU heads of state.[45] However it is actually a thin disguise for asserting the priority of sovereign rights over human rights in Africa.⌋

In the community of states, as noted, human rights law properly so-called is an expression of international constitutionalism: it imposes an external legal restraint on sovereign governments in relation to the population in their jurisdiction. If it is effective it ties the hands of governments which is undoubtedly why it is resisted. International constitutionalism is clearly evident in the European Convention for the

Protection of Human Rights and Fundamental Freedoms which is a legally binding instrument that provides comprehensive procedural safeguards to protect human rights. To be sure, it also permits derogation from these procedures in exceptional circumstances. For example, Article 15 provides that 'in time of war or other public emergency threatening the life of the nation any High Contracting Party may take measures derogating from its obligations'. These measures must be confined to those strictly necessary to deal with the crisis, however. Derogation clauses therefore define the precise grounds of exceptional state authority when human rights protections can be suspended temporarily for the sake of the greater good of all. However, they do not alter or even weaken the human rights provisions otherwise specified in the conventions.

The African Charter, by contrast, is not legally binding. There are not the same comprehensive procedural restraints on sovereigns in respect of basic human rights such as one finds in the European Convention. In the original draft, state parties were under an obligation to 'guarantee' the rights specified and 'ensure' respect for them. Evidently, in order to gain acceptance from African governments both of these vital words were eliminated from the final version.[46] The unrestraining character of the African Charter is strikingly evident in the absence of derogation clauses and the reliance, instead, on numerous clawback clauses which cripple many of the basic human rights enumerated. These entitle states to limit the specified rights by subjecting them to domestic law. For example, Article 9 (2) declares that 'every individual shall have the right to express and disseminate his opinions within the law'. Article 10 (1) provides every individual with 'the right to free association provided that he abides by the law'. Article 11 acknowledges 'the right to assemble freely' subject to 'necessary restrictions provided for by law, in particular those enacted in the interest of national security'. Article 12 recognizes mobility rights within countries, provided an individual 'abides by the law', and the right to leave and enter a country, subject to specified restrictions 'provided for by law'. Clawback clauses apply even to the fundamental right to liberty and security of person (Article 6).

Unlike derogation clauses, which do not limit specific enumerated rights, clawback clauses make them subject to the laws of the signatory sovereigns. If those laws uphold non-constitutional governments, which is usually the case in Africa, the clawback clauses nullify the human rights specified. Hence, they defeat the point of international constitutionalism and liberate African signatories from the most important restraints specified by the Charter. In other words, domestic

155

law takes precedence over the Charter and, since in Africa domestic law usually is authoritarian law, this means that the Charter actually acknowledges the priority of authoritarianism.

Furthermore, the Preamble of the African Charter makes reference to 'peoples' rights' which 'should necessarily guarantee human rights'. The vocabulary and grammar of the text indicate that 'peoples' are the populations of states (or colonies) considered as a collectivity whose rights are exercised by governments. For example, Article 19 specifies that 'all peoples' shall enjoy equal respect and equal rights and that 'nothing shall justify the domination of a people by another'. Article 20 expands on this by stating that 'all peoples shall have the right to existence' and the 'right to self-determination' and 'colonized or oppressed peoples' therefore have 'the right to free themselves'. Furthermore, peoples have the right to international assistance by other states in 'their liberation struggle against foreign domination'. Moreover, Article 21 declares that 'all peoples shall freely dispose of their wealth and natural resources'. At this point sovereign rights enter explicitly since 'states parties . . . exercise the right to free disposal of their wealth and natural resources' and 'enable their peoples to fully benefit from the advantages derived from their natural resources'. Likewise, Article 22 acknowledges that 'all peoples have the right to . . . development' and 'states . . . ensure the exercise of the right to development'. It is evident that 'peoples' rights' are, not only in effect but also intent, the rights of sovereign African governments.

Many of the 'peoples' rights' specified are identical to central principles of the OAU Charter which uphold the autonomy and jurisdiction of African sovereigns. That 'peoples' are synonymous with 'sovereigns' is particularly evident in Article 23 which declares as 'peoples' rights' the entitlements that sovereigns enjoy under the Charter of the OAU.[47] For instance, section (1) affords 'peoples' 'the right to national and international peace' governed by the UN and the OAU Charters. Section (2) provides that 'any individual enjoying the right of asylum under Article 12 of the present Charter shall not engage in subversive activities against his country of origin'. Section (2) also stipulates that 'their territories shall not be used as bases for subversive or terrorist activities against the people of any other State party to the present Charter'. This is virtually identical to language in Article 3 of the OAU Charter which is preoccupied with upholding the negative sovereignty of members.

It is clear that the term 'peoples' is a codeword for sovereigns. There are of course no ethnonational peoples, nor any other peoples, which are included, either directly or by implication, in the concept of 'peoples' rights' in the Banjul Charter. This language reflects the real concerns of African statesmen which are the protection of their jurisdictions not their populations. The new sovereignty game of post-colonial Africa, like the old sovereignty game of dynastic Europe, is a right of rulers rather than peoples. And it is generally respected by the community of states regardless of domestic human rights violations. In proclaiming 'peoples' rights' the African Charter has actually degraded human rights.

Sovereign rights are also unambiguously evident in the explicit duties of the individual to the state in the Charter. Political obligation, reminiscent of Hobbes and the age of absolutism, is definitely prior to civil or political rights. For example, Article 27 declares that 'every individual shall have duties towards ... the State ... and the international community'. Article 29 specifies the political duties of 'the individual': 'to serve his national community', 'not to compromise the security of the State whose national or resident he is', 'to preserve and strengthen the national independence and territorial integrity of his country', and 'to contribute' to 'African unity'. These duties, which also reflect basic OAU rules, are all owed to sovereign governments and disclose their preoccupation with security and unity. This facet of African international law mirrors and reinforces domestic laws of treason and sedition characteristic of authoritarian legal systems. In this regard the African Charter differs fundamentally from the European and American human rights covenants in which the notion of 'duty' refers exclusively to the State's obligation to the citizen including citizens of other states who are within its jurisdiction.

Finally, the supremacy of sovereign rights in the Banjul Charter is indicated by the subservient role given to the African Commission established ostensibly to promote human rights protection in Africa. (No provision is made in the African Charter for a human rights tribunal.) There is little resemblance to the European Commission which can not only investigate human rights complaints but also independently refer them to the European Court of Human Rights which is capable of ruling against state parties. According to Paul Sieghart, 'many individuals have found redress or compensation for their grievances, and many of the state parties have had to change their national laws, or their administrative practices, in order to comply with the [European] Convention'.[48] By contrast, communications made to the African Commission are considered only if they 'are compatible with the Charter of the OAU or with the present Charter' (Article 56). Moreover, any recommendations made by the Commission must have the prior approval of the OAU heads of state before they can be made public. The Commission is clearly the servant of the OAU with no authority of its own. There is virtually no possibility that it can serve as an independent protector of human rights.

In short, not only does the African Charter emasculate international human rights but it goes on to enshrine a category of 'peoples' rights' which are considered to be prior to human rights and which stand for nothing other than sovereign rights. Instead of promoting international constitutionalism by imposing civil restraints on African governments, the Charter by means of clawback clauses and individual duties to the state liberates sovereigns from the human rights it enumerates. The African commission ostensibly set up to police these rights is in fact the creature and servant of African governments. In other words, the African Charter is a reaffirmation of the OAU and its principles of negative sovereignty.

In a recent essay on the rule of law in postwar international relations Peter Calvocoressi considers the acceptance by European governments of decisions by the European Court of Human Rights as an historically significant 'curtailment of sovereignty in favour of the individual'. Any refusal 'would be cause for scandal not only in the Community at large but also in the country immediately concerned'.[49] In an argument reminiscent of Burke, he suggests that this accommodation of international constitutionalism is made possible by persisting family resemblances among West European states in terms of political ideas, institutional structures, historical experiences, jurisdictional theories and legal systems, education, and even language. Most of these states have enjoyed constitutionalism and the rule of law without interruption for a generation and many for a century or more. I believe the European human rights achievement has been possible because democracy is now entrenched in almost every signatory state. If this is valid it is a confirmation of Kant's belief discussed in chapter 7 that international humanitarianism is possible only in a league of constitutional – what he calls republican – states.[50]

Unfortunately, international constitutionalism is not urgent among such states which have civil and political liberties built into them and are statistically the least offensive to human rights. Where it is urgent, as in Africa and some other parts of the Third World, it is far less likely to be realized because domestic constitutionalism is comparatively weak. Pervasive authoritarianism – what Kant called despotism and saw as the enemy of the rule of law – driven by the insecurity of rulers obstructs it. Failure to subscribe to international human rights is no cause for scandal in Africa. Even the establishment of the African Charter which emasculates them has provoked no controversy. The weakness of the African human rights regime confirms an inference from Kant's belief, namely that international humanitarianism is likely to be obstructed by a league of authoritarian rulers who are preoccupied with their own security. This is the message of an African student of human rights: 'Few of these governments have given priority to any national principle other than their own survival. A considerable number of them have subordinated civil and political rights . . . Laws have been implemented in a discriminatory manner to reward citizens who support the rulers and to penalise those who do not.'[51]

INTERNATIONAL CIVILITY AND DOMESTIC INCIVILITY

Perhaps the threads of these remarks can be drawn together. It is evident that one cannot change significantly the rules of international society and expand and diversify its membership without affecting, directly or indirectly, not only that society but also the people who live within its member states. Decolonization clearly was an extension of self-determination and sovereign rights to numerous governments which previously had not been independent. But it was not always an extension of human rights to the populations under their jurisdiction. Only if those governments were prepared to protect the civil and political liberties of their subjects could it also be the latter. Some were prepared but many were not.

Sovereignty gave ex-colonial peoples a legitimate voice in world affairs and membership in international organizations, many designed expressly for underdeveloped countries. However, it could not give them domestic political and civil rights because these are not in the gift of international society. Departing colonial powers could not provide them not because they did not want to or did not try but because they ultimately were not theirs to give. International agencies have subsequently been unable to safeguard human rights for the same reason. They cannot arbitrarily intervene to protect citizens from their governments or from any other source of threat originating within sovereign states. Civil liberties can only be derived from effective state institutions such as free and fair elections, a constitutionally loyal military, independent courts, disciplined and uncorruptible police, and so forth. The effectiveness of such institutions depends more than anything else on the conduct of government and opposition and ultimately the character and virtue of leading political actors who are in the best position to support or undermine constitutionalism and the rule of law. Unfortunately, in circumstances of mass poverty, ethnic discord, and intense political struggle, common to many Third World states, government and opposition frequently are more inclined to pursue power at all costs than observe constitutional rules. Authoritarianism is likely to prevail whoever wins. And international society will respect the principle of nonintervention and support the winner whoever that may be.

In a global club of states whose members are divided into jurisdictions of widely varying cultural characteristics it is difficult to engage in humanitarian diplomacy even at the best of times. The large number of governments involved in human rights offences of one kind or another which in the late 1980s comprised approximately two-thirds of UN members obstructs international action to reduce them. Why should the United States intervene in Haiti to prevent electoral violence when the problem exists in many other countries as well? If humanitarian intervention was a policy where would it end in an international society containing many human rights offenders? This was the regrettable but realistic response of a US State Department official to a member of Congress who was shocked by the bloody suppression of democratic elections in that country in 1987 and felt something should be done about it. Not only is it more convenient to operate with a general prohibition against intervention but probably impossible to do otherwise without provoking serious international controversy which could threaten stability and adversely affect the foreign policy interests of the interventionists. In such circumstances it is not difficult to understand why sovereign rights have prevailed against human rights to date and why there is little chance this will soon change. International society requires and indeed depends on civility between all sovereign governments but this may have to be purchased at the price of tolerating incivility between some governments and their citizens.

Third World statesmen are fastidious in observing diplomatic codes and generally conducting their international relations in accordance with courtesy, dignity, honour, and other norms of civility. International organizations, public and private, constitute a worldwide network within which these norms are the operative code of conduct. The vast majority of such governments reciprocate politically and those which currently do not are few – Libya, Syria, Iran, and one or two others. This is surprising considering the traditional Western prejudice that non-European rulers could not be trusted to reciprocate and therefore should not qualify for membership in the community of states. They have in fact kept their promises as well as anybody. Decolonization has exploded this myth. Negative sovereignty has underwritten international civilization by Collingwood's definition of admitting strangers – in this case non-European governments – into the community of states. All countries are of course obliged to operate with civility internationally and it is also usually in their interests to do so. The same cannot be said of their domestic conduct. What seems noteworthy today is not merely the large number of places where the state is a threat to its own people or the fact that international society can do very little about it but the reality that certain recently adopted international norms actually contribute to this unfortunate state of affairs.

The standard of nondiscrimination is one such norm. Nowadays sovereign rights are reinforced by this standard which unintentionally acts as a bar to international criticism of certain abusive governments. The white critic of human rights violations by non-white regimes risks being accused of racism – which is about the most damning public accusation that can be suffered in the late twentieth century. Western politicians, diplomats, technical experts, academics, and others involved in international relations with non-Western states scrupulously avoid making any comments that might run the risk of inviting such a rebuke. The result has unfortunately been a very effective taboo on such criticism. During the terminal colonial period, as indicated, European powers with overseas dependencies were subjected to strenuous and articulate condemnation by whites and non-whites alike which made it more difficult for them to neglect the civil and even eventually the political liberties of their colonial subjects. By invoking self-censorship, however, the taboo effectively prevents condemnation of postcolonial governments equivalent to what was directed at their European predecessors and still is directed at the human rights abuses of South Africa. The society of states is thereby deprived of an important tool which otherwise might influence some governments to refrain from violating or neglecting the human rights of their own people. It is surely ironic that a new standard of nondiscrimination intended to repudiate racial prejudice has actually become a shield for certain abusive or negligent governments.

There is consequently a curious form of discrimination in international relations today in which the conduct of sovereign governments is subjected to different standards determined by race. Generally white governments are subjected to higher standards and expectations of domestic conduct. This is evident from the far more strenuous criticism applied to the government of South Africa as compared, say, to that of Sri Lanka despite the fact that human rights violations involving government or its agents are probably no greater in the former country and might be less. The beneficiaries of the

161

anti-racist taboo are not only decent governments but also those which engage in discriminatory, intolerant, and even inhumane practices. The losers are citizens of the latter. The double standard therefore punishes the very people that the international abolition of racial discrimination was intended to benefit. There is little to indicate that this twisted system of international nondiscrimination will soon end.

In a famous essay on non-intervention J. S. Mill argues that self-determination is the right of people 'to become free by their own efforts' and nonintervention is the principle guaranteeing they will not be prevented by foreign powers from attempting it.[52] However, it is not necessarily the case today that people everywhere are left to secure freedom on their own and that they have an international right not to be prevented by foreign powers from attempting it. They do have such a right under international law which is widely although not universally observed today. But prevention by foreign intervention is not usually the problem. Even where nonintervention is observed – which is most places – freedom is still very unlikely to be realized. This is because international relations have changed very significantly since Mill's time. Because they are already sovereign the longing for independence cannot serve as an incentive for incumbent rulers to mobilize and organize their populations to strive for freedom. On the contrary, sovereignty gives incumbent elites a strong incentive to maintain their privileges by preserving the *status quo*. It also gives rival elites an incentive to attempt to capture these privileges for themselves. This sets in motion the authoritarian struggle for power which is usually fatal to civil liberties. Furthermore, because most Third World countries are far more like internal empires than nation-states they cannot desire and strive for individual and national freedom in the same way as the subject nationalities of Central Europe which Mill had in mind. They are like the empires those nationalities were striving against. The authentic nationalities of the Third World which do possess such longings are effectively barred from acquiring statehood by international society. This barrier is higher than that which confronted the Balkan peoples in Mill's time because it is based ostensibly on 'self-determination' rather than 'imperialism' and is therefore upheld by current norms of international democracy.

To sum up. There is evidence of unprecedented civilization at the international level today. Third World statesmen are honourable members of international society who respect international law and morality as well as any others. Paradoxically, however, international civilization not only veils significant domestic incivility but actually contributes to it, albeit unintentionally. Under current norms of the negative sovereignty game the balance of advantage within states lies decidedly with sovereign governments and against their citizens. Perhaps this has always been the case but today it is reinforced by an elaborate international superstructure built and maintained very largely with the preservation of existing Third World jurisdictions in mind. The unintended consequence all too frequently is to uphold authoritarian violators of human rights. This is a curious reversal of civilization in the classical positive sovereignty regime.

7 QUASI-STATES AND INTERNATIONAL THEORY

CLASSICAL PARADIGMS OF INTERNATIONAL THOUGHT

A world containing both states and quasi-states is different from one containing only states, or states and formal dependencies, and if our theories are to be relevant they must be able to account for the difference. Can our classical theories of international relations make sense of the practices and institutions of the negative sovereignty game? Are their assumptions concerning the nature of states valid in the case of quasi-states? Or are amendments to them and possibly even new theories called for? Before these questions can be addressed it is necessary to be clear what is meant by 'international theory'. Martin Wight identifies three classical paradigms which have existed in different versions almost as long as sovereign states: 'realism', 'rationalism', and 'revolutionism'.[1] At the risk of oversimplification, these terms denote the contrasting ideas of national self-interest and prudent statecraft (Machiavellism), international law and civility (Grotianism), and global political community (Kantianism). They are categorically different modes of thought with their own logic and idiom.

Classical international theory, according to Wight, is preeminently a theory of survival. Being sovereign, states exist in a condition of anarchy and must in the last analysis depend on themselves to survive. Realism conceives of international relations as shaped predominantly if not exclusively by *raison d'état*: political right is the good of the state and sovereignty is the final word in such matters. Of course, it may sometimes be prudent to conduct foreign policy according to international ethics but they are not to be confused and the latter is merely a disguise. Since states are at liberty but exist in close quarters they cannot avoid coming into contact and are consequently bound together by fate although not by society. Machiavellism gives no credence to the idea of international morality and law. The international system is an arena where statesmen pursue their interests and period-

164

ically get into conflicts which may threaten the survival of some. The fundamental international relations problem is therefore preventing such conflicts from getting out of hand. International practices which address this problem include prudential diplomacy, national defence, military alliances, the balance of power, and other instrumental measures and calculations which disclose states as rival 'power-apparatuses' with an overriding interest in survival. The realist image consequently is that of sovereign states as free, competitive, and some-times combative egoists: international individualism.

A classical realist is also one who believes that the idea of national interest is a fixed datum of international relations which is affected neither by time nor by place. Perhaps this is why Machiavelli continues to be read today almost half a millennium after he wrote *The Prince*. This feature of realist theory also lends it 'scientific' status. However, it is not a scientific theory at all because its object is not a naturally occurring phenomenon but thinking, willing and acting human agents who have a habit of repeating themselves but are not slaves to forces beyond their control. They make mistakes. They change their minds. They lose their nerve. And they also sometimes learn from experience. International relations like all human relations are historical and not natural. Hans Morgenthau emphasizes this point: 'No formula will give the statesman certainty, no calculation eliminate the risk, no accumulation of facts open the future . . . his actual condition is more akin to the gambler's than to the scientist's.[2] In international relations, according to classical realism, there is no such thing as guaranteed security. Life is contingent. Survival is problematical. Statecraft is a world of uncertainty like a game of poker except it is governed by instrumental rules only.

Rationalism, by contrast, is a conception of international relations as a society shaped by a conversation between states and the rule of law. The root of the society of states is the sociability of man. The fact that international relations are anarchical does not rule out obligations between states which are bound together not only by fate or provi-dence but also by noninstrumental rules and practices such as equal sovereignty, mutual recognition, and reciprocity which they observe by and large – even during war which is a rule-based activity governed by the laws of war. The leading idea here is constitutionalism: observ-ing rules which apply equally to oneself as to others. Sovereign states are right-and-duty-bearing units and not merely instrumental agen-cies, other-regarding international citizens and not only self-regarding individualists. The international system is therefore a civil society of member states who have legitimate interests which may conflict but

165

who are also subject to a common body of international law which seeks to regulate such conflicts. International theory is still a theory of survival but the means of survival are social as well as individual.

Rationalism is a notion of states as freely consenting adults who form international society by making treaties, observing common customs and usages, attending conferences, founding organizations and engaging in other bilateral or multilateral activities which aim at moderating their relations and providing goods in common. Indeed, sovereign states not only contract international society but are inseparable from it. Since such ongoing activities change over time, rationalism is more explicitly historical and developmental than realism. Our own century has witnessed three reorientations of international society: the League of Nations, the United Nations, and the emergence of the Third World. A fourth is in the offing if Gorbachev is successful in reintegrating Russia into the comity of nations. Nevertheless, some international rules and institutions which are fundamental to any society of sovereign states – such as nonintervention – cannot be changed without destroying that society or rather transforming it into something else. Rationalism consequently is a theory open to some institutional reforms but also wedded in the final analysis to the practices of constitutionally independent states: international anarchy.

'Revolutionism' is the third paradigm of international theory identified by Wight and reflected in the Protestant Reformation, the French Revolution, the Communist Revolution, and by extension to the present day, the Islamic Revolution, the Green Revolution, and so forth. Revolutionists reject the existing sovereignty system in the conviction that it is an obstacle to the ultimate values of humankind. For Immanuel Kant sovereignty is a barrier in the path of enlightenment. The predominant revolutionist image is that of a community of mankind or *universitas*. Men always take precedence over institutions and consequently the sovereign state must be subject to a higher authority or *civitas maxima* of some kind.[3] A different revolutionist image associated with Marx and with some branches of political economy today is that of a globe divided into socioeconomic classes which are more fundamental than divisions between states: a wealthy and industrial centre and an impoverished and for the most part agrarian periphery with highly unequal and indeed imperial relations existing between the two.[4] This model is 'revolutionary' not only because sovereign states are less significant than classes and indeed are in certain respects the creatures and instruments of classes but also because the sought after future usually is a world free of class divisions and therefore free of the capitalist states which help to perpetuate them.

166

The remainder of this chapter is devoted to considering how far these classical theories can elucidate the relations and conditions of quasi-states. If the theory of an international system containing only states or states and colonies is a theory of survival, what is the theory of a system which contains many quasi-states and virtually no colonies? Is it still a theory of survival? Is it a theory of progress? Or is it something else? How do these notions of international theory square with the negative sovereignty game? I do not believe the institution of quasi-states 'refutes' any of these theories. It turns some on their head, however.

QUASI-STATES AND THE THEORY OF SURVIVAL

In conceiving of 'realism' Wight had theorists such as Machiavelli and Hobbes in mind so it may be appropriate to begin with them. Machiavelli is not the best example of a 'realist' because his thought only prefigures the modern theory of the sovereign state that emerges later in Bodin and Hobbes. There is no institutional theory of the state in *The Prince* but only an instrumental theory of personal rule. Even Machiavelli's analysis of the 'constitutional principality' is written from the singular viewpoint of becoming and remaining the ruler.[5] The principality is indistinguishable from the interest of the prince: a narrower conception than classical reason of state which allows for a public interest above and beyond that of the ruler. One cannot draw such a distinction in Machiavelli: the entire Machiavellian tool-kit of instrumental wisdom is calculated to serve the exclusive purpose of the will to rule. Machiavelli's theory consequently is more about personal political survival than survival of the state.

His emphasis on personal rule nevertheless is a particularly useful starting point for theorizing quasi-states. The domestic political life of many such states is evocative of *The Prince*: a place of insecurity but also opportunity where ambitious political actors struggle and conspire to control the government and the one with the strength of a lion and the wit of a fox usually prevails in the end.[6] Up to a point quasi-states are reversions to the early sixteenth century. But only up to a point, however, and that point is the late-twentieth-century society of states which underwrites their survival. The Third World prince must worry about losing his head but he need not be concerned about losing his principality. There is no King of France to threaten his sovereignty: his seat in the General Assembly is guaranteed. Although he must often be a lion and a fox domestically, he has an external insurance policy which permits him to be a statesman internationally. Quasi-states therefore introduce constitutional assumptions about international relations that are fundamentally at odds with the Machiavellian law of the jungle.

Hobbes' realism, unlike Machiavelli's, is founded solidly on a conception of sovereign statehood. In chapter 13 of *Leviathan* Hobbes calls attention to state frontiers bristling with guns and fortifications as evidence not only of an international state of nature but also of sovereign states. Sovereigns externally are in the same condition as men in the state of nature: naturally free and not merely independent. National defence is Leviathan carrying out according to the sovereign's judgement and commands (chapter 18, 6) that part of the social contract which relates to the external world: protecting the subject from foreign threat. This is the *office* of the sovereign. If he does not perform and the enemy invades, the covenant is dissolved and domestic civil society reverts to the state of nature which for Hobbes is the war of all. Sovereignty is consequently based on the sovereign's performance of his duty under the covenant: positive sovereignty. Although Hobbes is preoccupied with the problem of security and survival, he is concerned with the security and survival of subjects as well as rulers. Hobbes consequently goes far beyond instrumental Machiavellian statecraft and conceives of the sovereign state as an organized protectorate of its subjects. His political theory is a constitutional theory of the sovereign state and his international realism is a doctrine of reason of state and not merely of the prince.

Quasi-states possess arms but they usually point inward at subjects rather than outward at foreign powers which indicates that either no significant external threat exists or an internal threat is greater. Looking outward there can be no balance of power or international equilibrium based on the credibility of sovereigns. Quasi-states by definition are deficient and defective as apparatuses of power. They are not positively sovereign or naturally free. Instead, they are constitutionally independent which is a formal and not a substantive condition. Looking inward, there can hardly be a social contract since the ruler is threatening (at least some of) his subjects and evidently they him. This is an instance not of 'covenants, without the sword' being 'but words'[7] but of swords without a covenant signifying nothing but force and terror. The quasi-state is an uncivil more than a civil place: it does not yet possess the rule of law based on the social contract. The populations of quasi-states have not yet instituted a covenant. If no covenant exists, there can be neither subject nor sovereign nor commonwealth: no empirical state. But unlike Hobbes' realist scenario, the quasi-state cannot logically collapse into a state of nature because its sovereignty is derived not internally from empirical statehood but externally from the states-system whose members have evidently decided and are resolved that these jurisdiction shall not disappear. The quasi-state is upheld by an external covenant among sovereign states. This is not only ironical but also paradoxical in Hobbes' terms and inconsistent with his realist logic. Quasi-states turn Hobbes inside out: the state of nature is domestic, and civil society is international.

I hope it is clear from this brief summary that when it comes to quasi-states Machiavelli and Hobbes can be misleading. But what about classical realism as we understand it today? One might argue that even though quasi-states are organizationally impaired it does not contradict realist assumptions because their existence merely reflects indifference to them on the part of the real states of the world. The unconcern of the major powers enabled Third World states to become independent and they continue to exist for the same reason despite their disabilities and infirmities. 'Indifference' belongs to the vocabulary of power and therefore realism. Juridical statehood is only a façade: quasi-states are tolerated by real powers only because nothing vital is at stake. Where something is vital their ostensible independence is interfered with: as in Nicaragua, Grenada and Panama by the United States, Afghanistan by the Soviet Union, Lebanon by Israel and Syria, Angola and Mozambique by South Africa, Cambodia by Vietnam. Quasi-states therefore exist and survive by virtue of the East–West balance of power which has endured throughout the entire period of Third World decolonization and independence. This global contest in which the superpowers are checkmated has created international space to accommodate a nonaligned Third World of marginal states. Only a few strategic ex-colonies mainly in Asian and Middle-Eastern conflict zones have been drawn into alliances with the superpowers. The rest are bystanders.

The Soviet–American conflict undoubtedly created an international circumstance in which it was easier for quasi-states to be born and to survive. But it does not explain why many ex-colonial states which are marginal to power politics are not by any means ignored by the substantial states of the world including the superpowers. The latter can scarcely be interested in their own security so why do they entertain quasi-statesmen and their views? Perhaps it is because they are no less susceptible to international opinion than others: they desire prestige and seek the approbation of the statesmen of the world who give and withhold it. Power can deter rivals but it cannot procure good will. Although quasi-states have nothing substantial to contribute to the developed states, they can and do influence international opinion.

Quasi-statesmen have an articulate political voice which is registered in various international forums. Voice is significant only in a democratic society where opinion as well as power counts for something which is what international society has become since decolonization. Third World states consequently receive widespread and unceasing attention today. Realism underestimates the political significance of marginal states in international relations. It disregards the elaborate democratic ediface of international law, organization, and aid fashioned explicitly for such states. The novelty of this situation is emphasized by J. D. B. Miller: 'The general atmosphere of the international system is now more favourable to small states, and harsher towards the major powers, than at any time in the nineteenth and earlier twentieth centuries. This may seem a doubtful statement in the era of the superpowers, but the evidence suggests that it is true.'[8]

The contemporary realist might reply that political institutions and activities such as these are merely conveniences for the powerful states or at least are not inconvenient. This stems from a view of international law as fundamentally instrumental or economical rather than moral or obligatory: it is accepted and acknowledged only because it enables real states to get on with the business of international relations with greater predictability and confidence and perhaps less cost and effort than would otherwise be possible. Law is preferred to force in international relations because it is more cost effective. Consequently, the accommodation of quasi-states by international institutions which are underwritten by real states is consistent with realism and not in conflict with it. We come back to the realist point that quasi-states exist and are tolerated because they cannot interfere with the interests of real states. The international institutions which sustain them have utility to all states including the most powerful most of the time. In a democratic age nonintervention is less inconvenient than colonialism, giving states a place in the UN is easier than denying it, providing foreign aid costs little in national terms and might promote one's interests with the recipients, writing off the debts of the most impoverished countries is less disruptive than trying to collect them, and generally dealing courteously with marginal states is likely to work better than dictating to them or dismissing them as of no real consequence. I believe there is more than a grain of truth in this argument and to this extent realism provides an apt account of quasi-states.

However, it also misconstrues or overlooks some things. The key phrase 'in a democratic age' is not a statement of power but of legitimacy, of rights. Presumably in a nondemocratic age imperialism and colonialism were more convenient. The fact is that ideas change concerning what is not only instrumental or possible but also acceptable and justifiable. In finding convenience in these ways of operating the powerful states are acknowledging and observing important new normative precepts in their conduct. In short, classical realist theory does not altogether square with quasi-states as indicated, for example, by the following claim of Hans Morgenthau: 'Faced with the necessity to protect the hard core of the national interest, that is, to preserve the identity of the nation, *all governments throughout history* have resorted to certain basic policies, such as competitive armaments, the balance of power, alliances, and subversion, intended to make of the abstract concept of the national interest a viable reality.'[9] This is an apt summary of the traditional sovereignty game but if it were universally true today numerous states would be in grave jeopardy. Yet they are actually quite secure because they are not required to play this game at all. Their survival is guaranteed not by their own efforts or those of their allies but by the new democratic post-colonial international society most of which has arisen since Morgenthau wrote. Quasi-states are evidence not of traditional realism but of a novel kind of international idealism which has flourished in the last third of the twentieth century. And unlike the utopianism associated with the League of Nations this new idealism is confined only to the margins of international society where it can be sustained without presenting the same hazards as the earlier version.

This brings us to the implications of quasi-states for the rationalist conception of international theory. In conceiving rationalism Martin Wight had the classical international lawyers in mind. So perhaps it is appropriate to begin with brief remarks on Grotius.[10] One could consider Grotius a 'realist' insofar as he begins with the assumption of a plurality of sovereign governments that are free agents. However, international law is a response to the necessity of subjecting sovereign power to some workable standards of conduct. Grotius consequently takes issue with classical realists that states are a law unto themselves (Machiavelli) and that sovereignty is therefore absolute (Hobbes). On the contrary, it is limited by natural law – the dictate of right reason or morality to which statesmen are no less bound than others – and positive international law – treaties and customary practices – to which states consent. Sovereign states are therefore free to pursue their national interests but they are still subject to the international rule of law. They have no licence to disregard the legitimate interests of other states. The key to Grotius is the idea that international relations constitute a realm governed by law and morality and are not merely a cockpit of rival interests. Even warfare is bound by the laws of war. For Hobbes

171

sovereignty is free from external normative regulation, but for Grotius as for Locke it is held under law like 'property'.

Grotius expressly denies the Machiavellian doctrine 'that for a king or a state nothing is unjust which is expedient'.[11] International relations are not governed by the law of the jungle. Requirements of civility override considerations of expediency if they come into conflict. It would therefore be a distortion to claim that international relations are determined wholly by self-regarding behaviour of sovereign governments. On the contrary, they involve obligations: legal duties, honour, respect, courtesy, and other elements of civil conduct. The paradigm obligation and indeed the foundation of international law is the rule *pacta sunt servanda*. Hence the natural order of states is reciprocity rather than armed hostility. Grotius therefore acknowledges the reality of states as free agencies of power whose rivalries and conflicts could do enormous damage to persons and property either intentionally or inadvertently if they were slaves to their own self-interests and hubris. He was preoccupied with regulating this most awesome human power by the only rational means he could conceive: law. The fundamental predicament of international relations was not only subjecting such powers to the rule of law, however, but accomplishing it without the means of a superior authority.

How does classical rationalism square with quasi-states? Quasi-statesmen conduct their international relations with as much civility and forbearance as any others: they observe norms of international society, they avoid intervening in the domestic jurisdictions of other statesmen, they do not indulge in warfare. Indeed, they are champions of the law of nations and often seek an expansion and deepening of international obligations. This is entirely consistent with Grotianism but the facts may not be what they seem.

International civility presupposes the freedom to act otherwise. Quasi-states expect and demand forbearance from others because their survival depends fundamentally on nonintervention. However, they may not have to bear the burden of reciprocating because they are often in no position to do anything else. Their good conduct internationally may therefore spring more from necessity than virtue and indicate only the appearance of civility and not the reality. Furthermore, although they respect the rights of other sovereigns they often exercise only limited forbearance and civility in their relations with domestic rivals and subjects. Perhaps they cannot afford to be constitutionalists domestically because they cannot trust their domestic rivals and subjects to reciprocate. They are therefore obliged to be authoritarians. This is the reverse of their international survival which depends not on Machiavellian skills but on the willingness of others who could deprive them of their independence to refrain from doing so by observing the rule of nonintervention. In short, Grotianism makes assumptions about states as positively free yet mutually obligated international agents which cannot without distortion be made about quasi-states.

Rationalists today are called upon to theorize a novel international society with contradictory norms. As indicated in chapter 2, international law traditionally was conceived in procedural terms as a *societas* or civil association. It was 'adverbial' – as Oakeshott might put it – because it sought only to modify the self-chosen actions of statesmen in approximately the same manner as the rules of the road regulate drivers of motor vehicles (although it lacked an overarching office of rule and apparatus of enforcement).[12] It did not determine the destination or the route – legitimate national interests – but only the acceptable ways of proceeding – which were specified in its usages and practices. Public international law has retained this procedural feature in nonintervention and other rules of forbearance. However, it has also acquired purposive characteristics of a *universitas* or instrumental association which seeks to command and coordinate the actions and resources of states in the joint pursuit of common goals. Rationalism in the late twentieth century is therefore different from what it was in earlier times. It is no longer only a theory of international constitutionalism: the notion of states as free agents who are subject to normative restrictions and prohibitions of various sorts which reflect the *negative* character of classical international law. Contemporary international society in addition gives expression to 'rationalism' in Oakeshott's *positive* meaning: states as collaborators in a common engagement, for example, to develop the Third World or reduce environmental pollution or eradicate disease or prevent terrorism or combine in the joint pursuit of various other substantive purposes.[13]

QUASI-STATES AND THE THEORY OF PROGRESS

How well does revolutionism therefore square with the existence of quasi-states and the practices of the negative sovereignty game? Consider Kant's classical version which postulates a community of mankind that transcends the states-system and is prior to it.[14] The freedom of sovereign states presents a grave problem because they are capable of causing great destruction and suffering by their combative rivalries. Without a higher authority to curb them that is more effective than the feeble international rule of law theorized by Grotius the suffering will continue. (Kant is of course referring to civil and not socioeconomic hardship.) True freedom for mankind will be at hand only when the absolute freedom of states – a lawless condition – is transformed into *freedom under external laws*. This can be realized only by states entering a 'great federation' which must be a 'united power' which means that states must sacrifice their sovereignty. This development is the fulfilment of the 'enlightenment': the ascendancy of reason over man's 'baser instincts' which for so long has perpetuated the international state of nature. For Kant the problem of instituting political reason within states is therefore subordinate to that of establishing it between states. Only a league of constitutional states can ensure the civility of its members and bring into the light of day the universal community of humankind.

Although quasi-states generally are good citizens internationally many nevertheless operate contrary to the rule of law domestically. This might be read as a refutation of Kant's thesis concerning the humanizing effects of international constitutionalism. However, this would equate the UN with Kant's 'great federation' which would be erroneous since the UN is a creature of the states-system and no more. It nevertheless is tempting to speculate what might have been if all the victorious great powers in 1945 were constitutional states or if Gorbachev were to end Russian despotism and establish the rule of law in the Soviet Union and the same were to happen in China. Would the Security Council then perform a Kantian role in which member states are obliged to observe the categorical imperative of political reason and right domestically as well as internationally under enforcement by the great constitutional powers? But this is speculation and history has so far taken a different course.

As indicated in previous chapters, the UN accommodated as full and equal members all newly independent states regardless of their domestic conduct or characteristics. Authoritarian states eventually formed a majority of its membership. At the General Assembly in New York, Third World statesmen operated constitutionally: they were defenders of free speech and other rights of statesmen. But at home many if not indeed most were intolerant of the same rights for their own citizens. Today this inconsistency is taken entirely for granted as expected behaviour. Thus, the spread of international democracy has not usually been accompanied by a corresponding progress within newly enfranchised states where in many cases, if not most, mens' 'baser instincts' unfortunately continue to prevail. But Kant's theory cannot be evaluated because the practices it presupposes – unlike those of realism and rationalism – have never really been tried. The closest to it today is international human rights law which although subject like all

international law to the determination of independent states nevertheless discloses an image however shadowy of a community of mankind.
But, as noted in chapter 6, international humanitarianism is most
secure where domestic democracy is strong, and most vulnerable
where it is not.

In international theory today undoubtedly the most self-conscious
example of neo-Kantian revolutionism is the 'world order perspective'
best exemplified by the thought of Richard Falk who perceives intimations of an incipient movement away from the state-centric West-
phalian paradigm which has predominated for the past three and a half
centuries.[15] Although the new paradigm is not yet evident in practice it
is 'prefigured' in transnational problems which are rendering anomalous, obsolete, and even destructive the existing division of the planet
Earth into independent and self-serving territorial states. Global
problems such as the threat of nuclear destruction, poverty and underdevelopment, environmental degradation, the population explosion,
and so forth cannot be resolved by sovereign states and are indeed
exacerbated by their freedom which indicates that the state-centric
paradigm no longer 'works'. Since these problems are essentially
transnational they can only be addressed by international cooperation.
National governments must give up some of their sovereignty to both
higher and lower authorities which are better adapted and located to
deal with them. Falk foresees a new world order involving 'central
guidance' and 'non-territorial actors' in which the statist level of international society will weaken as the global and the local levels
strengthen: 'loyality and legitimacy are shifting away from the state . . .
toward the center of the globe and toward the local realities of community and sentiment'.[16]

The political future therefore envisaged by Falk is a global *universitas*
ironically reminiscent of the medieval world. But since mankind today
is not a positive political entity in itself the *universitas* model necessi-
tates a world body of some kind to give direction and animation to the
sought after global goals of mankind. This obviously would require a
lessening of the independence of sovereign states. On almost any
reading of contemporary world politics it is difficult to regard this kind
of forecast as anything but utopian and naive.[17] Developed states
certainly give little indication that such a prospect is even conceivable
let alone attainable. They would of course recognize the global
problems identified by Falk and possibly even agree with him that their
resolution is highly desirable but they also would almost certainly
insist they could only be addressed within the framework of the
existing states-system and would probably argue that sovereignty and

international cooperation are not incompatible. Falk seems to believe that the constraints of the existing divided world will thwart them and the negative externalities will eventually drive them to collaborate in the world order enterprise he foresees.

Falk makes a particular point of distinguishing the wellbeing of governments from that for peoples or countries. The separation is necessary because a decline of sovereignty need not entail a corresponding loss for peoples who according to Falk's reasoning would stand a chance of enjoying the values and goods already mentioned, particularly social justice and economic development, which the current regime denies to many. The only conceivable losers would be existing sovereigns. But quasi-states are creatures and indeed protectorates of the contemporary states-system and if that system is transcended in the manner prophesied by Falk their ruling elites will suffer a decline in status, privilege, and wealth. Furthermore, if the new world order promotes human rights and subnationalism – as Falk clearly implies – then we can be certain that most Third World statesmen will oppose it. A shortcoming of the world order perspective is its underestimation of the value of sovereignty to Third World governments which is extremely high because it is virtually the only source of their status and privileges. They are jealous of their sovereignty and are the first to complain at even the slightest hint of foreign interference. They are also the last to authorize international human rights covenants which might restrict their independency. In short, quasi-statesmen clearly desire development but it is doubtful they would embrace the sort of revolutionary change prophesied by Falk. What they demand from the international community is more contradictory: both guarantees of independence and rights to socioeconomic development.

This brings us to the neo-Marxist or structuralist variant of revolutionism. At first glance quasi-states appear consistent with many elements of structuralism: the socioeconomic division between the rich capitalist countries of the North and the poor proletarian countries of the South; the penetration of quasi-states by Multinational Corporations (MNCs); the dependency of many Third World states on economic decisions taken beyond their borders and for the most part within major capitalist states; the existence within quasi-states of small privileged elites and large oppressed classes of workers and peasants; the fact that the elites benefit from and indeed owe their existence and wellbeing to the states-system and consequently desire to conserve it rather than overthrow it; the tendency for the existing global capitalist order and its state auxiliaries to be perpetuated if undisturbed and the necessity of revolutionary action to change it. Independence hardly changed the material conditions of the Third World: it was a continuation of imperialism and colonialism under a different name which only revealed greater hypocrisy than before. The term 'quasi-states' therefore merely reiterates what is already well known: that most Third World states are not yet beneficial to the masses of ordinary people who inhabit them and whose living conditions have improved little if at all as a result of independence. After decolonization the levers of power and control remained exactly where they were before: in the hands of the major capitalist powers who were prepared to transfer sovereignty if that was all that was necessary to satisfy Third World elites clamouring for 'independence'. This is the familiar view of dependency theory. Hence, negative sovereignty is only another name for neocolonialism.

On closer analysis, however, quasi-states disclose a vision of international relations which is very far from viewing independence as little more than a veil on continuing dependency. To the contrary, it considers quasi-statesmen to be authentically independent in the classical legal sense of not being subjects of any higher authority. Within their jurisdictions they are at liberty to govern according to their own inclinations and decisions. No other authority can overrule them – as was the case under colonial rule. Hence there is a fundamental difference in presuppositions concerning 'independence': dependency theory sees it as a continuation of external compulsion by the structures of international capitalism and the major capitalist powers; the theory of negative sovereignty, however, understands it as a condition of authentic liberty which although obviously restricted by socio-economic and other circumstances leaves room for responsibility by post-colonial governments.

Independence is not trivial even if it is not harnessed to a capable and efficient state apparatus and ultimately a developed economy. Economic underdevelopment and technological backwardness do not mean that quasi-statesmen have any less right to make decisions than other statesmen. It means that they have far fewer means and resources with which to implement and enforce their decisions and consequently must face harder choices as to what they will concentrate their scarce resources and energies on. If a quasi-statesman is wise he will have an accute perception of what is important and what is not: a Machiavellian sense of priorities and the limits of power. If government capabilities and resources are not to be squandered decisions must be more intelligent. Scarcity makes it more difficult to achieve goals. There is less room for error. But less room is not the same as no

177

room: scarcity is a relative concept. Furthermore, responsibility in the realm of forbearance such as respecting human rights is not altered because of scarcity. At the end of the day independence is not freedom; but it is not slavery either. The term 'neocolonialism' conflates the distinction between the right to decide (authority) and the capacity to act (power) which is crucial in the theory of the state.

The significance of this distinction can be illustrated in connection with relations between MNCs and negatively sovereign statesmen. In the usual neo-Marxist model the Third World statesman is the handmaiden of the MNC which possesses most of the advantages in the relationship: it can threaten to locate elsewhere and its threat is credible; it has economic and technological resources which the country lacks; its investments and enterprise can consequently create employment, tax revenues, and other benefits of economic growth. In short, the quasi-statesman is presented with an offer that is difficult to refuse. Furthermore, if it is accepted the MNC can convert him into a 'comprador' or middleman whose role is essentially that of making the relationship between the MNC and the Third World state a smooth and workable one: the quasi-statesman and his associates can be bribed to serve the MNC rather than their own people.

However, the relationship contains less inequality than this implies. The quasi-statesman may indeed want or even need what the MNC has to offer. But he also possesses something which the MNC must have in order to operate: access to state jurisdictions. The post-colonial MNC confronts a globe more crosshatched by international frontiers and enclosed by local sovereignty than was ever the case during the colonial era when huge territories under the looser economic control of imperial powers were still open. International frontiers have also been expanded since decolonization to give sovereigns jurisdiction over offshore territories and resources. In short, more territory has become more subject to the sovereignty of more statesmen. MNCs must have access to sovereign territory to operate but they cannot gain access without a sovereign's authorization. They consequently must come to grips with the reality of sovereignty and make deals with sovereign governments in order to function. Whether there is a deal and what it might be depends on *both* parties. Perhaps a bargain will be struck and perhaps it will be a very bad one for the country involved. It is nevertheless still a deal. The rulers of quasi-states are of course at liberty to accept bribes or do the bidding of MNCs. But they are under no obligation to do so. They have the right to say no. MNCs realize this. The relationship is therefore less like rape or even seduction and more like legalized prostitution: the partners may be unequal in many substantial ways but any business they transact must involve the consent of both.

The point is therefore the following: the transnational capitalist game cannot override the territorial sovereignty game without the consent of sovereign governments. Structuralism has grave difficulty in theorizing quasi-states because of blindness to the significance of sovereignty and legal institutions generally. It thereby overlooks the reality of independent political choice and consequently some of the most important issues involved in the negative sovereignty regime. The source of this blindspot evidently is its socioeconomic determinism.

QUASI-STATES AND INTERNATIONAL JUSTICE

What therefore are the implications of quasi-states for international relations theory? Is it a theory of survival or a theory of progress or something else? Although realists and rationalists usually do not interrogate the notion of 'survival' but merely accept it as self-evident, it can only mean the long-term continuation of states as sovereign entities in more or less the same geographical location and shape. What if the independence of some states is guaranteed as a matter of right by the community of states? What becomes of the theory of survival if survival is no longer the defining international relations *problematique* it once was or must be defined in a radically different way? The theory of survival presupposes freedom, but quasi-states are not yet free and perhaps many of them never will be free. They enjoy an internationally guaranteed independence nonetheless which does not require positive sovereignty. This is the survival of citizens of an international community. The theory appropriate to it is not that of power politics or of classical international law but of international rights: a political theory.

Is the international theory of quasi-states therefore a theory of progress? Yes and No. Yes, in that such states demand and to some extent are accorded international development entitlements and assistance which is not reciprocated. No, in that they do not expect to surrender any of their independence to receive such assistance and they place a premium value on nonintervention. Quasi-statesmen are jealous of their sovereign rights and resistant to international human rights. They have no desire for an international revolution that would curb their prerogatives of sovereignty. The progress they seek is an international change that will assist them eventually to become developed without any sacrifice of their independence. This clearly is not revolutionism in Kantian or even Falkian terms. These changes are not

179

conceived to transcend the states-system. And although quasi-states-men are often openly critical of international capitalism they have little desire to participate in anti-capitalist activities beyond seeking international socioeconomic fairness through development diplomacy and law. Quasi-statesmen do not desire something radically new. They merely want what others already possess: positive sovereignty. But they want it by international right which is radically new. They consequently have contradictory expectations: the right of independence (reciprocity) but also the right to development (nonreciprocity). In short, they want to have their sovereignty and eat it.

This creates a constitutional dilemma for a society of sovereign states which international theory should try to explain. Since the dilemma involves contrary rules and rights the theory most appropriate to it is some version of rationalism. As indicated, quasi-states invoke two contrary modes of international association: negative rights consistent with the idea of a *societas* but also positive rights indicative of the contrary idea of a *universitas*. When theorists resort to such ideas they usually see international relations changing from the former arrangement to the latter. This is the view of Freidmann.[18] Terry Nardin, on the other hand, more accurately sees these two conflicting modes of international law as disclosing the 'incoherence' of the United Nations Charter. He also regards the demands of 'new states' for substantive international benefits as undermining the procedural or what he terms 'practical' mode of international law without overthrowing it.[19] However, as indicated in previous chapters, quasi-states are not only proponents of collective enterprise to enhance their welfare but are at the same time staunch defenders of nonintervention. They therefore promote these conflicting international norms which really disclose not only an 'incoherence' of international law but a dilemma of international justice.

Traditional international justice is commutative: it is premised on the moral and legal equality of states whatever may be the empirical differences between them and it consequently forbids the more powerful from doing down the less powerful. States have a right to exist and can only justifiably be interfered with if they have previously infringed upon the right of another state or violated the international rule of law in some equally offensive way . Commutative justice presupposes the intrinsic worth of all states, large and small, and therefore affirms international obligations such as the following: territorial jurisdiction shall not be violated, treaties should be kept, wars should only be fought to punish aggressors and restore the peace, innocent third parties should not be harmed in the conduct of war, and so forth.

Quasi-statesmen do not object to traditional commutative justice. On the contrary they invoke equal sovereignty, nonintervention, *pacta sunt servanda* and similar commutative claims of classical international liberalism. However, they do not stop at commutative justice but go on to demand distributive justice as well. They believe that the current distribution of the world's resources and opportunities is profoundly unjust not only because it registers in miserable standards of living for themselves but more importantly because it promises only to perpetuate this sorry state of affairs. They seek actively to correct by international means and endeavours this profound social injustice between the North and the South. And furthermore they do not see any contradiction between their claims to commutative and distributive justice.

There are at least three fundamental problems with the idea of international distributive justice in today's world, however.[20] I can only summarize them. First, there is no global organization that produces goods which could be distributed according to principles of social justice. The UN produces few if any such goods. The world economy is a huge abstraction and very far from a single organization of production and distribution. There are numerous economies in the world including national, transnational, and subnational, and countless producers and consumers. At what level should one expect distributive justice? Distributive justice within states is notoriously difficult but how much more difficult is it between states? And is there any reason to suppose that justice at one level will be compatible with justice at another? There is no conclusive moral reason why the international level should take precedence over the national or cosmopolitan levels or even be entitled to encroach on them. If any level can claim the moral highground it surely is the latter which is the basic morality of Kant's community of mankind. Without an association based on agreed principles and a central organization it is meaningless to talk of global distributive justice. Today distributive justice could only be provided internally – with very great difficulty and inadequacy – by individual states. But distributions of goods which may be just within states have no necessary connection with international distributive justice.

Second, unlike commutative justice which is universal, there are no agreed principles of international distribution. Should it be based on need, merit, effort, contribution, utility, or some other principle? In practice, need and to a lesser extent utility are usually singled out as the appropriate grounds. If merit, effort or contribution were taken into consideration the just distribution might favour the developed parts of the world. Moreover, these concepts are familiar to Western morality but are they known the world over? What additional principles exist in other parts of the world which ought to be taken into account? If distributive justice in Leningrad, Lima, Lagos, or Lahore does not mean the same as in London or Los Angeles what becomes of international distributive justice?

Finally, any system of distributive equity between states almost certainly would not be just for individuals living in them owing to the categorical differences between states and individuals. Persons are natural entities and more or less equal whereas states are artificial entities that are highly unequal in virtually every respect except legal status. Distributive equity between states even if it rested on a per capita basis would still not begin to achieve distributive justice unless a corresponding system of justice operated within states as well as between them that could insure a just domestic distribution of resources and opportunities. States are internally differentiated into rulers and ruled. The key to justice between states is the willingness and ability of sovereign governments to translate international justice into domestic justice. This is asking a great deal from even the best governments. Unfortunately, the governments of most states which would be entitled to international distributive justice on grounds of need are usually very far from the best. Distributive justice between states as seen from the outside might on closer examination be privilege for political elites who are strategically positioned to divert material goods to themselves or their supporters and are all the more likely to do so if they operate authoritarian regimes in poor countries. As J. R. Lucas puts it, 'justice does not require that rich nations provide poor nations with the wherewithal to buy arms or to subsidise national airlines which only a small minority of their peoples could ever afford to use'.[21] This could only be a travesty of justice. There might even be an international obligation not to provide such states with material goods in the reasonable belief that their governments would divert them to sustain their unjust authoritarian rule.

The very limited international redistribution we see today is, I believe, a reflection of such domestic difficulties and uncertainties. It is a genuine international predicament and not merely the absence of goodwill or generosity or decency or humanity or enlightenment. And it is fundamentally institutional. If we want greater equity in the global distribution of wealth and welfare we must accept some limitation of state sovereignty as Kant and Falk argue. We certainly cannot avoid looking inside of states. On the other hand, if we accept a world of states we must also accept the possibilities and limitations of such a world which are those of sovereignty. Justice between independent states can only be commutative: keeping one's agreements. And that is what international justice has been since the beginnings of the states-system: *pacta sunt servanda*. The fact that most quasi-statesmen cannot accept this and continue to seek both forms of justice at the same time does not falsify the argument although it does underline the difficulty of their position.

The international normative dilemma presented by quasi-states does not end with distributive justice, however, but extends to commutative justice which makes the same fundamental assumption about states that it makes about individual humans: their intrinsic value. Both natural rights and civil rights presuppose what Gregory Vlastos terms 'individual human worth'.[22] Kant expressed the same thought by claiming that humans are 'ends in themselves' and can therefore never be treated merely as means: the authoritarian temptation. This foundational idea in the theory of rights is carried over into international theory via the domestic analogy which attributes the moral capabilities of individual persons to sovereign states. The assumption that sovereign states possess intrinsic value is embedded in both realism and rationalism. Defending the national interest makes sense only if that interest entails value. The state being defended must be assumed to be valuable or worthwhile. There is no point in the 'hard shell' of the modern territorial state – to use the image of John Herz – if there is nothing valuable behind it.[23] This proposition is not affected by the particular shape of national values but only by the existence of them. Consequently, it can embrace the liberal-constitutional and socialist-welfare as well as any other form of state – providing it is of authentic worth to the populations involved which is the usual justification of statehood. One can make a similar argument about rationalism. Regulating states by international law to avert or reduce the incidence or extent of damaging collisions between them also makes sense only if those entities are valuable in themselves: collisions would result in harm to persons and property, perhaps bloodshed and destruction on a large scale. International civil society and its law – *societas* – therefore exists primarily to provide for the autonomy of implicitly valuable states and to cushion their relations.

These value assumptions are turned upside down by quasi-states which by definition are not yet valuable places for their populations. Their good life is something which must still be built possibly with international assistance and support. Whether it is built or not is an empirical question that need not concern us. What is at issue are the normative assumptions involved. Insofar as quasi-states claim international assistance on grounds of underdevelopment they must be assumed incapable as yet of providing their populations with the goods associated with developed statehood. Otherwise they could not claim aid on such grounds. Indeed, as Mohammed Bedjaoui points out, constitutional independence can be considered little more than the beginnings of their self-determination which can be fulfilled only by their eventual development: the realization of authentic international freedom or positive sovereignty.[24] And this can only be realized if the rules of international relations are changed to make it possible. The elaborate ediface of international development which caters for quasi-states is therefore indicative of their incompleteness and still limited value to their populations. This limitation is the moral ground of their claims to social justice.

However, the same limitation undermines in the same proportion their moral claims to nonintervention and commutative justice because there is less public value in such states. Intervention might conceivably result in greater dividends than nonintervention for the population at large. Demands for human rights protections in such states cast further serious doubt on their intrinsic worth. In short, the real value of states varies enormously compared to the intrinsic worth of persons which does not vary at all. Consequently, quasi-states raise value questions not only about distributive justice but also commutative justice because intrinsic worth cannot be applied to states as categorically as to humans and the easy transition from one to the other via the domestic analogy is problematical to say the least.

The international theory of J. S. Mill and Michael Walzer on the question of nonintervention is useful for analysing this problem as regards quasi-states.[25] Mill argues that individuals and states should not be interfered with providing they respect the rights of others and the (external) rule of law. Negative liberty and negative sovereignty should be respected even if one has good reason to believe that intervention would prevent self-inflicted harm. This rules out any form of paternalism to promote the welfare of another agent. Although Mill justifies international paternalism (see below) he is sceptical of the ability of civilized states to bestow permanent freedom on any people who are not determined to possess it even by fighting if necessary: the mark of authentic self-determination. Positive sovereignty like positive liberty can only be achieved by oneself.

Mill therefore had a very great reluctance to give any latitude to paternalism. However, children and other persons who patently are not yet prepared for liberty have to be interfered with for their own good. Likewise, although intervention cannot be justified in relations with 'civilized nations' it is justified in regard to 'barbarous nations' since 'it is likely to be for their benefit that they should be conquered and held in subjection by [civilized] foreigners'. The question of intervention in such nations has to be determined according to 'totally different principles'. A 'barbarous nation' is defined by Mill as an illiberal government which inflicts adversity on its subjects and therefore can not legitimately claim any rights of international liberty and reciprocity including nonintervention. On the contrary, nations which have no knowledge of liberty can rightfully be made wards of an existing sovereign. 'Despotism is a legitimate mode of government in dealing with barbarians, provided the end be their improvement, and the means justified by actually effecting that end.'[26] Colonialism in Mill's international theory performs the same role as paternalism in his political theory: a defensible and indeed responsible method of dealing with agents deemed not yet fit for self-determination. Nonintervention is not an obligation, therefore, when it comes to illiberal states and indeed international support for such a government is repugnant to civilized values. 'The only moral laws for the relation between a civilized and a barbarous government, are the universal rules of morality between man and man.' In other words, such a government has no rights as a sovereign and the intervening state has only to respect the human rights of the local population.

Our negative reaction to this paternalistic argument indicates how far international moral practice has changed since Mill's time. International paternalism has fallen into disrepute because adults everywhere today are assumed to be equal politically and therefore equally entitled to self-government regardless of their actual circumstances or capacities. Mill's 'solution' is therefore not available today and most people probably believe this to be a good thing. But the problem of competence and responsibility has not disappeared simply by the reformation of international legitimacy and the ending of colonialism. The international community has merely pursued new ways of dealing with it which are compatible with equal sovereignty. Typical of these are assistance to improve the socioeconomic conditions of countries and exhortations that their sovereign governments protect human rights which the latter are at liberty to accept or not. Hence, contemporary practice has not resolved the problem Mill is wrestling with. It has only reversed in an ironical fashion his observation concerning human rights: today nonintervention protects constitutional and authoritarian governments alike and human rights violations are no justification for interfering with sovereign rights.

Michael Walzer has adapted Mill's argument to contemporary international society. The paternalist downside is abandoned and the liberal upside that foreign powers cannot force peoples to be free is elaborated. Nations can only become free by their own efforts: 'self-determination is the school in which virtue is learned (or not) and liberty is won (or not)'. Independence cannot make people free but it can give them an opportunity to become free which is its fundamental justification: it can establish 'an arena within which freedom can be fought for and (sometimes) won'. Nonintervention is the guarantee of this possibility. Therefore, although negative sovereignty cannot presuppose the same as negative liberty – intrinsic worth – it can nevertheless postulate the possibility of achieving the good life in the future. Exceptional circumstances such as revolution, civil war, massacre, enslavement, or mass expulsion can perhaps justify intervention. 'Ordinary' oppression clearly cannot, however. The main thrust of the argument is to rule out intervention in the vast majority of cases. This is conventional international libertarian doctrine.

The usual criticism of Walzer's thesis is that it restricts unduly the human rights grounds of justifiable foreign intervention and therefore leaves millions at the mercy of governments which usually are not legitimate domestically and often are prepared to go to almost any length to remain in power.[27] The problem with such criticism, however, is its underestimation of the moral standing of states: it does not face up to the authentic international relations dilemma between the legitimate rights of states and those of humans. It sidesteps the problem by disparaging the moral claims of sovereign states which is something Walzer is not prepared to do.

The theory of quasi-states suggests a different line of criticism connected with the contemporary community of states which is far more elaborate than the relatively simple nineteenth-century international regime Mill had in mind and more significant than Walzer's analysis implies. Walzer underestimates the weight and scope of the rights and immunities that sovereign states enjoy today which derive from the constitutional fact that international society is now far more democratic and rights-based than it has ever been. And he overestimates the possibilities of popular self-determination against oppressive regimes. Numerous new states have been enfranchised by the revolution of decolonization. Democratic franchises, once granted, are almost impossible to withdraw or even curtail. International democracy therefore probably is not any more likely to be revoked or even revised than domestic democracy. And although these franchises are justified as belonging to the populations of new states they are in fact held and exercised by rulers. In practice international democratization has validated all governments without any regard to their subjects which usually amounts to the underwriting of authoritarianism within states. Furthermore, international enfranchisement undermines if it does not eliminate altogether the competitive game which in the past gave governments an incentive to improve the domestic conditions of their states in order to elicit taxation, conscription, and other forms of legitimacy and support from their populations. The deck of international relations today consequently is stacked in favour of sovereigns and against citizens more than it was in the past. In short, Walzer's libertarian solution expects too much virtue from populations who are up against not only the local despot but also an international society which accords him far more respect and support than his historical counterpart would have enjoyed. We cannot therefore avoid Mill's argument from paternalism quite as easily as Walzer implies.

Does paternalism have any place in international relations today? If by 'paternalism' is meant relations in which some states assume a positive regard for other states and provide them with assistance then of course paternalism is evident in relations between states today. Indeed there is more of it now than ever before. Much of the international superstructure outlined in this book could be considered an expression of informal paternalism. The relationship of France to the French-speaking states of sub-Saharan Africa has this character: the President of France is the 'father' figure of Francophone African heads of states. The numerous patron-client ties evident between developed and underdeveloped countries is strongly suggestive of the same. However, if the term 'paternalism' is to retain its original meaning – which is the moral and legal responsibility of one agent for another agent on the grounds of the latter's inability to bear that responsibility – then international paternalism is rare today. It has been supplanted by egalitarianism. France is no longer responsible for its former African colonies. Very few states today have responsibility for other states. Colonialism and all other authentic forms of paternalism have been ruled out of international relations. The theory of paternalism therefore does not fit the reality of quasi-states any more than the theory of freedom.

The key to quasi-states is their independence and survival regardless of their comparative lack of power and agency in an international system which also contains many 'real' states. What sort of international relations could exist between real states and quasi-states which makes the survival of the latter conceivable and justifiable? The prevalent justification currently is based on the possibility that such

187

states will eventually develop into livable countries and independence is the opportunity for this to happen. This obviously is neither wholly the international ethics of rationalism nor of revolutionism but something ambiguously in between. Sovereignty can no longer postulate the good life. Instead, it is the basis of a novel claim to overcome the bad life. It is the ethic of progress within the juridical status quo: an anomalous sort of progressive conservatism. This is rationalism turned on its head.

CONCLUSION

THE FUTURE OF QUASI-STATES

Will quasi-states continue to be a major feature of the international landscape in the decades to come as they have been in the past thirty years? Speculation about what might be is a hazardous enterprise and often avoided by scholars who perhaps like myself find it hard enough to grasp what is and what has been. There nevertheless can be value in contemplating the future of quasi-states if only to draw some conclusions from the foregoing analysis. Such an exercise might even be timely at the start of the last decade of the twentieth century when significant and perhaps momentous changes affecting East–West relations are underway.

The prospects for quasi-states hinge generally on two things: whether they develop to the point of no longer depending on the negative sovereignty game, and if they do not whether it will continue to be possible to play that game in the future. The development outlook for quasi-states is of course extremely difficult to establish owing to the particular circumstances of each country which vary enormously. The twentieth century already has witnessed profound international changes and not least the independence of the Third World and so we ought not to rule out the possibility of further change. We should expect some Third World countries to achieve significant developmental breakthroughs as the NICs recently have. Democratization is also a possibility. History is a contingent and not a determined process of change and the future is therefore open and not closed. However, if reports of the World Bank are anything to go by we should also expect economic poverty and technological backwardness to characterise a large number of independent countries and probably the majority in the foreseeable future as in the recent past. And Amnesty International gives no indication that it plans to go out of business because it anticipates an end to human rights violations. Consequently, I shall assume the adverse civil and socioeconomic conditions of many states are likely to continue.

189

The question I address therefore is whether in the years to come the rules of the negative sovereignty regime which quasi-states depend upon are likely to be supported by the community of states as they have been since decolonization. The fundamental rule that inaugurated quasi-states is categorical self-determination of ex-colonial territories which is now an historical event. The deck of overseas colonies has been dealt, virtually every colony of any significance has acquired independence, and no more cards remain. The possibility that the issue of self-determination will be reopened in those ex-colonies where it continues to provoke controversy seems very slim indeed. Apart from the Palestinians who are an exceptional case, no group which currently claims a right of self-determination against an existing ex-colonial sovereign has received international backing. The governments which exercise jurisdiction over the territories in question must recognize such claims before anyone else will. There are obvious reasons why we should not expect this. Sovereignty today as in the past is a status which attaches itself to territory. Sovereign governments are usually prepared to repatriate disaffected or disruptive populations but not to accept changes that would incur any loss of territory. Even minor boundary disputes often prove difficult to resolve. Furthermore, if such claims were allowed in some cases they could very easily encourage demands for the same elsewhere and therefore threaten the territorial integrity of many other states with dissident regions. International order could be put at risk if this happened. All sovereign governments realize this and all except the very few that stand to gain territory from irredentism naturally wish to avoid it. Consequently, there is international determination to retain the existing political map and to reject virtually out of hand any belated demands for self-determination, however worthy or just the cause may be. The conservatism of international society on this question is profound.

Self-determination involved constitutional independence of colonies on a basis of equality with former colonial masters and all other sovereign states: negative sovereignty. It is not difficult to see why equal sovereignty was adopted instead of some other international status. Who would accept second or third-class citizenship? What criteria could be used to determine it? And who would make the decision? Legal equality is the easiest principle to accept even by states which are profoundly unequal in most other respects. Anything else provokes controversy and uncertainty. Moreover, once rights are granted particularly in an age of democracy they become entrenched and are almost impossible to withdraw. This is a stabilizing mechanism of international society but it entails other consequences as well. Equal sovereignty for all states makes it impossible to address the domestic problems of some states by international means without the consent of their governments. Alternative arrangements which could supply greater expertise, responsibility, and probity in government decision-making are not only impossible without the permission of the government whose authority they would undermine but also unthinkable because they touch directly on a crucial issue which is ruled out of order by post-colonial international society: the domestic behaviour of independent governments. This issue cannot be raised internationally without inviting accusations of paternalism, neocolonialism, and even racism and so international society for the most part remains silent.

Quasi-statesmen have taken the opposite approach. They have tried to expand their equal sovereignty into areas from which it has until now been excluded, such as international economic bodies like the IMF or the World Bank where the financial contributions of states roughly determine their voting rights. The chances they will be successful at instituting majority rule based on one state, one vote are slim owing to a similar conservative bias in these positive sovereignty rules and an unwillingness of economic powers to surrender any authority to Third World governments whom they probably believe privately are not sufficiently competent or responsible to be entrusted with it. How long would the capital of any bank last if it were run by borrowers? This continues to be the predominant reasoning of the leading OECD states.

Consequently, instead of radical changes either in the direction of trusteeship or greater equality the current stalemate in North–South relations will almost certainly continue. Giving aid will probably still be a badge of good citizenship of developed states and receiving it a moral if not a legal entitlement of underdeveloped countries. Development assistance will also remain a useful device by which rich states promote their international standing among poor clienteles. A few developing countries and perhaps more than a few might 'graduate' from the nonreciprocial development regime either as a result of economic fortune – such as the discovery of oil – or their own efforts. But most will not. International development assistance will also continue to be restricted by the sovereignty of recipients. The chance that the IMF and the World Bank will intrude into domestic jurisdiction beyond the current lawful policy of restructuring is unlikely. The anticipated international outcry that it would provoke effectively prevents it. Perhaps more likely is the expansion of debt relief for the poorest countries. However, this would in effect forgive the past mismanagement and corruption of governments and would consequently reinforce rather than undermine their negative sovereignty. Aid transfers will probably continue to be too small to improve the general welfare but large enough to be of definite interest and value to ruling elites who are strategically placed to channel them.

This brings us to the pivotal rule which upholds quasi-states: nonintervention. Despite the enormous inequalities of power between states today and the fact that some powers could if they desired forcibly intervene virtually at will in the affairs of other states, it usually has not happened. In sub-Saharan Africa, for example, most significant interventions have been invoked by the sovereign government involved and not imposed by the intervening power or solicited by anti-government rebels. There is evidently a great reluctance on the part of major military powers to infringe upon the jurisdiction of even the least substantial sovereign state. Nonintervention is the foundation of international society and there would have to be very compelling reasons of state to disregard this general prohibition. In recent decades only intense regional superpower rivalry has provoked dictatorial intervention in Third World countries considered to be of significance to the East–West contest. Forcible intervention in today's democratic international society is construed as bullying and widely condemned. Moreover, it is far easier and possibly cheaper to bribe governments than to coerce them and such influence also is entirely consistent with international law.

This raises the issue of human rights which is of course contrary to the negative sovereignty game. If offences against humanity even to the point of genocide in a few cases have not been sufficient justification to override sovereign rights until now we probably should not expect it to be any different in the future. This assumes that current international toleration of sovereign governments which fail to adequately protect human rights will not decrease. International awareness, organization, and action concerning human rights have nevertheless been increasing in recent decades and there is no reason to expect this to stop either. Any future success of international humanitarianism, however, will depend in the final analysis on the inclinations and abilities of independent governments to prevent human rights violations. If international human rights awareness increases perhaps their humanitarian inclinations will increase also. But unless there is far more willingness in the future to effectively censure human rights offenders than there has been up to now this seems unlikely to happen. As I indicate below, there is one significant possibility of such a development stemming from human rights reform in the Soviet Union and Eastern Europe which could have a demonstration effect elsewhere.

However, even if increased pressure were placed on Third World human rights offenders it might still have limited effect owing to domestic political conditions. Quasi-states as a rule are places where incivility is by no means confined only to governments but extends to their opponents both of whom are usually prepared to engage in such behaviour if it is considered politically necessary. Unfortunately, incivility in such countries is usually tolerated or at least expected by many people inside government and outside. It consequently is difficult to curtail let alone eliminate. Even if international pressure is exerted against the governments of such states and they attempt to respond positively, their ability to do so may be limited by these circumstances. This argument should not be carried too far, however, because in all societies civil and uncivil behaviour is at the end of the day a matter of choice. Even in corrupt societies governments can set standards of probity and try to enforce them. The same is true of human rights. Government usually is the most important agency that can create expectations about social conduct. Securing a responsible government is probably the crucial step in fostering not only a less corrupt but also a more humane society. Unfortunately international influence to promote responsible government is strictly limited under conditions of negative sovereignty. Whether it happens or not depends mainly on those in control of government. In summary, there is more reason to expect the negative sovereignty game to continue in its present shape than to change into something else.

Dramatic new international circumstances could intervene to revise this forecast, however. At the start of the 1990s the most significant and indeed fascinating international development is undoubtedly the Gorbachev phenomenon and its unsettling effects on the East–West status quo. We are witnessing an unprecedented reappraisal and perhaps readjustment of East–West relations which is propelled by equally remarkable reform movements in the Soviet Union and other East European countries. This astonishing development has already brought about agreements to reduce if not to resolve regional conflicts in Western Asia, Southeast Asia, and Southern Africa in which superpowers have been involved. Significant balanced reductions in both nuclear and conventional weapons between NATO and the Warsaw Pact are underway. One can only speculate about what might happen to international relations if the current Soviet leadership remains in power and continues to pursue its declared policies of *glasnost* and *perestroika*. What would be the effect on the negative sovereignty game of a *rapprochement* between the Soviet Union and the United States or a Soviet Union which complied with the spirit and the letter of the Helsinki accords on human rights? Would such international developments be more likely to increase or decrease the political space of quasi-states?

Since the Third World initially emerged and survived under Cold War conditions any change which moved East–West relations some distance along the road from conflict to cooperation might be expected to reduce its political space accordingly, just as the non-Western world had less autonomy when something resembling a Concert of Europe existed in the nineteenth century. How much movement would be necessary for such an effect is of course impossible to say. On the other hand, East–West détente could also conceivably increase the indifference of the superpowers to the Third World which would perhaps be left more to itself than during the era of Cold War rivalry. If the Soviet Union became a member of the international economic establishment it and other parts of Eastern Europe might henceforth become a major focus of international development perhaps to the detriment of the Third World. This is not the kind of indifference which quasi-statesmen would wish to see. Only rather later could a reformed Soviet economy begin to make a contribution to overseas development. This is highly speculative, of course, but it is not inconsistent with the logic of a conceivable readmission of Russia to the comity of nations after many decades as a hostile outsider. On balance quasi-statesmen would probably prefer a continued divide between East and West which gives them greater latitude to play off one side against the other in a sort of reverse international version of imperial divide and conquer. Whatever the effects might prove to be, however, such momentous changes could scarcely leave quasi-states untouched.

If despotism could finally be brought to an end in Russia after centuries would it not also become more vulnerable elsewhere? The cessation of Soviet human rights offences would probably make it rather easier to criticize humanitarian abuses by other states. The argument that human rights are merely capitalist ideology would certainly be more difficult to sustain if the world's socialist superpower publicly avowed their moral and legal validity. A preliminary statement to this effect was made by President Gorbachev in a speech at the United Nations in 1988. If the Soviet Union re-entered the comity of nations not only by joining ruling international economic bodies but also by observing human rights conventions it might create an expectation of similar conduct by other states which do not currently respect human rights. Soviet protection of human rights might encourage greater compliance with international humanitarian standards. Democratic reforms in Hungary, Poland, Czechoslovakia and other East European countries could only add to these expectations. The United States would no longer perhaps feel obliged to turn a blind eye to humanitarian offences by some of its clients out of concern that otherwise they might go over to the Soviet side. In other words, reasons of state might intrude less into humanitarian issues and consequently it would not be as easy to get away with human rights abuses as it has been. For the first time since decolonization there would be a converging view of acceptable and unacceptable conduct concerning human rights by the world's most prominent and influential states. In other words, the standard of civilization might again become an acknowledged principle of international relations.

Would not Soviet entry into the international establishment therefore be as momentous an international event as 1919 or 1945 or 1960? Possibly yes but probably no. For even if the USSR became a 'civilized' nation by traditional standards it still seems unlikely that this could undermine the basic international conditions which support quasi-states. Negative sovereignty would in all likelihood still be not only a legitimate but also a useful institution of international society. It has successfully filled the juridical void in the non-Western world left by the ending of Western empire. No developed government today will publicly question the wisdom or justice of the post-colonial regime whatever their private opinions might be. It is difficult to believe that the imaginary future scenario outlined above could change this. Even if the Soviet Union instituted domestic human rights reforms it would still want to enjoy the good opinion of as many states as possible including those of the Third World. It would not receive this if it stood in judgement of their domestic conduct. Indeed, it would be resented as unwarranted intervention and angrily opposed. The same normative restraint would apply no less to the United States, Japan, the Western European states, and indeed all states.

In summary, there are two compelling reasons why the negative sovereignty game will almost certainly continue to be played. The first is instrumental. There is in most institutions to which individuals or states become attached a powerful conservatism. This is owing in no small part to unreflective habit or lack of imagination that things could conceivably be other than they are. But it is also because of a conviction that the devil we know, as the saying goes, is almost always preferable to the devil we do not know. The costs of alternative arrangements may turn out in the end to exceed the benefits. The process of change itself may prove costly. Better to leave well enough alone. Statesmen as a rule desire stability before all else in their external relations. They wish to avoid unnecessary difficulties in pursuing their national interests and concerns with other states. This usually rules out or at least curtails severely any questions about the domestic character and conduct of other statesmen which are almost bound to be disruptive or at least productive of ill will. Diplomacy is an established and successful institution only because statesmen are prepared for the sake of good international relations not to look very closely at each other's domestic affairs. Agnosticism or live and let live is the religion of international relations: *cujus regio, ejus religio*. If domestic considerations were taken into account diplomacy itself would probably be the first casualty. The expansion of international society across all domestic societies and cultures makes toleration and agnosticism more imperative than ever. It also reduces to a minimum the number of issues about which diplomats can expect to agree and increases to a maximum those about which they must simply agree to disagree and leave it at that. One can therefore see the negative sovereignty game as an institution which accommodates the instrumental requirements of diplomacy in what is today a far flung society of states with exceedingly diverse characteristics. In other words it has utility both for existing states individually and for international society at large.

The second reason is normative. Statesmen do not merely confront each other from the narrow perspective of their own national interests. They also engage in broader dialogue from a position of equal legal status with its attached rights and duties. No permanent and stable system of human relations including international relations could be based on power and interest alone. It also requires not only law but consideration, respect, courtesy, honour, dignity, decorum, and similar norms which are usually observed by statesmen despite the enormous inequalities of power and wealth between them. International relations in this regard have the character of a 'club'. Members are honourable fellows. Membership has its privileges. Once granted it is rarely withdrawn or even questioned. Provided members conform to club rules in their outward conduct, their private lives are their own. Even skeletons in closets are their own affair providing they are not those of some other members. Statesmen who break club rules usually cannot be deprived of sovereignty. But they can be cast out of international society: condemned, ostracized, isolated and in rare cases sanctioned – as happened to South Africa. This action it should be emphasized was for violating a cardinal rule of the negative sovereignty game: self-determination for the black majority in South Africa. The white South African government could not accept black self-determination and expect to remain in control of the state, so it was reconciled to almost universal condemnation by the international community as the necessary price it had to pay for pursuing its self-interest in survival. The South African state continued to have more than adequate power to survive and it is unlikely that sanctions fundamentally altered this. It possessed positive sovereignty based on empirical statehood. Its isolation was not a question of power, however, it was a question of legitimacy.

Quasi-statesmen in black Africa are supported by the same principle of racial sovereignty which isolated white South Africa. While this principle cannot make a contribution to their empirical statehood it can underwrite their negative sovereignty by censuring external criticism of their domestic conduct which in some cases involves discrimination against ethnic segments of their own populations which is not fundamentally different from that of South Africa. Racial sovereignty constitutes a powerful taboo against even the mildest questioning of their conduct. The taboo operates silently as a form of self-censorship by virtually all agents and representatives of states and international organizations and adds decisive normative sanction to the traditional reluctance of diplomats to engage in public criticism of each other's domestic affairs. The result is a form of reverse discrimination in international relations in which the Soviet Union, other East European states, and South Africa have deservedly come in for strenuous human rights criticism from the international community but numerous equally deserving non-white violators usually receive at most only a mild rebuke almost always tempered by an understanding of the difficult circumstances they face.

This taboo seems unlikely to be merely temporary because it is rooted in a fundamental historical change of public values (although not necessarily private attitudes) concerning race relations which has occurred in Western countries and particularly the United States after a lengthy political struggle for racial equality. It has been institutionalized in public law, shapes public policy and could hardly now be reversed. Furthermore, it is reinforced by the doctrine of cultural relativism which has displaced ethnocentrism and forbids negative evaluations of nationalities, societies, or cultures different from one's own. Fortunately it is today difficult and unusual for defamatory remarks against people of non-European descent to be made in public particularly by state authorities. Unfortunately, it is equally difficult because of this to condemn the domestic conduct of certain statesmen

197

if it is warranted but they happen not to be of European race. The cultural remoteness of non-Western governments reduces further and probably eliminates any expectation that they should observe the same domestic standards. This narrowing of moral evaluation and widening of toleration in international relations is also a consequence of the globalization of international society. Diplomacy in such a society could not operate on any other basis. It is therefore one thing to ostracize the South African government. It would be something entirely different to isolate every sovereign government that could justifiably be accused of offences against human rights. International society would become a club of outcasts. In short, there is an ironic and tragic but probably necessary form of discrimination in the nondiscrimination practices of contemporary international relations which protects non-European sovereign governments from justifiable public criticism and condemnation. It is difficult to see human rights norms overcoming these barriers.

INSTITUTIONAL FATE

At the time of decolonization decisions were taken which instituted the negative sovereignty regime as the sole successor to colonialism. This ruled out alternative institutional arrangements which might have been better suited to the different circumstances and needs of particular colonial populations. In brief, legal uniformity triumphed despite the fact that the emerging world of states was anything but uniform and was indeed highly pluralistic in almost every respect. This institutional outcome deserves some concluding comments from the perspective of international jurisprudence.

No doubt it was hoped that changing the international status of territories from dependency to independency would prove to be generally beneficial for peoples who previously had been denied sovereignty. After all most independent countries at the time enjoyed far higher standards of living than most colonies. Why should everybody not be entitled to the same opportunity? It was possible to believe not only that independence and higher living standards were positively related but even that the former would produce the latter. Increased prosperity has indeed resulted in many former colonies sometimes exceeding what would have been expected whether or not decolonization had occurred. But there have also been many other ex-colonies in which independence was followed by increased adversity also beyond what might otherwise have been. If anything is clear from the post-colonial experience it is that sovereignty and development are not necessarily collaborators and can be antagonists.

Both prosperity and adversity should have been expected because in the sovereignty game as in any other not everybody can play equally well and some can scarcely play at all. Rules of the game place a premium on certain talents and resources while devaluing or ignoring others. Games are not democratic by definition: if everybody can play well it is not much of a game. To assume that every country can take equal advantage of sovereignty is to ignore the huge differences in talent, skill, experience, discipline, dedication, training, education, perseverance, equipment, opportunities, and so forth which inevitably discriminate between not only individuals but also national populations. Yet this is the assumption (usually unstated) of the negative sovereignty game. The fact that ex-colonial populations have benefited unequally from equal sovereignty and that some have suffered under independent governments is indicative of the contrary assumption which is consistent with games in general.

Constitutional choices always involve opportunity costs: alternative arrangements are ruled out. And for such choices unlike ordinary decisions the costs are borne for as long as the institutions are in effect. This institutional maxim is applicable to European colonial disengagement from Asia, Africa, and Oceania. The adoption of negative sovereignty precluded other conceivable arrangements some of which might have been more appropriate to the circumstances. From a backward looking Burkean perspective, for example, decolonization was an indiscriminate abandonment of traditional territorial statuses of which some might have proved adaptable to the particular circumstances or needs of ex-colonial populations and territories. Residual sovereignty, condominia, trust territories, and various other arrangements which limit independence were discarded and a solitary institution which was blind to sociological diversity was adopted instead. For those who question the utility of tradition in general or the foregoing arrangements in particular this argument will not be persuasive. But even from a forward looking Benthamite perspective independence was a blinkered change which failed to consider new institutional arrangements for a radically different post-colonial international society which embraced all the peoples of the world. Independence was not the innovative moment it might have been if novel territorial statuses suited to the special circumstances and needs of ex-colonial states and aimed at increasing the prosperity of their populations had been fashioned. The moment was lost and the one-dimensional negative sovereignty game was established instead.

From either perspective the decision was not rational so much as rationalist. The episode is an instance of 'rationalism' in Michael

199

Oakeshott's meaning insofar as it was the shortest possible distance or rather the quickest move from colonialism to noncolonialism: 'politics as the crow flies'. The problem with rationalism as a political process is its lack of empirical adjustment to the circumstances of particular cases. 'There is no place ... for a "best in the circumstances", only a place for "the best".'[1] The various circumstances and needs of different colonial populations were ruled out by the universalist ideology of self-determination: the rationalists easily defeated the empiricists.

The effect of establishing negative sovereignty across the board was to create an artificial institutional levelling of a world which in actual fact was and is anything but level. There are basically two opposing views about how best to accommodate the diversity of the world by institutional means. The first perspective again associated with Burke and later with British imperial constitutionalism but by no means confined only to colonial arrangements is that societal and cultural differences among nations and peoples are to be expected and should be recognized and reflected in specially adapted rules and institutions. Thus, in a post-colonial but highly unequal world such as ours, there ought to be various international statuses ranging from outright independence to associate statehood to international trusteeship which are determined by the circumstances and needs of particular populations. Only one institution or rule for all cases is *prima facie* not only irrational but also inequitable. The obvious and apparently insurmountable problem with this argument, as indicated above, is determining the appropriate legal arrangement in the circumstances. Who would merit independence? Who must settle for associate statehood or some other nonindependent status? Who would make the decision? How should it be made? If it were a referendum, who would frame the question? The prevailing and undoubtedly justified belief is that it is impossible although it is fascinating to speculate about what ex-colonial peoples would decide if given a real choice in a fair referendum on the question. Having experienced the bitter harvest of independence would some now choose a reduced status if it promised improved living conditions through greater international involvement and supervision?

The second view associated with Michael Walzer and international liberalism is that sovereign statehood is the best way of guaranteeing the national freedom that is necessary to secure and protect the diverse cultures and societies of the world.[2] Sovereign statehood leaves people at liberty to determine their own fate according to their own values and beliefs. Alternative arrangements including international human rights provide an opening for outsiders to interfere and impose their values: cultural imperialism. The contemporary world is organized exclusively on the second basis and there is little doubt that negative sovereignty accommodates cultural diversity internationally. Within many quasi-states, however, plurality often is not encouraged or even tolerated: minority cultures and populations not to mention political oppositions are under some measure of threat from sovereign governments. Domestic plurality may therefore be sacrificed for the sake of international plurality by the existing framework of universal sovereign statehood.

Current international practice operates with the aim of recognizing and accommodating diversity *within* this framework. Hence, states which are underdeveloped are reconciled by new institutions and practices of international development. Problems of incivility are addressed by international human rights. Previous chapters have outlined how these institutional arrangements have fared to date and it is not necessary to repeat what has already been written. In general they have run up against the immovable object of contemporary international society: equal sovereign statehood. These arrangements are only effective if sovereign governments are willing and able to make them effective. They cannot overrule sovereignty and consequently cannot compensate for alternative institutions which were ruled out of consideration at the time of decolonization. The possibility of going further within the existing sovereignty framework as advocated by proponents of a New International Economic Order is definitely limited.

Once institutional arrangements become set they are difficult to change: one is saddled with them for better or worse. This is desirable if on balance they contribute to the wellbeing of those subject to them. For populations of countries whose governments regularly protect civil rights and provide socioeconomic welfare it is a blessing that the institutions of sovereignty are difficult to alter. Outsiders cannot interfere and perhaps threaten their good life. But for populations whose governments do not provide such goods the institutional fate of sovereignty is less kind. Quasi-states are now a settled feature of the international landscape. Third World rulers enjoy the full complement of sovereign rights including the most important one: nonintervention. Their international liberty and formal equality with all other statesmen is underwritten by the community of states. But many Third World populations find themselves confined within jurisdictions of questionable value and limited promise under governments which frequently are incompetent and corrupt and sometimes abusive also. This is their institutional fate. And Michael Walzer is right; it is up to them to change it. But this is difficult because sovereign statehood works in favour of governments; sovereign rights continue to prevail over human rights in international relations. This institutional predicament of many Third World populations is reinforced by some of the most powerful taboos of our time which make it a moral offence to evaluate negatively the domestic conduct of nonwhite governments or criticize the international institutions which support them. Once taboos invade issues such as these the room for subsequent rational discussion is strictly limited.

It is perhaps appropriate to end on the ironic note that has sounded throughout this book: the same institution which provided international recognition, dignity, and independence to all colonized populations could be exploited to deny domestic civility, liberty, and welfare to some. And the exploitation this time was by their own governments. International liberation could therefore be followed by domestic subjugation. Alternative institutions which provided for international review or supervision might have prevented such adversities or at least reduced them. Of course they would have fostered unintended consequences of their own not all of which would have proved desirable. However, a greater variety of international statuses including more intrusive forms of international trusteeship might have rendered the post-colonial situation less unsatisfactory than it proved time and again to be under the one-dimensional negative sovereignty regime.

NOTES

Introduction

1 Peter Worsley, *The Third World* (London, 1964).
2 See especially Ralph Pettman, *State and Class* (London, 1979) and Robert W. Cox, 'Social forces, states and world orders', *Millennium*, vol. 10 (1981), pp. 126–55.
3 Some legal scholars also take a broader view. G. Schwarzenberger and E. D. Brown conceive of international law as consisting of not only 'rules', such as exclusive domestic jurisdiction, but also 'principles', which are abstractions and 'provide the common denominator for a number of related rules'. See *A Manual of International Law*, 6th edn (London, 1976), pp. 33–6. Similar distinctions are drawn in jurisprudence. See, for example, R. M. Dworkin, *Taking Rights Seriously* (Cambridge, Mass., 1978), chs. 2 and 3.
4 See, for example, Ian Brownlie, *Principles of Public International Law*, 3rd edn (Oxford, 1979).
5 *Ibid.*, p. 515.
6 I cannot consider the jurisprudential problem of establishing the character of rules in human relations, but see the famous analysis by H. L. A. Hart, 'Analytical jurisprudence in mid-twentieth century', *University of Pennsylvania Law Review*, vol. 105 (1957), pp. 953–75. Also see G. Marshall, 'The role of rules', in D. Miller and L. Siedentop (eds.), *The Nature of Political Theory* (Oxford, 1983), pp. 183–97.
7 Dorothy Emmet, *Rules, Roles and Relations* (Boston, 1966), p. 12. Emmet is a philosopher but her definition is virtually identical with a recent one by two lawyers: ' "Rule" is . . . a general norm guiding conduct or action in a given type of situation.' W. Twining and D. Miers, *How To Do Things with Rules*, 2nd edn (London, 1984), pp. 126–7.
8 Emmet, *Rules, Roles and Relations*, p. 11 (original emphasis).
9 K. R. Popper, *The Open Society and Its Enemies*, vol. 1: *Plato*, 5th edn (London, 1966), ch. 5.
10 Jacob Burckhardt, *The Civilization of the Renaissance in Italy*, vol. 1, *The State as a Work of Art* (New York, 1958).
11 Edmund Burke, 'First letter on a Regicide peace', in F. W. Rafferty (ed.), *The Works of Edmund Burke VI* (Oxford, 1928).
12 See Hedley Bull, 'The theory of international politics 1919–1969', in Brian Porter (ed.), *The Aberystwyth Papers* (London, 1972), p. 32.
13 See chapter 3.

14 I am inspired by Hedley Bull's remark: 'My book [is] . . . an attempt to deal with a large and complex subject simply by thinking it through.' See Hedley Bull, *The Anarchical Society* (London, 1977), p. x.

15 E. E. Schattschneider, *The Semisovereign People* (New York, 1960), p. 71.

16 This view of international relations theory is attributed to Martin Wight. See Hedley Bull, 'Martin Wight and the theory of international relations', *British Journal of International Studies*, vol. 2 (1976), p. 115.

17 A. D. Lindsay, *The Modern Democratic State* (London, 1943), pp. 37–8.

18 Oakeshott has expressed this point as follows: ' "Experience" stands for the concrete whole which analysis divides into "experiencing" and "what is experienced". Experiencing and what is experienced are, taken separately, meaningless abstractions; they cannot be separated. Perceiving, for example, involves a something perceived, willing a something willed . . . These two abstractions stand to one another in the most complete inter-dependence; they compose a single whole.' *Experience and Its Modes* (Cambridge, 1933), p. 9. Also see R. G. Collingwood, *An Autobiography* (London, 1970), ch. 12.

19 R. G. Collingwood, *The Idea of History* (London, 1956), pp. 315, 316.

20 See in particular, Hans J. Morgenthau, *Scientific Man Versus Power Politics* (Chicago, 1965).

21 R. A. Mortimer, *The Third World Coalition in International Politics*, 2nd edn (London, 1984).

22 Adam Watson, *Diplomacy* (London, 1982). On diplomacy as a characteristic of international society see Martin Wight, *Systems of States* (Leicester, 1977), pp. 141–2.

23 The distinctions between 'realism' and 'rationalism' are discussed in Hedley Bull, 'Martin Wight and the theory of international relations', *British Journal of International Studies*, vol. 2 (1976), pp. 104–5.

24 F. W. Maitland, 'Moral personality and legal personality', reprinted in David Nichols, *The Pluralist State* (London, 1975), p. 159.

25 Isaiah Berlin, *Four Essays on Liberty* (Oxford, 1969), ch. 3. See chapter 1.

1 States and quasi-states

1 Margery Perham, 'Our task in Africa', *The Times* (10, 11, 12 February 1936), reprinted in Margery Perham, *Colonial Sequence* (London, 1967), pp. 140–54.

2 Sir Donald Cameron was Governor of Nigeria between 1930 and 1935. This is discussed in Margery Perham, *Native Administration in Nigeria* (London, 1937), chs. 20 and 21.

3 'Oceania' hereafter refers to small island jurisdictions in not only the Pacific but also the Indian and Caribbean Oceans.

4 John Plamenatz, *On Alien Rule and Self-Government* (London, 1960), pp. 21–3.

5 *Ibid.*, p. 28.

6 See J. Crawford, 'The criteria for statehood in international law', *British Yearbook of International Law 1976–1977* (Oxford, 1978), pp. 116–17.

7 The term 'quasi-state' is used by H. Bull and A. Watson, *The Expansion of International Society* (Oxford, 1984), p. 430. Also see Robert H. Jackson, 'Quasi-states, dual regimes, and neoclassical theory', *International Organiz-*

ation, vol. 41 (Autumn 1987), pp. 519–49. The rather different legal concept of 'quasi-sovereignty' ('quasi-international law', 'quasi-personal jurisdiction', and 'quasi-territorial jurisdiction') is discussed in Schwarzenberger and Brown, *A Manual of International Law*.

8 Sir Lewis Namier, *Vanished Supremacies* (New York, 1963), p. 33.
9 R. W. Tucker, *The Inequality of Nations* (New York, 1977).
10 H. J. Morgenthau, *Scientific Man Versus Power Politics* (Chicago, 1946) and M. Wight, 'Why is there no international theory', in Sir H. Butterfield and M. Wight (ed.), *Diplomatic investigations* (London, 1966), pp. 17–34. Also see chapter 7.
11 See A. Ryan, *J. S. Mill* (London, 1974), p. 214.
12 See chapter 3.
13 Plamenatz, *On Alien Rule and Self-Government*, pp. 22–3.
14 See Francis Snyder and Peter Slinn (ed.), *International Law of Development* (Abingdon, 1987).
15 See chapter 5.
16 Berlin, *Four Essays on Liberty*, ch. 3.
17 *Ibid.*, p. 122.
18 'The only purpose for which power can be rightfully exercised over any member of a civilised community, against his will, is to prevent harm to others'. J. S. Mill, *On Liberty*, reprinted in H. B. Acton (ed.), *J. S. Mill: Utilitarianism, On Liberty and Considerations on Representative Government* (London, 1972), p. 73.
19 This is the usual legal concept. See Schwarzenberger and Brown, *A Manual of International Law*, pp. 54–5. Schwarzenberger's conception of negative and positive sovereignty overlaps with my own at several points but is not identical to it.
20 *Ibid.*, pp. 52, 564. By political sovereignty Schwarzenberger means 'independence in fact, not merely in law'.
21 *Ibid.*, p. 53f. Schwarzenberger considers positive sovereignty to be an absolute rather than a relative condition, and negative sovereignty the reverse. But this is logically inconsistent if positive sovereignty is a substantive condition and negative sovereignty a formal-legal one, as he also seems to suggest.
22 See Ian Brownlie, 'The Expansion of international society: the consequences for the law of nations', in Bull and Watson, *The Expansion of International Society*, ch. 24.

2 A new sovereignty regime
1 Alan James, *Sovereign Statehood* (London, 1986), p. 25.
2 *Ibid.*, p. 39. The analysis in this paragraph is based on chapter 3 of James' book.
3 *Ibid.*, p. 48.
4 Gilbert Ryle, *The Concept of Mind* (Harmondsworth, 1968), ch. 2.
5 Crawford, 'The criteria for statehood in international law', p. 96. Also see Wight, *Systems of States*, p. 27.
6 H. Kelsen, *General Theory of Law and State* (Cambridge, 1945), p. 29.

7 See Michael Oakeshott, 'The rule of law', *On History and Other Essays* (Oxford, 1983), pp. 125–8.

8 Hugo Grotius, *De Jure Belli Ac Pacis Libri*, trans. F. Kelsey (Oxford, 1925).

9 P. Calvocoressi, 'The frailty of internationalism', *International Relations*, vol. 8 (1986).

10 See Heinz Lubasz (ed.), *The Development of the Modern State* (London, 1964), p. 3.

11 Hobbes, *Leviathan*, Michael Oakeshott (ed.) (Oxford, 1946), ch. 13.

12 Bodin, *Six Books of the Commonwealth*, M. J. Tooley (ed.) (Oxford, n.d.), book 1.

13 Also see chapter 7.

14 M. Oakeshott, *On Human Conduct* (Oxford, 1975), Part 3.

15 T. Nardin, *Law, Morality and the Relations of States* (Princeton, 1983).

16 See G. Murdock, *Africa: Its Peoples and the Cultural History* (London, 1959).

17 H. Shue, *Basic Rights* (Princeton, 1980), ch. 1.

18 See, among others, C. R. Beitz, M. Cohen, T. Scanlon, and J. Simmons, ed. *International Ethics* (Princeton, 1985), Part 5, C. R. Beitz, *Political Theory and International Relations* (Princeton, 1979), parts 2 and 3 and Shue, *Basic Rights* parts 1 and 2.

19 See S. I. Benn, 'Human rights-for whom and for what?' in E. Kamenka and A. E. Tay (ed.), *Human Rights* (London, 1978), p. 65. Also see D. M. Trubek, 'Human rights law and human needs programs', in T. Meron (ed.), *Human Rights in International Law* (Oxford, 1985), ch. 6.

20 The European Convention on Human Rights makes provision for derogation in exceptional circumstances, such as during national emergencies. See Rosalyn Higgins, 'The European Convention on Human Rights', in Meron, *Human Rights*, ch. 13.

21 See, for example, *Amnesty International Report 1986* (London, 1986).

22 See the balanced discussion in Jack Donnelly, 'Humanitarian intervention', *Journal of International Affairs*, vol. 37 (Winter 1984), pp. 311–28.

3 Sovereignty regimes in history

1 E. L. Jones, *The European Miracle* (Cambridge, 1981), pp. 106, 118–19.

2 M. Wight, *Power Politics*, 2nd edn (London, 1986), p. 25.

3 H. Lauterpacht, 'The Grotian tradition in international law', *The British Year Book of International Law 1946* (Oxford, 1947), pp. 28–9.

4 J. Burckhardt, *The Civilization of the Renaissance in Italy*, vol. 1 (New York, 1958), p. 22.

5 C. H. McIlwain, *The Growth of Political Thought in the West* (New York, 1982), p. 268.

6 Bodin, *Six Books of the Commonwealth*, book 4, ch. 1, p. 109.

7 Hobbes, *Leviathan*, p. 83.

8 S. Pufendorf, *De Jure Naturae et Gentium Libri Octo* (1672), C. H. and W. A. Oldfather, trans., (Oxford, 1934), book 7, ch. 3, para 690.

9 F. H. Hinsley, *Sovereignty*, 2nd edn (Cambridge, 1986), p. 185.

10 Schwarzenberger and Brown, *A Manual of International Law*, p. 44.

11 J. L. Brierly, *The Law of Nations*, 2nd edn (London, 1936), pp. 102–3.

12 John Austin, *The Province of Jurisprudence Determined*, H. L. A. Hart (ed.) (London, 1954), p. 194 (original emphasis).

13 Bull, *The Anarchical Society*, pp. 8–9.

14 C. de Visscher, *Theory and Reality in Public International Law*, P. E. Corbett, trans. (Princeton, 1968), pp. 174–5.

15 Wight, *Systems of States*, p. 128.

16 The closest to it is Bull and Watson, *The Expansion of International Society*.

17 Alfred Cobban, *The Nation State and National Self-Determination* (New York, 1969), ch. 4.

18 Adam Watson, 'European international society and its expansion', in Bull and Watson, *The Expansion of International Society*, p. 18.

19 *Ibid.*, pp. 25–6.

20 Charles H. Alexandrowicz', 'New and original states', *International Affairs*, vol. 45 (July 1969), pp. 470–1. Also see his *Introduction to the History of the Law of Nations in the East Indies* (London, 1967).

21 See the discussion in A. P. d'Entreves, *Natural Law*, 2nd edn (London, 1970), pp. 53–56.

22 Alexandrowicz, 'New and original states', pp. 469, 479.

23 See, for example, Martin Wight's criticism of Alexandrowicz's thesis in *Systems of States*, pp. 117–28.

24 Patrick O'Brien, 'Europe in the world economy', in Bull and Watson, *The Expansion of International Society*, p. 60.

25 Grotius, *The Law of War and Peace*, pp. 190–91.

26 A. H. L. Heeren quoted by Watson, 'European international society and its expansion', p. 25.

27 *Letters on the Regicide Peace* reprinted in F. W. Raffety (ed.), *The Works of the Right Honourable Edmund Burke*, vol. 6 (Oxford, 1928), pp. 156–7.

28 Michael Howard, 'The military factor in European expansion', in Bull and Watson, *The Expansion of International Society*, p. 38.

29 J. S. Mill, 'A few words on non-intervention', reprinted in G. Himmelfarb (ed.), *Essays on Politics and Culture by John Stuart Mill* (New York, 1963), pp. 368–84.

30 Quoted by Wight, *Systems of States*, p. 115.

31 Hedley Bull, 'The emergence of a universal international society', in Bull and Watson, *The Expansion of International Society*, pp. 121–2.

32 Alexandrowicz, 'New and original states', p. 467.

33 C. H. Alexandrowicz, *The European–African Confrontation* (Leiden, 1973), p. 125.

34 See T. Naff, 'The Ottoman Empire and the European states-system', in Bull and Watson, *The Expansion of International Society*, pp. 153–69.

35 See Gerrit W. Gong, 'China's entry into international society', in Bull and Watson, *The Expansion of International Society*, pp. 171–83.

36 See Hidemi Suganami, 'Japan's entry into international society', in Bull and Watson, *The Expansion of International Society*, pp. 185–99.

37 Charles C. Griffin, 'The states of Latin America', in F. H. Hinsley (ed.), *The New Cambridge Modern History*, vol. 11 (Cambridge, 1976), p. 516.

38 Quoted by J. C. Beaglehole, 'The British Commonwealth of Nations', in David Thomson (ed.), *The New Cambridge Modern History*, vol. 12 (Cambridge, 1960), p. 540.
39 See Chapter 4.
40 Peter Lyon, 'New states and international order', in A. James (ed.), *The Bases of International Order* (London, 1973), p. 45.
41 J. Westlake, *International Law*, part 1 (London, 1904), pp. 40–1.
42 The definitive legal study of the process refers to these territories as 'backward'. See M. F. Lindley, *The Acquisition and Government of Backward Territory in International Law* (London, 1926).
43 Western powers bought and sold territories as late as the present century. For example, Denmark sold the Danish West India Islands to the United States in 1916 for $25,000,000. See Lindley, *The Acquisition and Government of Backward Territory* p. 167.
44 J. Vansina, *Kingdoms of the Savanna* (Madison, 1966), pp. 155–6. Also see Lucy Mair, *African Kingdoms* (Oxford, 1967), ch. 1.
45 M. Fortes and E. E. Evans-Pritchard (ed.), *African Political Systems* (Oxford, 1940), pp. 6–7.
46 Jacques Richard-Molard as quoted by A. B. Bozeman, *Conflict in Africa* (Princeton, 1976), pp. 131–3.
47 Bozeman, *Conflict in Africa*, p. 143.
48 Lindley, *Backward Territory in International Law*, pp. 43–4.
49 Alexandrowicz, *The European–African Confrontation*, ch. 7.
50 Lindley, *Backward Territory in International Law*, ch. 21.
51 M. Wight, *British Colonial Constitutions 1947* (Oxford, 1952), p. 10.
52 A. C. McEwen, *International Boundaries of East Africa* (Oxford, 1971), p. 14.
53 'In 1831 Chief Justice Marshall, delivering judgement in a case entitled "The Cherokee Nation versus the State of Georgia", defined the position of the Federal Government as one of trustee for the lands held by Indians. It is certainly the fact that in 1837 a committee of the British House of Commons, appointed to consider "the treatment of aboriginal tribes in British territories", explicitly adopted this formula.' Lord Hailey, *The Future of Colonial Peoples* (London, 1943), p. 15.
54 Quoted by H. A. C. Cairns, *Prelude to Imperialism* (London, 1965), p. 95.
55 Lindley, *Backward Territory in International Law*, pp. 329–30.
56 G. L. Beer, *African Questions at the Paris Peace Conference* (New York, 1923), p. 117.
57 See C. W. Jenks, *The Common Law of Mankind* (London, 1958), pp. 43–4, and G. W. Gong, *The Standard of 'Civilization' in International Society* (Oxford, 1984), pp. 14–15.
58 Lindley, *Backward Territory in International Law*, p. 327.
59 L. H. Gann, 'The Berlin Conference and the humanitarian conscience', in S. Forster, W. J. Mommsen, and R. Robinson (eds.), *Bismarck, Europe, and Africa: The Berlin Conference 1884–1885, and the Onset of Partition* (Oxford, 1988), pp. 330–1.
60 According to Brierly, Article 22 was one of the successful functions of the League of Nations. See J. L. Brierly, 'The League of Nations', in Thomson,

The New Cambridge Modern History, vol. 12, p. 498. It is sometimes forgotten that the principle of trusteeship was also enshrined in Article 23 of the Covenant under which signatories accepted the duty of securing 'just treatment of the native inhabitants of [existing] territories under their control'. Lindley argues that trusteeship therefore applied *both* to mandates and to ordinary colonies and protectorates. See Lindley, *Backward Territory in International Law*, p. 336.

61 Schwarzenberger, *A Manual of International Law*, pp. 14–15.

62 Mill, *Utilitarianism*, p. 361.

63 M. N. Shaw, *Title to Territory in Africa* (Oxford, 1986), p. 59.

64 The majority opinion of legal commentators is that Articles 1 (2) and 55 do not create a binding legal obligation. For a review of this controversy see Shaw, *Title to Territory in Africa*, ch. 2.

65 A. Mazrui, *Towards a Pax Africana* (London, 1967), p. 39.

66 Wight, *Systems of States*, p. 41.

67 Ibid., p. 118.

68 Alan James, 'The emerging global society', *Third World Affairs*, vol. 7 (1986), p. 467.

69 Alexandrowicz, *The European–African Confrontation*, p. 6. Also see by the same author 'The new states and international law', *Millennium*, vol. 3 (1974), pp. 226–233.

70 Alexandrowicz, *The European–African Confrontation*, p. 125.

71 Ibid., pp. 5, 112–13. Also see Alexandrowicz, 'New and original states,' pp. 465–80, and N. L. Wallace-Bruce, 'Africa and international law: the emergence to statehood', *The Journal of Modern African Studies*, vol. 23 (December 1985), pp. 575–602.

4 Independence by right

1 The Middle East and North Africa are excluded from this analysis.

2 See Hedley Bull, 'The revolt against the west', in Bull and Watson, *The Expansion of International Society*, note 45, ch. 14.

3 Geoffrey Barraclough, *An Introduction to Contemporary History* (Harmondsworth, 1967), p. 106.

4 See D. J. Morgan, *Guidance Towards Self-Government in British Colonies, 1941–1971, The Official History of Colonial Development*, vol. 5 (London, 1980); A. N. Porter and A. J. Stockwell, *British Imperial Policy and Decolonization: 1938–64*, vol. 1 (Cambridge, 1987); John Gallagher, *The Decline, Revival and Fall of the British Empire* (Cambridge, 1982); R. F. Holland, *European Decolonization 1918–1981* (London, 1985); and P. Gifford and W. R. Louis (eds.), *The Transfer of Power in Africa* (London, 1982).

5 Holland, *European Decolonization 1918–1981*, p. 300.

6 Ronald Robinson, 'Andrew Cohen and the transfer of power in Tropical Africa', in W. H. Morris-Jones (ed.), *Decolonization and After* (London, 1980), p. 52.

7 Porter and Stockwell, *British Imperial Policy*, p. 69.

8 Peter Calvocoressi, *World Order and New States* (London, 1962), p. 34.

9 Hailey, *The Future of Colonial Peoples*, pp. 40–1.

10 The Netherlands administered West New Guinea until 1962.

11 Holland, *European Decolonization*, p. 73.

12 The major exceptions were Algeria and to a far lesser extent Guinea-Bissau, Angola, Mozambique, and Zimbabwe (Rhodesia).

13 Hailey, *The Future of Colonial Peoples*, p. 24.

14 Lord F. D. Lugard, *The Dual Mandate in British Tropical Africa* (Edinburgh, 1922), pp. 94–5, 103–4.

15 Quoted by Kenneth Robinson, *The Dilemmas of Trusteeship* (London, 1965), p. 91. As indicated, the 'Colonial Empire' did not include British India or Burma.

16 Quoted by J. M. Ward, *Colonial Self-Government 1759–1856* (Oxford, 1976), p. 1. Those who were not refers to French-Canadians.

17 Perham, *Colonial Sequence*, p.255.

18 *The Colonial Problem: A Report by a Study Group of Members of the Royal Institute of International Affairs* (Oxford, 1937), p. 255.

19 Quoted by Porter and Stockwell, *British Imperial Policy*, p. 29.

20 Reprinted *ibid.*, pp. 104–5.

21 He went on to say that 'a declaration by us must lead off with those resounding statements of principle on which America insists – for to Americans a declaration of this nature is rather of the nature of an advertisement of the character of the party making it than a guarantee of performance'. Quoted *ibid.*, p. 155.

22 Quoted *ibid*, p. 35.

23 Hailey, *The Future of Colonial Peoples*, p. 24.

24 Quoted by Porter & Stockwell, *British Imperial Policy*, pp. 120–1.

25 Quoted *ibid.*, p. 156.

26 Quoted by Morgan, *Guidance Towards Self-Government*, p. 11.

27 Perham, *Colonial Sequence*, p. 267.

28 Quoted by Porter and Stockwell, *British Imperial Policy*, pp. 322–30.

29 Perham, *Colonial Sequence*, pp. 295, 336–7.

30 Quoted by Porter and Stockwell, *British Imperial Policy*, p. 233.

31 Quoted *ibid.*, p. 338.

32 *Ibid.*, p. 36.

33 Quoted *ibid.*, p. 124.

34 Quoted *ibid.*, p. 255.

35 Quoted *ibid.*, p. 277.

36 See *ibid.*, p. 202.

37 First Letter on a Regicide Peace, in Rafferty, *The Works of Edmund Burke*, vol. 6.

38 Reprinted in Bruce Fetter (ed.), *Colonial Rule in Africa* (London, 1979), p. 36.

39 Barbu Niculescu, *Colonial Planning: A Comparative Study* (London, 1958), p. 60.

40 Quoted by Niculescu *ibid.*, p. 61.

41 D. J. Morgan, (ed.), *A Reassessment of British Aid Policy 1951–1965, The Official History of Colonial Development*, vol. 3 (London 1980), p. 339.

42 Quoted by Morgan, *Guidance Towards Self-Government*, p. 312.

43 Quoted *ibid.*, p. 21.

44 Porter and Stockwell, *British Imperial Policy*, p. 28.

45 Quoted by Morgan, *Guidance Towards Self-Government*, p. 21.
46 Quoted by Colin Cross, *The Fall of the British Empire, 1918–1968* (London, 1968), p. 262.
47 Morgan, *Guidance Towards Self-Government*, p. 102.
48 Quoted by Morgan *ibid.*, p. 342.
49 *Ibid.*, p. 97.
50 *Ibid.*, p. 98.
51 Quoted by Morgan *ibid.*, p. 117.
52 *Ibid.*, pp. 213–14.
53 According to General Principle XIV of the first UNCTAD 'complete decolonization ... is a necessary condition for economic development and the exercise of sovereign rights over natural resources'. The role of the conference in promoting North–South politics is discussed by Robert A. Mortimer, *The Third World Coalition in International Politics*, 2nd edn (London, 1984), p. 16.
54 Sir Andrew Cohen, *British Policy in Changing Africa* (Evanston, Ill., 1959).
55 See the analysis in Wight, *British Colonial Constitutions*, ch. 2.
56 J. M. Lee, *Colonial Development and Good Government* (Oxford, 1967), pp. 204, 215.
57 Morgan, *Guidance Towards Self-Government*, p. 218.
58 Lee, *Colonial Development*, p. 281.
59 Peter Lyon (ed.), *The Round Table: Special Edition on Small States and the Commonwealth* (London: 1985), p. 3.
60 Perham, *Colonial Sequence*, p. 338 (emphasis added).
61 John D. Hargreaves, *West Africa: The Former French States* (Englewood Cliffs, 1967), p. 155.
62 M. E. Chamberlain, *Decolonization: The Fall of the European Empires* (Oxford, 1985), pp. 55–6. Thomas Hodgkin writes of French 'Cartesianism'. *Nationalism in Colonial Africa* (London, 1956), pp. 33–40.
63 Hailey, *The Future of Colonial Peoples*, p. 45.
64 Ruth Schachter Morgenthau, *Political Parties in French-Speaking West Africa* (Oxford, 1964), p. 56.
65 Quoted *ibid.*, p. 74.
66 Chamberlain, *Decolonization*, p. 68.
67 J. Stengers, 'The Congo Free State and the Belgium Congo before 1914', in L. H. Gann and Peter Duignan (ed.), *Colonialism in Africa: 1870–1960*, vol. 1 (Cambridge, 1981), p. 305.
68 Quoted by Stengers, 'The Congo Free State', p. 314.
69 Roger Anstey, 'Belgian rule in the Congo and the aspirations of the *évolué* class', in Gann and Duignan, *Colonialism in Africa*, vol. 2, p. 218.
70 Stengers, 'The Congo Free State', p. 329.
71 Crawford Young, *Politics in the Congo* (Princeton, 1965), p. 160.
72 Stengers, 'The Congo Free State', p. 325.
73 Quoted by Wilfred Benson, 'The international machinery for colonial liberation', in Arthur Creech-Jones (ed.), *New Fabian Colonial Essays* (London, 1959), p. 227.
74 Morgan, *Guidance Towards Self-Government*, p. 18.

75 Quoted *Ibid.*, p. 218.
76 Quoted *Ibid.*, p. 184.
77 Quoted *Ibid.*, p. 218.
78 Quoted *Ibid.*, p. 215.
79 *Ibid.*, p. 184.
80 *Ibid.*, p. 204.
81 *Ibid.*, p. 105.
82 See I. Claude, 'Domestic jurisdiction and colonialism', in M. Kilson (ed.), *New States in the Modern World* (London, 1975), pp. 121–35.
83 Quoted by Claude *ibid.*, p. 130.
84 *Ibid.*, p. 132.
85 Fawcett cites the following examples: several Latin American countries, India, Burma, Afghanistan, the Philippines, Iraq, Syria, Saudi Arabia, Liberia, and the Soviet Union. See James Fawcett, *Law and Power in International Relations* (London, 1982). One could undoubtedly cite many others.
86 Claude, 'Domestic jurisdiction and colonialism', pp. 125–6.
87 Quoted by Leo Gross, 'The right of self-determination in international law', in Kilson, *New States in the Modern World*, pp. 153–4.
88 Fawcett, *Law and Power*, pp. 19–20.
89 Crawford, 'The criteria for statehood', p. 162.
90 *Ibid.*, pp. 144, 164.

5 Sovereignty and development

1 See World Bank, *World Development Report 1988* (New York, 1988), Table 1: Basic Indicators, pp. 222–3.
2 Kabir-ur-Rahman Khan, 'International law of development and the law of the GATT', in F. Snyder and P. Slinn, *International Law of Development* (Abingdon, 1987), p. 194.
3 P. T. Bauer, *Equality, the Third World and Economic Delusion* (Cambridge, Mass., 1981), p. 87.
4 Evan Luard, *International Agencies* (London, 1977), p. 242.
5 Eugene R. Black, *The Diplomacy of Economic Development and Other Papers* (New York, 1963), p. 23.
6 International Labour Organization, Food and Agriculture Organization, UN Economic and Social Council, UN Educational, Scientific and Cultural Organization.
7 UN Conference on Trade And Development, UN Development Programme, UN Industrial Development Organization, UN Economic Commission for Asia and the Far East, UN Economic Commission for Africa, UN Economic Commission for Latin America.
8 Luard, *International Agencies*, pp. 320–1.
9 Martin Wight, *Power Politics*, 2nd edn (Harmondsworth, 1986), p. 238. Also see S. D. Krasner, *Structural Conflict: The Third World Against Global Liberalism* (Berkeley, 1985).
10 M. Bedjaoui, 'A Third World view of international organizations', in Georges Abi-Saab (ed.), *The Concept of International Organization* (Paris, 1981), p. 219.
11 *World Development Report 1988* (New York, 1988), Table 21.

12 *World Development Report 1988*, Table 17.
13 *Partners in Development: Report of the Commission on International Development* (New York, 1969), pp. 127–8.
14 *North–South: A Program for Survival* (Cambridge, Mass., 1981), p. 10.
15 *Ibid.*, pp. 17–18.
16 See the documents published in Philippe Braillard and Mohammad-Reza Djalili (eds.), *The Third World and International Relations* (London, 1984), part 3.
17 Wang Tieya, 'The Third World and international law', quoted by Alain Pellet, 'A new international legal order', in Snyder and Slinn, *International Law of Development*, p. 119.
18 Pellet, 'A new international legal order', p. 126.
19 Mohammed Bennouna quoted by Maurice Flory, 'A North–South legal dialogue', in Snyder and Slinn, *International Law of Development*, p. 12.
20 Maurice Flory, *Droit International du Developpement* (Paris 1977), p. 16.
21 Pellet, 'A new international legal order', p. 119.
22 Schwarzenberger and Brown, *A Manual of International Law*, p. 34.
23 W. Friedmann, *The Changing Structure of International Law* (New York, 1964), p. 5.
24 Antony Allott, 'The law of development and the development of law', in Snyder and Slinn, *International Law of Development*, p. 82.
25 B. V. A. Roling, *International Law in an Expanded World* (Amsterdam, 1960), p. 83.
26 Friedmann, *The Changing Structure of International Law*, p. 62. Also see H. Suganami, 'International law', in J. Mayall (ed.), *The Community of States* (London, 1982), pp. 67–8.
27 Kabir-ur-Rahman Khan, 'International law of development and the law of the GATT', in Snyder and Slinn *International Law of Development*, p. 176.
28 *Ibid.*, pp. 175–6.
29 Mohammed Bedjaoui, 'Some unorthodox reflections on the "right to development"', in Snyder and Slinn, *International Law of Development*, p. 94.
30 Bedjaoui, 'Some unorthodox reflections on the "right to development"', p. 94 (original emphasis).
31 Reprinted in Braillard and Djalili, *The Third World and International Relations*, pp. 226–36.
32 Reprinted *ibid.*, p. 232.
33 Khan 'International law of development and the law of the GATT', p. 182.
34 The latter 'gives to a contracting party automatically any rights in the same field already granted, or to be granted at a future date, to any third State. Thus, most-favoured-nation treatment . . . creates equality with third parties.' The former 'does not aim at equality . . . but at discrimination in favour of those entitled to invoke it'. Schwarzenberger and Brown, *A Manual of International Law*, pp. 87–8.
35 Khan, 'International law of development and the law of the GATT', p. 179.
36 See *World Development Report 1988*, tables 17–19.
37 See Peter Korner, Gegro Maass, T. Siebold and R. Tetzlaff, *The IMF and the Debt Crisis* (London, 1987), pp. 23–4.

38 *The Globe and Mail* [Toronto], *Report on Business* (3 October 1987).
39 G. K. Helleiner, 'Economic crisis in sub-Saharan Africa', *International Journal*, vol. 41, no. 4 (Autumn 1986), p. 759–66.
40 *Report on Business* (16 June 1988).
41 Trevor Parfitt and Stephen Riley, 'The international politics of African debt', *Political Studies* (1987), 35, p. 5.
42 I. V. Gruhn, 'The recolonization of Africa', *Africa Today*, vol. 30, no. 4 (1983), pp. 37, 48.
43 Tim Congdon, *The Debt Threat* (Oxford, 1988), p. 156.
44 J. R. Lucas, *On Justice* (Oxford, 1980), pp. 211–12.
45 Section 15 (2).
46 See A. H. Goldman, 'Affirmative action', *Philosophy and Public Affairs*, vol. 5 (1976), pp. 178–95.
47 This point was suggested by Alan Cairns.
48 Affirmative action programmes based on gender discrimination – against women – for this reason may not prove to be as workable.
49 See N. Glazer, *Affirmative Discrimination* (New York, 1975).
50 *Report on Business* (19 December 1987).
51 Stephen Haggard, 'The politics of adjustment: lessons from the IMF's Extended Fund Facility', *International Organization*, vol. 39, no. 3 (Summer 1985), pp. 505–6.
52 T. M. Callaghy, 'Africa's debt crisis', *Journal of International Affairs*, vol. 38, no. 1 (Summer 1984), pp. 70.

6 Sovereign rights versus human rights

1 See *Amnesty International Reports* (published in London annually).
2 *Refugees: A Report for the Independent Commission on International Humanitarian Issues* (London, 1986), p. 9.
3 *Political Killings by Governments: An Amnesty International Report* (London, 1983).
4 L. Kuper, *Genocide: Its Political Use in the Twentieth Century* (Harmondsworth, 1981).
5 *Disappeared: A Report for the Independent Commission on International Humanitarian Issues* (London, 1986), p. 29.
6 *Torture in the Eighties: An Amnesty International Report* (London, 1984).
7 See Barry Buzan, *People, States and Fear* (Brighton, 1983), ch. 1.
8 Worsley, *The Third World*.
9 See H. L. A. Hart, *The Concept of Law* (Oxford, 1961), pp. 189–95.
10 See R. G. Collingwood, *The New Leviathan* (New York, 1971), part 3.
11 *Ibid.*, pp. 291–9.
12 *Remarks on the Policy of the Allies*, quoted by Martin Wight, 'Western values in international relations', in H. Butterfield and M. Wight (eds.), *Diplomatic Investigations* (London, 1966), p. 124 (original emphasis).
13 Collingwood, *The New Leviathan*, p. 332 (original emphasis).
14 See the analysis in Michael Walzer, *Just and Unjust Wars* (New York, 1977), pp. 289–96.
15 G. W. Gong, *The Standard of 'Civilization' in International Society* (Oxford, 1984), pp. 90–2.

16 P. Sieghart, *The Lawful Rights of Mankind* (London, 1986), p. vii (original emphasis).

17 See Brownlie, *Principles of Public International Law*, p. 513, and R. B. Lillich, 'Civil rights', in Meron, *Human Rights in International Law*, pp. 117–18.

18 Sieghart, *The Lawful Rights of Mankind*, p. 68.

19 The literature is too vast to cite. For a useful source of pertinent articles consult the *Human Rights Quarterly*.

20 Immanuel Kant, 'Perpetual peace: a philosophical sketch', in Hans Reiss (ed.), *Kant's Political Writings* (Cambridge, 1977), pp. 107–8.

21 'Sed quis custodiet ipsos Custodes?' Juvenal, as quoted by *The Oxford Dictionary of Quotations* (2nd edn) (Oxford, 1955), p. 283.

22 *Amnesty International Report 1986*, pp. 6–7.

23 David Goldsworthy, *Colonial Issues in British Politics 1945–1961* (Oxford, 1971), p. 385.

24 C. Wilfred Jenks, *The Common Law of Mankind* (London, 1958), p. 4.

25 J. L. Brierly, 'The League of Nations', in David Thomson (ed.), *The New Cambridge Modern History*, vol. 12 (Cambridge, 1960), p. 498.

26 Keith Hart, *The Political Economy of West African Agriculture* (Cambridge, 1982), p. 104.

27 Sir. W. Ivor Jennings, *The Approach to Self-Government* (Cambridge, 1956), p. 162.

28 See the special issue devoted to this topic by *Third World Quarterly*, vol. 10 (1988).

29 See S. P. Huntington, *Political Order in Changing Societies* (Yale, 1968).

30 See the comprehensive survey by D. L. Horowitz, *Ethnic Groups in Conflict* (Berkeley, 1985).

31 Collingwood, *The New Leviathan*, p. 299.

32 Zdenek Cervenka, *The Unfinished Quest for Unity* (New York, 1977), p. 77.

33 For a study of such episodes see Kuper, *Genocide*.

34 Alan Dowty, *Closed Borders* (London, 1987), p. 142.

35 *Refugees*, p. 9.

36 Bill C89 as reported in *The Globe and Mail* (4 June 1988).

37 Brownlie, *Principles of Public International Law*, p. 515.

38 Wight, *Systems of States*, ch. 6. The notion of 'territorial vicinage' is from Edmund Burke, 'First letter on a regicide peace', in Rafferty, *The Works of Edmund Burke*, vol. 6, p. 159, note 3.

39 Mazrui, *Towards a Pax Africana*, ch. 2.

40 Wight, *Systems of States*, note 5, pp. 170–2.

41 See Ian Brownlie (ed.), *Basic Documents on African Affairs* (Oxford, 1971), p. 3.

42 See the analysis in A. C. McEwen, *International Boundaries of East Africa* (Oxford, 1971), p. 22.

43 Quoted *ibid.*, p. 24.

44 Arnold Wolfers, *Discord and Collaboration* (London, 1962), pp. 239–40.

45 Reprinted in Claude E. Welch, Jr, and Ronald I. Meltzer (ed.), *Human Rights and Development in Africa* (Albany, 1984), pp. 317–29.

46 See Richard Gittleman, 'The Banjul Charter on Human and Peoples' Rights:

a legal analysis', in Welch and Meltzer, *Human Rights and Development in Africa*, p. 159.

47 The Preamble reaffirms the African states 'adherence to the principles of human and peoples' rights ... adopted by the Organization of African Unity, the Movement of Non-Aligned Countries, and the United Nations'.

48 Sieghart, *The Lawful Rights of Mankind*, p. 99.

49 Calvocoressi, 'The frailty of internationalism', *International Relations*, p. 588.

50 Kant, 'Perpetual peace', pp. 99–102.

51 G. W. Kanyeihamba, 'Human rights and development with special reference to Africa', in Snyder and Slinn, *International Law of Development*, p. 225.

52 Mill, 'A few words on non-intervention', in Himmelfarb, *Essays on Politics and Culture by John Stuart Mill*, ch. 10.

7 Quasi-states and international theory

1 M. Wight, 'An anatomy of international thought', *Review of International Studies*, vol. 13 (1987), pp. 221–7. Also see Bull, 'Martin Wight and the theory of international relations', pp. 101–16.

2 Morgenthau, *Scientific Man Versus Power Politics*, p. 221.

3 See A. Linklater, 'Men and citizens in international relations', *Review of International Studies*, vol. 7 (1981), pp. 23–37.

4 See R. Pettman, 'Competing Paradigms in international politics', *Review of International Studies*, vol. 7 (1981), pp. 39–49.

5 N. Machiavelli, *The Prince*, George Bull, trans., (Harmondsworth, 1961), ch. 9.

6 Machiavelli, *The Prince*, ch. 18.

7 Hobbes, *Leviathan*, ch. 17.

8 J. D. B. Miller, 'The sovereign state and its future', *International Journal*, vol. 39 (1984), p. 292.

9 Hans J. Morgenthau as quoted by P. Gellman, 'Hans J. Morgenthau and the legacy of political realism', *Review of International Studies*, vol. 14 (1988), p. 254 (emphasis added).

10 This brief analysis is derived mainly from H. Lauterpacht, 'The Grotian tradition in international law', *The British Year Book of International Law*, vol. 23 (1946), pp. 1–53.

11 Lauterpacht, 'The Grotian tradition in international law', p. 31.

12 M. Oakeshott, 'The rule of law', *On History and Other Essays* (Oxford, 1983), p. 129. Also see chapter 2.

13 M. Oakeshott, *Rationalism in Politics and Other Essays* (London, 1962), pp. 1–36.

14 This summary analysis is based on Kant's essays 'Idea for a universal history with a cosmopolitan purpose', 'On the common saying: "this may be true in theory, but it does not apply in practice"', and 'Perpetual peace: a philosophical sketch', in Reiss, *Kant's Political Writings*, pp. 41–53, 61–92 and 93–130.

15 Richard Falk, 'A new paradigm for international legal studies', in R. Falk, F. Kratochwil, and S. H. Mendlovitz (eds.), *International Law: A Contemporary Perspective* (London, 1985), pp. 657–93.

16 *Ibid.*, p. 690.

17 See the discussion in Bull, *The Anarchical Society*, p. 302–5.

18 See Friedmann, *The Changing Structure of International Law*.

19 For a criticism of the UN in these terms see Nardin, *Law, Morality and the Relations of States*, p. 110.

20 For an analysis along these lines see Lucas, *On Justice*, ch. 15.

21 *Ibid.*, p. 256.

22 G. Vlastos, 'Justice and equality', in J. Waldron (ed.), *Theories of Rights* (Oxford, 1984), p. 55.

23 J. H. Herz, 'Rise and demise of the territorial state', *World Politics*, vol. 9 (1957), pp. 473–93.

24 Bedjaoui, 'Some unorthodox reflections on the "right to development"', pp. 87–116.

25 Unless otherwise indicated the following analysis and quotations are from Mill, 'A few words on non-intervention', pp. 368–84, and Walzer, *Just and Unjust Wars*, ch. 6.

26 Mill, *Utilitarianism*, p. 73.

27 See D. Luban, 'The romance of the nation-state', in Beitz, *International Ethics*, pp. 238–43.

Conclusion

1 Oakeshott, *Rationalism in Politics and Other Essays*, p. 5.

2 M. Walzer, 'The moral standing of states', in Beitz, Cohen, Scanlon and Simmons, *International Ethics*, pp. 223–4.

INDEX